# The Routledge Critic Adoption Studies Reader

*The Routledge Critical Adoption Studies Reader* presents a central source of scholarly approaches arranged around fundamental questions about how adoption, as a complex practice of family-making, is represented in art, philosophy, the law, history, literature, political science, and other humanities. Divided into three major parts, this volume traces the history of adoption and its analogues, identifies major movements in the practice, and illuminates comprehensive disciplinary frameworks that underpin the field's approaches. This key scholarly and pedagogical tool includes excerpts from scholars such as Judith Butler, Dorothy Roberts, Margaret Homans, Margaret D. Jacobs, Arissa Oh, Marianne Novy, and Kori Graves. It explores a variety of representations of adoption and embraces interdisciplinary discussions of reproduction as it intersects race, ethnicity, power relations, the concept of nation, history, the idea of childhood, and many other contemporary concerns. *The Routledge Critical Adoption Studies Reader* provides a single-volume resource for instructors or students who want a convenient collection of foundational materials for teaching or reference, and for researchers newly discovering the field. This volume's humanities perspective makes it the first of its kind to collect secondary materials in Critical Adoption Studies for researchers, who, in taking up cultural representations of adoption, examine cultural contexts not for their impact on the practice over time but for their richness of engagement with the human experience of belonging, kinship, and identity.

**Emily Hipchen** received her PhD in literary studies from the University of Georgia. She is a Fulbright scholar, the editor of *Adoption & Culture*, co-editor of the book series *Formations: Adoption, Kinship, and Culture*, and an emeritus editor of *a/b: Auto/Biography Studies*. She is also the author of a memoir, *Coming Apart Together: Fragments from an Adoption* (2005). She's an editor of *Inhabiting La Patria: Identity, Agency, and Antojo in the Works of Julia Alvarez* (2013) and *The Routledge Auto|Biography Studies Reader* (2015), as well as five special issues, "Adoption Life Writing," "Adoption Studies Research," "Critique as a Signature Pedagogy," "What's Next? The Futures of Auto|Biography Studies," and most recently, "The *Dobbs* Issue." She directs the Nonfiction Writing Program as a faculty member in the Department of English at Brown University, where she teaches nonfiction writing and editing.

# The Routledge Critical Adoption Studies Reader

## Edited by Emily Hipchen

NEW YORK AND LONDON

Designed cover image: Getty

First published 2024
by Routledge
605 Third Avenue, New York, NY 10158

and by Routledge
4 Park Square, Milton Park, Abingdon, Oxon, OX14 4RN

*Routledge is an imprint of the Taylor & Francis Group, an informa business*



ISBN: 978-1-032-06783-4 (hbk)
ISBN: 978-1-032-06782-7 (pbk)
ISBN: 978-1-003-20382-7 (ebk)

DOI: 10.4324/9781003203827

Typeset in Galliard
by Apex CoVantage, LLC

For my mother, Martha "Dody" Josephine Rich Hipchen (May 1, 1932–April 11, 2023)

# Contents

# Acknowledgements

There would be no *Reader* without the support of several institutions, including Brown University, its Department of English, and the Nonfiction Writing Program, which have sustained and encouraged me and this project. I am grateful for the support of The Ohio State University Press, but particularly that of Kristen Elias-Rowley, Emily Taylor, and Tony Sanfillipo. I owe to The Alliance for the Study of Adoption and Culture, its conferences, journal, and book series years of conversations about our mutual intellectual obsessions. I am thankful in particular to The OVPR Salomon Grant, which underwrote the cost of permissions to reprint the excerpts in this volume. I am grateful to the publishers and authors who granted permission.

I mention here the support of my four parents, in the ways possible to them: Donald Eugene Hipchen (June 30, 1932–Sept. 1989) and Martha Hipchen; Anna Eleanor Govern Mauro (July 16, 1945–February 3, 2011) and Joseph Charles Mauro (July 7, 1944–March 30, 2023).

The people who have supported me and the project are almost innumerable. These include my brothers and sisters and their spouses: Karl, Chris, Missy, Tom, John, Tracey; my nieces and nephews, Brian, Chloe, Jack, Hayden, Madison; and their children: Emmy, Harper; Caroline, Oliver; Andrew, Ryan, Joey, Jeffrey, Shelby, Heather, Brittany, Bryan, and the rest of the clan. Among my friends and colleagues, I thank especially Mary-Kim Arnold, Tim Bewes, Amy Cuomo and Stephen McConnell and Dixie and Chloe, Carol DeBoer-Langworthy, Jim Egan, Shelly Ellman, Steve and Martha Goodson, Kristen and John Griffin, Ed Hardy, Becky and Joe Hogan, RaeAnna Hogle, Catherine Imbriglio, Austin Jackson, Nell Lake, Naomi and Lilo Pariseault, Jon Readey, Ravit Reichman, Rick Rambuss, Elizabeth Rush, Kate Schapira, Larry Stanley, Grace Talusan, Felix Tweraser, Colleen Vasconcellos, Rob Ward.

Among my adoption studies cohort, I am immensely grateful for the work and friendship of Lucy Curzon, Alice Diver, Sally Haslanger, Kimberly Leighton, Kim McKee, Claudia Nelson, Kim Park Nelson, Martha Satz, and

Carol Singley; especially for the work and friendship of Margaret Homans, John McLeod, and Marianne Novy; and that of all the authors whose writing appears in this volume. For their intimate friendship and for the years of meeting twice a week as we worked on our projects together, great thanks to Marina Fedosik and Cynthia Callahan. For their help preparing this manuscript, I thank Ellen Viola, RaeAnna Hogle, and Lily Lustig.

For all her good care over the decades, I am grateful to Rusti Klein.

Finally, I want to attend to those who in an absolute sense I live with, even if they are not exactly nearby: Ollie, Darby, Selkie, and Sedna, for their affection; Sayres, for his kind and unceasing caring, for asking the hard questions (asking me to ask them, better and better) and for helping me think and feel and try to love this world. And Bowie, just "Bowie." His delight in this volume would have been celebrated in dance and song and feasting. (Perhaps it is, in the elsewhere.)

# Note on the Text

This text is composed of excerpts from writing about family creation and kinship outside that formed through biological or blood ties, which includes adoption, artificial reproduction technologies, and fostering in private homes, boarding schools, and orphanages. In their approaches to these subjects, authors are broadly critical, and their materials are not usually in the sciences or social sciences but instead address cultural productions (archives, literature, films, art) that represent adoptive practices. Because so many of these authors come from different disciplines with differing citation styles, where these styles include full bibliographical notes, I have left them and not produced a Works Cited. Where the citation style is parenthetical or bibliographical notes are not full, I have added a Works Cited to the original text. For consistency's sake, all Works Cited conform to MLA 9th edition style.

# Note on the Text

# Introduction

## Belonging

This book has been on my mind a long time, certainly since the first Conference on Adoption and Culture in 2005 showed me both that we had a field and some of its potential futures. Over the nearly twenty years of my editorship of *Adoption & Culture*, the journal of the Alliance for the Study of Adoption and Culture, I have seen increasing engagement in our subject but continuing difficulties identifying and accessing our materials. Despite the journal and biennial conferences, it's still hard to locate our conversations, situated as they usually are in separate disciplines like literary studies, media studies, law, art, or philosophy and made searchable with headings, titles, and keywords that don't speak to their connection to each other. Thus, this volume, which I hope provides the beginnings of a textual home, a kind of jumping-off point for Critical Adoption Studies (CAS) scholars, to familiarize us with each other and reach out to those who want to join us or who already have without realizing it. As such, it's a welcoming book, a field-gathering start, a place where our scholars might understand they belong.

It has been difficult to locate CAS as a field given scholarly lack of awareness of it and unhelpful search parameters; that difficulty has been magnified by its internal tensions and irresolutions. This volume necessarily mirrors that complexity. In order to choose materials for this book, I initially searched bibliographies of recent publications to see who and what people most cited, but because the field is so diffuse and so large, this produced hundreds of non-repeating references. Thus, I decided to build something more gestural and reflective that laid out as clearly as possible what concerns us, where we come from, who we (think we) are. Some of this work began in 2018, in a special issue of *Adoption & Culture* edited by Margaret Homans and devoted to defining Critical Adoption Studies as an approach, a "fielding." In her introduction, Homans outlines some of the questions we might be addressing:

> Is the goal of critical adoption studies to critique (either to analyze for better understanding or to reform or to bring to an end) the practice of

DOI: 10.4324/9781003203827-1

> adoption and related practices such as fostering and surrogacy? Or is its purpose to use adoption (and related practices) as a critical lens through which to see, in new ways, such central features of human existence as race, identity, kinship, heritage, nationality, sexuality, and gender? Is the focus of adoption studies the rights-bearing individual whose subjection within unequal relations of power calls out for justice? Can the critical study of adoption expose the structural inequities—of race, of gender, of economic access, of geopolitics—that not only render contemporary adoption intrinsically unjust, but that also characterize global social relations more generally? Alternatively yet simultaneously, does adoption's exposure of bionormativity in kinship and in subject formation mobilize alternative conceptions of the human and therefore alternative pathways to justice? Modern adoption has been described as an "as if" family formation, in which relations between parents and children mimic biological ties, but the nuclear family that adoption mimics is itself an imaginary ideal, as is the individual whose identity would be wholly accounted for by biogenetic origins. Can the critical study of adoption help to crack open regulatory regimes premised on biogenetic essentialism?
>
> (3)

In what follows Homans's framing, CAS scholars describe the field as "embrac[ing] . . . methodologies and research designs that best illuminate complicated issues and problems within adoption policy, practice, and culture" (Park Nelson 20); as concentrating on questions such as "how . . . we know what we know and [whether there] . . . are alternative forms of knowledge and practice" (Myers 18); as "forc[ing] us [to] tell stories from the inside out[,] . . . political stories about state practices, war, refugees, visas and immigration, the economics of whose children are adopted or fostered and whose are not, work and wages, judges and social workers, racism, Indigeneity, misogyny, rape and abortion, feminism and those who loathe it, policing and prisons" (Briggs 22). Peggy Phelan suggests that the "critical" of critical adoption studies "should help differentiate [the field from] . . . data-driven research and encourage interest in the messier affective, economic, narratological, and geopolitical consequences of the adoption complex" (7).

The examples collected in this volume (like *Adoption & Culture*'s presentation of CAS) underscore how variously scholars perceive the work. But that variety produces an unsettled "field" that can seem, and be, messy and incoherent. In fact, choosing pieces for this volume presented significant representational challenges, some of which frankly belong to a discipline that has not yet contested many of its positions and central terms (for example: *origins*, *family*, *roots*, *kinship*, *reproduction*, *natural*—among many others). Even the terms of our field name have not quite condensed. *Adoption* itself seems easily defined, but it isn't. We struggle to understand whether adoption includes, for instance, foster care or alternative reproduction technologies (ARTs). We try to assess whether birth is an important distinction in the field, if you can adopt the pre-born, whether permanent as opposed to temporary placement outside the natal home makes a difference or what sort of difference it might make. We ask whether "real" adoption is a visible/visual phenomenon—whether, if you or your family can "pass" as biogenetically kinned, your family is more or less adoptive than one that can't hide its adoptiveness. We wonder about the way in which adoptive difference is coded outside the rhetorics of sameness common to pro-adoption advocates. We want to address how and whether nonbiogenetically created families cohere, what makes those relationships sticky or not. We ask whether the *feeling* of adoptive difference (what John McLeod frames as "adoptive being" in transcultural adoption) is substantive enough for distinct inquiry. We want to figure how adoption trauma matters, to whom, and why—whether anyone can experience adoption meaningfully without being traumatized or without living among or coming from either personally or systemically traumatized people. We aren't yet sure, either, what it means to be a field, especially in the humanities, separate from but still beholden intellectually to the work of social scientists and psychologists trying to describe or imagine the relationships in and between families created biogenetically and otherwise. Even the terms by which we address each other aren't settled yet and are a subject for contention. For example, relinquishing parents might be called, among other designations, *real*, *natal*, *natural*, *birth*, *first*, or simply *parents*. People who were adopted might be adopted *children* all their lives, or *the adopted* or *adoptees*, or not be recognized as different at all, just like adoptive parents, who often enough fight to feel or be seen as *real*, *natural*, or *parental*.

The unsettled nature of the field reflects and responds to the unsettled times in which we think and write about the language and practice of making families. Examples of this general struggle abound. In 2022, the US Supreme Court's overturning of years of federal oversight of reproductive rights brought again to the foreground conversations about what happens to children conceived outside the desire for them—children, as the decision notes, who might be available for adoption, should they be born. But everywhere, the family is now being boundaried and stretched simultaneously in ways that CAS speaks to, in the pieces collected in this volume and elsewhere. Politicians have proposed and sometimes passed restrictive legislation concerning trans healthcare, drag queens, gay marriage, access in public school classrooms and gymnasiums to books and ideas about family creation. This legislation has appeared amid various, less codified erosions of family reinvention, such as COVID-fueled returns to traditional family roles, judicial and non-legislative attacks on access to birth control and abortion, and other shorings-up of traditional, gendered kinship and clan forms. But these are happening alongside opposite pressures and changes, including the opening of marriage to same-sex partners and the reimagining of gay/queer identity as potentially reproductive through ARTs and adoption, the increase in blended family visibility, and the adoption of (old) non-nuclear family forms as a response to the housing crisis and jobs crisis that keep home young people without jobs, the elderly, the unhoused or unhousible aunts, uncles, and cousins for whom independent living is economically or emotionally impossible. Indeed, "family" is now flexible enough to include "work wives" and "work husbands" or "those one lives with," who are not necessarily consanguineous relatives but who identify as family—"chosen family" as an echo of the chosen child of adoption—in a time when marriage is on the steep decrease and, in many Western countries, childbearing has fallen below replacement levels.

The continuing whiplash around the correct constitution and behavior of family comes with increasing cultural attention to adoptive family-making, ARTs, foster care, family separation as both a historical and present-tense practice, and the reproductive rights of LGBTQ+ people; it is this manifestation in cultural productions that is the especial subject of CAS scholars. In contemporary books, especially memoirs and histories; in recent film, television, episodic visual media, and comics; and on social media, representations of relinquishment and adoption proliferate (in speculative fiction, technology and science produce "children" and "families" that can productively challenge our notions of both). Representations featuring the real (but mediated) lives of people in adoption in the news are also frequent: in 2013, Reuters prepared a report on the phenomenon of "re-homing" unwanted adoptees; in reports from the US Southwestern border, children continue to be separated from their parents, caged, and then moved into US foster and adoptive families—a practice condemned, but not begun, in the Trump regime and continuing at this writing; attention to the psychological damage done to children separated from their natal families is an ongoing research project outside the humanities; in recent years have come revelations about the mass graves of infants and children at homes for unwed mothers in Ireland and at such homes and at boarding schools for the Indigenous in the US and Canada (and, in some cases, official apologies for this practice). These and many other stories of families created outside biogenesis have been common but come more and more to our notice as such, among increasing numbers and increasing awareness of stories of abortion, miscarriage, infant and maternal death, and the medical abuse of mothers and children, including work by the winner of the 2022 Nobel Prize for Literature, the French writer Annie Ernaux. This is the near-dizzying cultural moment into which CAS scholars can and do step with their questions about how we see, and what we might do with, current ideas of family formation.

Much of this ferment is localized in the West, and many CAS scholars are located there as well, mostly in the US. There are two reasons for this: the field was generated by and is still largely populated by English-speaking US scholars, and the kind of adoption we study is particularly linked to Euro-American and US ideologies and narratives. The humanities approach to adoption studies rests initially on a pair of books that look at adoption in literature—Marianne Novy's *Imagining Adoption* (2001), an edited anthology of essays, and her monograph, *Reading Adoption* (2005)—and three histories of adoption: E. Wayne Carp's *Family Matters: Secrets and Disclosure in the History of Adoption* (1998), Barbara Melosh's *Strangers and Kin: The American Way of Adoption* (2002), and Ellen Herman's *The Adoption History Project* (2003). Essays in the special issue on adoption of *Tulsa Studies in Women's Literature* (vol. 21, no. 2, 2002), edited by Holly Laird, began the field's theoretical framing—especially Margaret Homans's "Adoption and Essentialism" and Susan Bordo's "All of Us Are Real: Old Images in a New World of Adoption"—as did *Adoption Matters: Philosophical and Feminist Essays*, edited by Sally Haslanger and Charlotte Witt, in 2005. Many early humanities-oriented scholars in CAS were trained in literary studies (and sometimes feminism) in the last quarter of the twentieth century (such as Carol Singley, Marianne Novy, Martha Satz, Claudia Nelson, Margaret Homans, Jill Deans, and myself); our approaches differ from social science ones in that we attend to adoption in the symbolic and representational spaces of literature, film, art, theater, and theory. This shift from data-based research to representational analysis marks the shift into CAS as we know it and away from an adoption studies that addresses data about living subjects. Most CAS scholars are, however, indebted to decades of work in the social sciences and history. Early on, psychologists, historians, and social workers, such as Erich Wellisch, H. J. Sants, and Jean Paton and, later, Florence Fisher and Betty Jean Lifton, registered alarm about the perceived harm for adopted people and their families of adoption secrecy and adoptee alienation from natal families. Paton provided a place for adopted people to speak about their experiences, particularly their sense of their difference; Fisher and Lifton developed life narratives and organizations that helped adoptees search for their parents (and manage the process and aftermath). Such writers began or codified our speaking of adoption as traumatizing, especially of adoptee estrangement and secrecy as a source of mental illness and family dysfunction. Harms to the adopted person and to the adoptive family through adoption became a hallmark of the conversation about adoption and of "being adopted" as an identity category: to be adopted was *de facto* to identify as traumatized through banishment from the maternal body (really or through analogy, where relinquishment extends to include maternal race and geography) and/or difference from the "normative" or "traditional" look-alike, consanguineous family.

Framing adoption difference as harmful and preferring blood ties in making family coherent were part of a larger set of ideas about the importance of heredity in the late nineteenth and early twentieth centuries in the West, just as one current iteration of adoption developed—plenary adoption, the one that most frequently comes to mind in thinking of the word. Residues of the tendency to privilege heredity are visible in racialized thinking about identity and origins while, at least in theory, adoption de-emphasizes the role of genetics in the manifestation of selfhood or social value, asserting that people can usually become whatever they want to, given opportunity, education, and advantages—especially wealth. This is, after all, the idea at the base of most US literature—indeed, most American ideology. In coming (or being brought) to the US, people leave their roots behind and discover themselves, so the story goes, a process very like having lost one's natal family and starting anew among strangers—adoption—as Carol Singley has noted. Thus, CAS's positions, like adoption's, find common ground not just in the representations scholars tend to address, but in the tensions and ideologies common to, and apparent in, "American-ness."

The field's interaction with Western texts, practices, and ideologies is one feature of its current state. There are parts of the world, of course, where adoption is rare or adoption narratives are infrequent, appear in languages outside English, or don't follow the most common forms of such stories in the West. We look forward to these as they come to our attention and, in the meantime, are cognizant of the way in which their absence magnifies the politics and the political silences of adoption practice. That is, in speaking of transnational adoption, the US and Europe were and still are the largest receivers of children from outside the country, usually from the Global South. But even domestic adoption reflects central inequities in power, a subject of frequent concern for those in CAS who are looking at representations of adoption in the context of data about living people to make those inequities apparent in order to correct them. In the usual narrative, as in the frequent practice, empowered, rich White people who covet them abet the removal of children, for the purposes of raising them as kin, from their natal families and geographies. These practices are suspect as exercises of consumption clothed in often self-serving rescue narratives and in neoliberal ideas of the possibility of overcoming race and class through re-classing and/or re-racing children in the middle-class White home. A significant strand of CAS is rooted in reproductive justice activism, and part of what CAS can do is provide thoughtful, impassioned attention not just to overt abuses such as Indian boarding schools, re-homing, or foster-care neglect, but also to the way in which breaking up families is tactical, political, and intended to maintain an existing class and race structure through intimidation and violence. The adoption abolition movement springs from this attention, part of a continuum of critique that frames the practice of placing children outside their natal families as essentially flawed. However, the field is capacious enough that we can, and do, ask less absolute questions about the practice—if there's a better way to meet the needs of children for homes (where there's honestly a need); if we can discriminate systemic abuses from individual ones in adoption; ultimately, if we should celebrate adoption, reform it, or discard it.

The most ambitious collection of these various concerns in the field so far is a bibliography, published in 2014 as volume 4 of *Adoption & Culture*. There, Cynthia Callahan and I asked scholars to propose sections in whatever way it seemed best to them. They built their bibliographies along racial or national lines, grouped by positions on the adoption triad, along genre lines, or along disciplinary lines. We found the volume fascinating as it came together, given not just the differences in approaches and groupings we saw, but also the way in which the canon began to cohere to that point—what mattered, what was useful, who was doing what, and how that material might be accessed. I call your attention to it as a resource, a supplement to the text you're reading. The present *Reader*, however, rather than being a list of citations subdivided by any of the categories our contributors used in that journal issue, has three parts containing thirty-three short excerpts from texts representing perspectives, voices, concerns, and questions in the field as it stands in 2023. The first of these groups includes excerpts from work that presents foundational positions or questions upon which or against which lines of thinking in CAS have been developed. These include questions about adoption history (where did "adoption" come from?); about key terms such as *roots* and *origins* and their meanings and place in our discussions; about secrecy and its importance (or not) to identity; about policies that free children for removal from their natal families or geographies; about the racialization of adoption; about the intersections of eugenics and disability in representations of and thinking about adoption; about immigration and citizenship; about what is and isn't natural in family formation and how adoption might make visible the difference; about the ubiquity of adoption in American literature, identity, and ideology. In the second part, I've clustered work that addresses the body in CAS—the natural and unnatural, gendered, sexed, raced, technologized, reproductive or infertile, endangered, needy, commodified body not just of the adopted person, but of all those involved in representations of adoption practices, policies, and connections. In the third section are grouped texts that treat adoption as a narrative experience, something CAS notices differently than other fields that analyze data about living persons. Here, adoption is encountered as story, something inside time, with setting, scenes, characters (fictive, even when based on the living). This section presents idealized stories of adoption in which the family is home and a hopeful nurturing space and critical stories that reveal how difficult adoption can be or how delusional those who hope for coherent adoptive—or, indeed, natal—families might be.

In the end, I hope this volume is simply a start or a gesture that invites readers to probe further, to recognize their work and their questions as belonging to ours, to interest new scholars or scholars who want to try new questions in those that we're asking. I hope it collects voices foundational to the field as it is and to what it may become. We have passed through periods of scholarship focused on opening adoption records, recording the trauma of secrecy and shame, adopting these as identities, revealing corporate and political abuses, delving into our anger or sadness or grief. CAS scholars are working on projects in film, with poetry, with the law and history, and with affect theory and disability theory as well. Looking at representations of adoption in speculative fiction, horror, and science fiction could prove enlightening since it's there, far from the practical and the real, that CAS scholars may discover new and better questions about our field. We are seeing more work from outside the US—from Europe, but also from scholars in sending countries—and I hope this continues to grow so that it can challenge narratives that are sometimes taken now to be all there is. And though I am not particularly sure how it will form up in scholarship, however exciting it is to find and to read sometimes in digital social spaces, young people in adoptions very different from their parents' and grandparents' are adding their voices to the mix, questioning expectations that coerce them into identities that don't fit, truisms that are no longer and may never have been universally true. Not, at least, the kind of universally true that films, television, and books have insisted they are. It's my hope that we begin to encounter new, larger, meatier, more global, more surprising stories and approaches to them as the field continues to mature.

## Works Cited

Briggs, Laura. "Adoption, from Private to Public: Intimate Economies." *Adoption & Culture*, vol. 6, no. 1, 2018, pp. 22–24.

Callahan, Cynthia, and Emily Hipchen, editors. "The Bibliographies Issue." Special Issue of *Adoption & Culture*, vol. 4, 2014.

Carp, E. Wayne. *Secrecy and Disclosure in the History of Adoption*. Harvard UP, 2000.

Fisher, Florence. *The Search for Anna Fisher*. A. Fields, 1973.

Haslanger, Sally, and Charlotte Witt, editors. *Adoption Matters: Philosophical and Feminist Essays*. Cornell UP, 2004.

Herman, Ellen. *The Adoption History Project*. 2003. Updated 2012. https://pages.uoregon.edu/adoption/.

Homans, Margaret. Introduction. "Critical Adoption Studies." Special Issue of *Adoption & Culture*, vol. 6, no. 1, 2018, pp. 1–4.

Laird, Holly, editor. "The Adoption Issue." *Special Issue of Tulsa Studies in Women's Literature*, vol. 21, no. 2, 2002.

Lifton, Betty Jean. *Twice Born: Memoirs of an Adopted Daughter*. McGraw-Hill, 1975.

McLeod, John. *Life Lines: Writing Transcultural Adoption*. Bloomsbury, 2015.
Melosh, Barbara. *Strangers and Kin: The American Way of Adoption*. Harvard UP, 2002.
Myers, Kit. "Marking the Turn and New Stakes in (Critical) Adoption Studies." *Adoption & Culture*, vol. 6, no. 1, 2018, pp. 17–20.
Novy, Marianne, editor. *Imagining Adoption: Essays on Literature and Culture*. U of Michigan P, 2001.
———. *Reading Adoption: Family Difference in Fiction and Drama*. U of Michigan P, 2005.
Park Nelson, Kim. "Critical Adoption Studies as Inclusive Knowledge Production and Corrective Action." *Adoption & Culture*, vol. 6, no. 1, 2018, pp. 20–21.
Paton, Jean M. *The Adopted Break Silence*. Life History Center, 1954.
Phelan, Peggy. "Letter to the Special Issue Editor." *Adoption & Culture*, vol. 6, no. 1, 2018, pp. 5–9.
Sants, H. J. "Genealogical Bewilderment in Children with Substitute Parents." *British Journal of Medical Psychology*, vol. 37, no. 2, 1964, pp. 133–141.
Singley, Carol. *Adopting America: Childhood, Kinship, and National Identity in American Literature*. Oxford UP, 2011.
Wellisch, Erich. "Children Without Genealogy—A Problem of Adoption." *Mental Health*, vol. 12, no. 1, 1952, pp. 42–42.

# Part 1

# Foundations, Histories, Frames

## Introduction: Beginnings

In this section of the volume, readers will encounter approaches in the field that are foundational, are framing, and/or provide historical context for a practice and a set of cultural representations that are far from static—that have their own genealogies. We start with an excerpt from one of the three most frequently cited histories of adoption in the West: *Family Matters*, by E. Wayne Carp. Carp not only presents us with several corrections to general assumptions—we learn that secrecy was never ubiquitous and was a later development in adoption practice, tied largely to fears of stigma for the presumed-illegitimate adoptee; that adoption has had many formal and informal iterations; that the scarcity of children freed for adoption began in the first third of the twentieth century, for example—and a neat timeline for adoption's history, at least as a domestic practice. Readers here will also encounter the idea that, in the US at least, "biological kinship was superior to adoptive kinship and that adoption was an inferior type of kinship relation" but that this preference for the biological would "wax and wane throughout American history." Here, too, Carp lays out the connection between religion, politics, and adoption as a historical phenomenon and touches on eugenics and race as they intersect and inform adoption. Then, in Judith Modell's work, readers find engagement with legal thought—what is legal and illegal about adoption and especially reform and search movements?—as well as the trace of thinking genetically about "an integrated identity" ("the significance of genetics to who one is and will become") that haunts current adoption and reunion narratives: "the concept of roots," she writes, "justified the search for one's own ethnic and ancestral past and for, ultimately, the sources of one's being. . . . Not precisely defined, 'biology' stood in for the aspect of one's identity linked to genes and the physical traits one inherits from blood relatives." Kim Leighton's essay introduces anonymous gamete donation (AGD) as a kind of adoption, noting AGD's claim that anonymity "borrow[s] the language" of genealogical bewilderment

DOI: 10.4324/9781003203827-2

("what children suffer from when they do not know their genetic parents"), observing that the diagnosis of genealogical bewilderment seems "to displace former worries about the harmful effects of illegitimacy onto the effects of adoption itself." In its questioning of both the twinning of artificial reproductive technologies (ARTs) and adoption and the idea that ignorance of origins produces harm, Leighton's work provides counterpositions to other claims that ARTs are adoptive and that the lack of genetic origins is harmful, but this work also notices her source's (Erich Wellisch, in this case) concerns about the reproduction of race. That is, "there is also in us a drive to sexually reproduce something that is born into us, i.e. to reproduce our race." The harm in not knowing our natal parents, she writes, is that, without that knowledge, "we can't know what we are reproducing. . . . [W]ithout knowing what my real race is, I could be passing—and so could my child—as a member of the race I think I am," but am not.

Leighton's sense of the way in which adoption and non-biogenetic forms of kinship meet introduces readers to one of the intersections of CAS and ideas of race and racialized reproduction, an observation that is centered in Dorothy Roberts's most recent book. Roberts's concern is to expose injustices in order to correct them, and in her text, we see the expansion of our subject matter to foster care (often a prequel to plenary adoption) as the natural subsequent of child-taking as a systemic, raced, and classed project. She notes how "sometimes all three systems—child protection, criminal, and immigration—conspire to tear families apart." Her particular concern in this excerpt is for women in abusive relationships and for children taken at the border, but that concern extends to all families; Roberts's central critique is of the "good family" or "good parent" model that is raced, classed, oppressive, and harmful when abetted by systems of surveillance and control that tear children from families. Roberts's criticism of systemically supported child-taking shows up in discussions of transnational and transracial adoption but is also clear in Sandra Sufian's examination of the way in which disability has been framed to "disable" families and children. In her look at the effect of the US's War on Drugs, particularly in the last quarter of the twentieth century, on families, particularly poor families or families of color, Sufian finds that the "pejorative notion of dependency and its racial, class, and disability axes during this time, [meant that] many Americans conceptualized these children [in narratives of addicted mothers and babies] as inherently a burden, a lack, and risky candidates for family life." In the context of movements in the 1980s and 90s arguing that doctors and parents should let fragile infants die, adoption steps in when natal families can't care for such children as "a better alternative than death by starvation, permanent institutionalization, or physical abuse. Children had a right to this option rather than death," Sufian notes of thinking at the time. In her work is apparent not only this strand of imagining the value of a child—what's in its best interest, a common defense of adoption in social work—but also of the way in which alternatives are conceptualized as irremediably dire and adoption as salvific. It was ever thus in narratives of adoption, as CAS scholars often remind us.

In both Roberts's and Sufian's addressing of adoption practice and narrative, the value of a child—to whom, how, in what way—is a key issue. Viviana Zelizer's book *Pricing the Priceless Child* provides one history of the issue, cataloging historical changes in "pricing" children, from that based on their use as labor to those that privilege their affective worth. "Child welfare workers [in the late nineteenth century] sought to replace mercenary foster parenting of any kind with a new approach to adoption more suitable for the economically 'useless' child," Zelizer writes; "the shift in social class [of adopters, from mostly farmers to mostly business men] . . . was tied to the sentimentalization of adoption," which in turn shifted the way in which the relative value of infants and older children was framed. That is, when children were mostly thought useful as laborers, infants were not in demand, but as "sentimental adoption" became more prevalent, adopters begged for babies: little blonde, blue-eyed girls who would love their new parents as sweetly as they looked, who would (it was thought) be most pliable and grateful for their homes.

Kim Park Nelson's work registers both a major shift in adoption practice, beginning in the middle of the twentieth century, and a concomitantly significant object of study in CAS: Korean transnational, transracial adoption. The attention here is both to the harm done to adoptees and to the way in which adoption and adoptees are instrumentalized and metaphoricalized to produce or reproduce conflicted national and race relations amid the opposite: talk of salvation, peace, and unity through color-blindness. Park Nelson notes how "Korean adoptees' assimilation into the family is followed by assimilation into racial and cultural identities of Whiteness," which produces adopted people who are "generally accepted as 'culturally White' and often assume roles as racial and cultural bridge-makers." But for the adoptee, who is "always going to be in between, . . . not Asian enough, . . . not White enough," this is an unbearable liminality that, when it produces ingratitude, "potentially threatens family systems and relationships, the multi-million dollar transnational adoption industry, and paternalistic relations between the United States and the nations that supply adoptable children." Korean adoptees and transracial and transnational adoption are simply overborne with signification. Where—and to whom—do we belong? This question is central to Marilyn Strathern's work here, which addresses ARTs—surrogacy and IVF in particular—as practices that ask us to think about what nature is and what technology can do, should do, can't do. Strathern describes shifts in thinking about the "naturalness" of technologically enhanced reproduction (surrogacy as a kind of technology as well), noting that "by the 1980s, . . .

debates were less about the animality of the procedures than about the intrusion of technology into biological process, less about the lawfulness of a union than about the kind of contract the parties should make with each other, and less about the property claims to bastards than about rights to the products of one's body." Quoting Naomi Pfeffer, she writes that "handling human gametes and embryos outside of the body raised the problem of moral responsibility and legal ownership." Strathern's work helps us ask not just about whether ARTs are sufficiently "adoptive" but about what role discourses of nature and technology play, how our fears influence our kinship practices and what we say about them, whether our notions of ownership and power distort our understanding of ourselves and our families. Carol Singley's essay argues for the natural alignment of American culture and adoption ("adoption speaks to the American experience") as borne out in looking for, and at, adoption in the American literature classroom. She describes the "deeply rooted, historical definition of identity as derived only through bloodline, and an equally strong belief in self-improvement and the power of individuals to define and shape their own lives." This central "tension" is captured in adoption stories, which connect nation and family, macro- and microcosm: "[O]n a small scale, adoption narratives dramatize the struggle of individuals and families to draw and redraw lines of bonds and affection; on a larger scale, they portray a nation wrestling in multiple ways with conflicting notions of citizenship in which belonging and entitlement are bestowed by birthright and by ideology." Thus, in addressing stories of adoption in the literature classroom, Singley argues, we can get at the push-pull of national identity in the same moment we engage discussions of individuation, family formation, and kinship.

Cynthia Callahan's contribution here is a reminder of the costs—and who pays—in the struggles, wrestling, and tensions of an America that, as Singley describes it, is "capable of extending its boundaries and absorbing new ideas and individuals." "The [American Indian] boarding schools," Callahan writes, "were part of a larger, assimilationist strategy that included, in particular, the division of collectively held tribal lands." This strategy, at a time when hunger for adoptable children and the loosening of social workers' dedication to matching adoptive parents and children freed Indigenous children for transracial placements, meant the taking of children as a resource and a deliberate destabilization of tribal sovereignty: "[T]he primary concern for tribes was not racial integrity as such, but national sovereignty." In essence, Callahan argues, in the pressures to preserve tribal identities and power, tribes submerged racial difference at the same moment white families were submerging it for other reasons. This observation points to another set of questions CAS scholars engage: how are narratives of difference manipulated to create categories of adoptability? How do civilizing discourses such as those used to tear Indigenous children from their families and house them in boarding schools look like the rescue narratives behind child removal policies that move children out of their natal homes into adoptive or foster ones? How do these narratives intersect ideas about what is innate and inherited and what is learned or learnable? In Sarah Potter's treatment of the Great Migration and black adoptive practices in Chicago, families are again microcosms of greater political movements, here out of the terrors of the post-Reconstruction and Jim Crow South and towards greater (not absolute) safety that's figured in not just the tightening of black family bonds, but also in the way in which those bonds became foundational to the movement itself.

In this section, then, readers will encounter many of CAS's most prominent themes, including: are we made or do we become, and what's the relationship between heredity and learning made clearer (or not) in adoptive families? What is the history of family-making outside the biogenetic, and why have things changed and for whom? What is the connection between adoptive family-making and citizenship, immigration, race, national identity, sovereignty, religion, class, and other markers of individual identity? How do adoption narratives help us see who we are, what we might become, where we belong?

# From Carp, E. Wayne. *Family Matters: Secrecy and Disclosure in the History of Adoption.* Harvard UP, 1998.

At the beginning of the seventeenth century, the institution of adoption hardly existed. There were no established legal processes, no confidential court records, birth certificates, or adoption case records, no social workers, no standards for determining the best interests of the child or, for that matter, any criteria of what constituted desirable qualities in adoptive parents. And in place of secrecy, there existed an ethos of openness, a bias toward disclosure, for most of the people directly involved in adoption. How American adoption went from its initial climate of openness and disclosure, which lasted until the end of the Second World War, to one of secrecy in the post-war era, and how it then began to return to openness in the 1970s cannot be understood unless these issues are first set into their broadest historical context.

Adoption, the method of establishing by law the social relationship of parent and child between individuals who are not each other's biological parent or child, is doubtless as old as humanity itself. It appears in the Code of Hammurabi, drafted by the Babylonians around 2285 B.C., which provided that "if a man has taken a young child 'from his waters' to sonship and has reared him up no one has any claim against the nursling." Adoption was practiced in ancient Egypt, Greece, Rome, the Middle East, Asia, and the tribal societies of Africa and Oceania. But there are many differences between modern adoption and its counterpart in the past, when the purpose of adoption was not the welfare of the child but the needs of adults, whether for the purpose of kinship, religion, or the community.[4]

****

By the seventeenth century, the West's emphasis on the primacy of biological kinship and the concomitant prejudice against adoption resulted in the demise of adoption in most European countries. The virtual disappearance of adoption in the West was also the result of a number of specific factors. For centuries, the Church had discouraged adoption as a strategy

DOI: 10.4324/9781003203827-3

for inheritance. Adoption was also denounced by sixteenth-century Catholic and Protestant reformers who, in their insistence that marriage should be the sole arena for sexual activity and procreation, wanted to stop the long-standing practice of fathers bringing their illegitimate sons surreptitiously into the family. Fears of adoption were spread by stories of accidental incestuous unions between unsuspecting blood relatives. As a result, people hesitated to adopt: childless couples who adopted invited public scrutiny of their infertility; other presumptive adoptive families worried that neighbors might perceive them as challenging the natural order. In short, by the early modern period adoption had almost died out in Europe, being judged "unchristian" and "unnatural."[6]

England, whence the American colonists derived their culture and laws, emulated European attitudes and practice toward adoption. English common law did not recognize adoption. This legal opposition to adoption stemmed from a desire to protect the property rights of blood relatives in cases of inheritance, a moral repugnance of illegitimacy, and the availability of other quasi-adoptive devices such as apprenticeship and voluntary transfers. Not until 1926 did England enact its first adoption statute.[7]

The history of adoption in early America reveals a past that initially broke away from Europe's and England's prohibition against adoptive kinship. Although the United States would eventually manifest typically Western attitudes toward adoption—that biological kinship was superior to adoptive kinship and that adoption was an inferior type of kinship relation—these would wax and wane throughout American history. What is noteworthy about the history of adoption in America is that at its beginning, colonial Americans showed little preference for the primacy of biological kinship, practiced adoption on a limited scale, and frequently placed children in what we would call foster care. This was primarily due to the multifaceted functions of the colonial American family: it was the cornerstone of church and state, the center of all institutional life, and the fundamental unit of society. As Lawrence Cremin has noted, the family "provided food and clothing, succor and shelter; it conferred social standing, economic possibility, and religious affiliation; and it served from time to time as church, playground, factory, army, and court."[8]

Most important, the family served as a school and as a system of child care for dependent children through the institution of indenture or apprenticeship. Colonial America inherited from England a three-tier system of apprenticeship, by which children of all classes were placed in families to learn a trade. Merchants paid fees to apprentice their adolescent sons to lawyers or doctors or silversmiths. Middle class parents voluntarily entered into contracts to "put out" their children to learn a craft and ease their economic burden, or as an alternative for parents "who did not trust themselves with their own children" because they were "afraid of spoiling them by too great affection." And church and town authorities involuntarily "bound out" orphans, bastards, abandoned children, and impoverished, neglected, or abused children to families to labor and be educated.[9]

Involuntary or compulsory apprenticeship stemmed from the Elizabethan poor laws that had been designed to suppress vagrancy and idleness and provide for the relief of poverty. Under the legal doctrine of *parens patriae*, derived from the belief that the king is the father and protector of his people, the role of the state included the right to intervene, on behalf of the child, in the biological family. It was not unusual for English Overseers of the Poor to remove children from impoverished families and place them with those more fortunate, saving the taxpayers from additional financial burdens. Similarly, Parliament, under Henry VIII, saw nothing wrong with passing an act ordering that all vagrant children between the ages of five and fourteen be arrested and bound out as apprentices. Compulsory apprenticeship was designed to relieve the community from the cost of supporting vagrant or impoverished children while at the same time ensuring that they received the basic necessities of life—food, clothing, and shelter.[10]

Colonial Americans copied the English poor law system when it came to caring for children born out of wedlock, orphaned, or neglected. Statutes permitted town and parish authorities to remove children from pauper families and place them with masters who, in exchange for their labor, would provide them with an adequate maintenance. Thus, for example, in 1648, at a town meeting, the inhabitants of Salem, Massachusetts, resolved that "the eldest children of Reuben Guppy be placed out, the boy till the age of 21 years and the mayd till the age of 18 years." Nearly a century later, Boston town officials authorized the overseers of the poor to bind out children whose parents were unable or neglected to support and educate them. During the 1750s, the churchwardens of Virginia's Frederick County removed 7.3 percent of the children from their families and bound them out as apprentices.[11] Primarily as a result of the indenture system, both voluntary and involuntary, colonial American family life was far from the stable, nuclear family so idealized by many twentieth century Americans: a substantial number of colonial American children grew up in families other than their own, many with the consent of their parents.

The fluid boundaries between consanguine and nonconsanguine families in colonial America led in some cases to the adoption of children, particularly in Puritan Massachusetts and Dutch New York. Informal adoption occurred when children were adopted without a legal proceeding. In 1658 in Plymouth Colony, for example, Lawrence Lichfeild, while lying on his deathbed, adopted out his youngest son to John and Ann Allin "for ever." Colonial Americans also practiced testamentary adoption, by which childless couples used their wills to provide generously for young relatives or children who had been "put out" to service in their homes. The most famous example and "the first known case of adoption" in colonial Massachusetts, as Jamil S. Zainaldin has noted, occurred in 1693 when Governor Sir William Phips mentioned his adopted son in his will. The adopted son was Phips's nephew, who legally changed his name in 1716. The concept of adoption also appeared in the more informal device of the godparent-godchild relationship, in which godparents not only bequeathed part of their estate but also frequently their names.[12]

By the middle of the nineteenth century, the number of adoptions increased, though it is impossible to know precisely by how much. In addition to informal and testamentary adoption, many private bills providing for the adoption of children by adults were enacted by state legislatures. Parents who sought a change of name for their adopted children often had recourse to these private legislative enactments. For example, a 1848 Pennsylvania statute directed that "henceforth the name of David Richardson Blair, an adopted son of Thompson Richardson . . . shall be David Richardson . . . and he is hereby in vested with all the legal rights of a legitimate son of said Thompson Richardson." In Massachusetts between 1781 and 1851, the General Court enacted 101 private name-change acts, compared to just four in the previous century.[13]

The increased incidence of private legislation legalizing informal adoptions reflected profound changes occurring in American society. By the mid-nineteenth century, under the impact of large-scale immigration, urbanization, and the advent of the factory system and wage labor, the compact, stable, agricultural communities of colonial America were giving way to crowded, sprawling, coastal cities. One of the effects of these wrenching economic and social transformations was that both urban and rural poverty became major problems. Consequently, humanitarian and religious child welfare reformers all over the United States turned to large-scale institutions such as public almshouses and private orphanages to reduce the expense of poor relief and, with utopian expectations, to reform, rehabilitate, and educate paupers.[14]

Although private orphanages had existed in six cities before 1800, urban poverty, cholera and yellow fever epidemics, and evidence of child abuse in almshouses provided the impetus for the founding of an additional 164 orphan asylums in the next half-century, 75 of them between 1831 and 1851. In the following twenty years, another 126 private institutions came into existence. Before 1850, the primary aims of these institutions were to withdraw their charges from association with harmful adult influences, tutor boys and girls separately in practical and moral instruction, and then indenture them for apprenticeship or, less typically, place them out for adoption. In the first forty-five years of its existence, for example, the Boston Female Asylum adopted out 4.9 percent of its children.[15]

In the decades that followed, neither almshouses nor orphanages lived up to reformers' expectations. In almshouses, where conditions were abysmal, orphaned, impoverished, abandoned, neglected, or delinquent children were routinely housed with adult criminals, paupers, and the insane. A select committee of the New York State Senate in 1857 reported on the state's almshouses and condemned their "filth, nakedness, licentiousness, general bad morals and disregard of religion and the most common religious observances, as well as a gross neglect of the most ordinary comforts and decencies of life." Similarly, many child welfare reformers became disillusioned by the failure of orphan asylums to reform or rehabilitate their charges. They began attacking these institutions for their high expense, rigid routines, harsh discipline, and failure to produce independent and hard working children. In contrast to the artificial environment of the institution, these reformers extolled "God's orphanage," the family, and its natural ability to produce sociable, independent, and industrious citizens at little expense. Changing attitudes toward the nature of children reinforced reformers' renewed appreciation of the family. Supplanting older Calvinist views of innate evil, infant depravity, and original sin, more optimistic doctrines derived from John Locke and Horace Bushnell emphasized the malleability of children and the importance of the environment in shaping their character. Child reformers' disillusionment with institutions and their newfound belief in the ability of a family environment to shape and reform dependent children lay behind the full-scale home-finding movement (which included foster care, boarding out, and adoption) that gained increasing momentum with child welfare reformers throughout the second half of the nineteenth century.[16]

****

The large-scale placing-out movement inaugurated by the widely imitated CAS had enormous consequences for the history of adoption. The origins of America's first adoption laws can be traced to the increase in the number of middle-class farmers who wished to legalize the addition of a child to the family. By the mid-nineteenth century, state legislatures began enacting the first general, as opposed to private, adoption statutes. These were designed to ease the burden on legislatures caused by the many private adoption acts and to clarify inheritance rights. First enacted in Mississippi in 1846 and Texas in 1850 (states that were originally subject to the laws of France and Spain, respectively), the general adoption statutes were influenced by the civil law tradition embodied in the Napoleonic Code. They merely provided a legal procedure "to authenticate and make a public record of private adoption agreements," analogous to recording a deed for a piece of land.[22]

Alongside adoption by deed, state legislatures began to enact a second type of general adoption statute. The 1851 Massachusetts law, "An Act to Provide for the Adoption of Children," is commonly considered the first modern adoption law. It codified earlier state court decisions that had transformed the law of custody to reflect Americans' new conceptions of childhood and parenthood, which emphasized the needs of children and the contractual and egalitarian nature of spouses' rights of guardianship.[23] The Massachusetts statute differed from all earlier statutes in its emphasis on the welfare of the child—it made the adopted person the prime beneficiary of the proceeding—and the evaluation of the adopters' parental qualifications. The Massachusetts Adoption Act, as it was commonly called, was the first statute to establish the principle of judicial supervision of adoptions. It required the judge to ascertain that the adoptive parents were "of sufficient ability to bring up the child, before issuing the decree, and furnish suitable nurture and education," and that in general the magistrate was satisfied that the adoption was "fit and proper." The concern for the child's welfare drew on the "best interests of the child" doctrine, which had been evolving slowly in custody cases since the early 1800s, and which would become the cornerstone of modem adoption law. The statute also required the written consent of the natural parents, if living, or of the guardian or next of kin if the parents were deceased. The law also ended the power of natural parents over the children they relinquished by severing the legal bonds between them and freeing the child from all legal obligations to them. The enactment of the Massachusetts Adoption Act marked a watershed in the history of Anglo-American family and society. Instead of defining the parent-child relationship exclusively in terms of blood kinship, it encouraged adoptive parents to build a family by assuming the responsibility and emotional outlook of natural parents. In the next quarter-century, the Massachusetts Adoption Act came to be regarded as a model statute, and twenty-five states enacted similar laws.[24]

* * * *

Beginning at the end of the depression of the 1890s and extending to the conclusion of World War I, many Americans responded to the profound strains, widespread misery, and deep class divisions produced by a new industrial society by demanding reforms. Progressivism took the form of a political movement that sought by collective action and government intervention the reorganization and improvement of American life. Originating among a shifting coalition of mostly Protestant, newly professionalized, middle-class men and women, these "evangelistic modernizers," according to John Whiteclay Chambers, "wedded a quasi-religious idealism and scientism in a movement that worked for specific reforms while seeking to restore [America to] a sense of community and common purpose." Progressive reformers engaged in countless national and local campaigns to mitigate the impact of brutal factory conditions, concentrated economic power, corrupt politics, crowded and unsanitary cities, and a newly arrived, heterogeneous immigrant population. In reality members of a set of loosely connected movements, Progressives set about to regulate big business, democratize and reform the political system, aid the urban poor and exploited workers, and impose homogeneous cultural values on the entire population, especially Catholic and Jewish immigrants and blacks.[28]

Progressive reformers were particularly concerned with protecting women and children from the harsh effects of urban and industrial changes. From the 1909 White House Conference on the Care of Dependent Children that proclaimed "home life is the highest and finest product of civilization . . . Children should not be deprived of it except for urgent and compelling reasons" to the 1921 Sheppard Towner Infancy and Maternity Protection Act that provided for federal spending to promote infant and maternal health, the Progressive Era witnessed a flurry of child welfare reforms instituted by Congress and state legislatures. Prominent among these reforms was the establishment of the U.S. Children's Bureau and legislation providing for mothers' pensions. It was also during the Progressive Era that a number of innovative institutions and practices first appeared in the field of adoption. The first private adoption agencies were created; social workers began the long process of professionalization; and social workers sought the aid of the state to regulate adoptions.[30]

Paradoxically, the number of dependent children in institutions nearly doubled during the first three decades of the twentieth century, while adoptions increased slowly. By 1900, breaking up families had become practically taboo, at least in theory, and family preservation had become a fundamental principle among all child-savers. This social work ideal would continue to be axiomatic among professional social workers until the end of World War II. As Galen A. Merrill, a child welfare reformer, noted in 1900 at the twenty-seventh annual meeting of the National Conference of Charities and Correction, ". . . the permanent separation of a child from its natural parents is such a grave matter that it should be permitted only when parents cannot be helped or compelled to meet their obligations as parents."[31] By the early twentieth century, in the effort to prevent Brace's reckless child placing policies, child welfare experts and social workers went to the other extreme and stressed the cultural primacy of the blood bond in family kinship. While they continued to extol the family as superior to the institution, the "family" they now meant was the child's *natural parents*, the family of origin.[32]

It is this emphasis on the preservation of the biological family that above all explains why the number of adopted children failed to increase significantly during the first third of the twentieth century. Rather than break up families, child welfare experts' new strategy was to emphasize the prevention of the causes of child dependency in the first place. To this end, they stressed that families should not be broken up merely because of poverty and that children should be separated from their natural families only as a last resort, for reasons of "inefficiency and immorality."

****

Although the first generation of state laws provided a mechanism for legalizing adoption, they did not compel the state to regulate the transfer of children from one family to another. Consequently, the first private adoption agencies, created at the beginning of the twentieth century, were largely unsupervised by federal or state agencies. Moreover, these amateur child-placing institutions were staffed by nonprofessional volunteers. Wealthy, socially prominent women with little social work training volunteered to care for homeless infants. They soon found themselves running adoption agencies, initially supplying their friends' requests for babies and later expanding their operations to meet childless couples' demands for infants. A number of these private adoption agencies first sprang up in New York City. One of the first was the Alice Chapin Adoption Nursery, started in 1911 by the wife of the prominent pediatrician Dr. Henry Dwight Chapin. Five years later, Mrs. Louise Wise, the wife of the famous Reform rabbi Stephen Wise, sought assistance from three wealthy members of her husband's Reform congregation, the Free Synagogue of New York, to expand and systematize her ad hoc adoption activities. Their financial assistance led to the incorporation of the Child Adoption Committee, which eventually became the largest Jewish adoption agency in New York City, the Louise Wise Services.[38] Similarly, in Chicago, several wealthy businessmen donated the money that permitted Mrs. Florence Dahl Walruth to purchase the residence that became The Cradle Society, Chicago's first adoption agency. Unlike professional social workers, these upper-class female amateurs made little effort to keep families together. They vigorously recommended adoption for children born out of wedlock and, on this issue, were sometimes supported by the influential print media.[39]

A host of other institutions seeking to place for adoption children born out of wedlock engaged in similar dubious practices. These included private maternity homes, family welfare agencies, hospital social service departments, state court probation departments, child protective agencies, and legal aid societies. Doctors and lawyers facilitated private nonagency or independent adoptions, acting as liaisons between childless couples and unmarried mothers trying to avoid social stigma. In many states only a minority of adoptions were regulated. Studies conducted in Massachusetts and New Jersey during the 1920s revealed that only one-quarter to one-third of children adopted in those states were placed by state-licensed child-placing institutions. Moreover, many parents succeeded in circumventing all institutions, whether licensed by the state or not, by advertising in newspapers that their infants were available for adoption. Adding to the disreputable aura of adoption were the commercial maternity homes and baby farms that sold infants born out of wedlock to childless couples. A 1917 study, commissioned by Chicago's Juvenile Protective Association, investigated adoptions and confirmed the worst fears of Progressive reformers. It found that there was "a regular commercialized business of child placing being carried on in the city of Chicago; that there were many maternity hospitals which made regular charges . . . for disposing of unwelcome children; and that there were also doctors and other individuals who took advantage of the unmarried mother willing to pay any amount of money to dispose of the child. No name, address, or reference was required to secure the custody of a child from these people." The combination of cultural, medical, and social stigma surrounding adoption during the first quarter of the twentieth century kept the number of potential adoptive parents relatively low and thus depressed the number of children who were adopted.[40]

* * * *

The initial sign that the old order was changing was the decline during the 1920s and 1930s of the stigma of eugenics surrounding adopted children. In 1924, Sophie van Senden Theis published her pioneering study, *How Foster Children Turn Out*, which reported that 88.1 percent of 269 children placed out for adoption by the New York State Charities Aid Association had made a "capable" social adjustment in adult life, thereby repudiating the eugenicists' claims about the "menace of the feebleminded." By then, medical authorities had distanced themselves from the "science" of eugenics and were embracing the new theories of psychiatry and mental hygiene. Also by the 1930s, adoption agencies routinely administered to children the Stanford revision of the Binet-Simon intelligence test, while popular magazines assured prospective adoptive parents that "the 'danger' of adoption has been largely obviated by scientific advance."[55]

Not only were children represented as "safer" to adopt after 1940, but there were also more of them to adopt. In addition to the continued large number of homes broken by death, divorce, and desertion, there was a veritable demographic revolution in the number of children born out of wedlock. With social bonds loosened by wartime, illegitimacy rates, especially among nonwhites, began to soar and continued their upward flight for the next fifty years. In 1938, 88,000 children were born out of wedlock; a decade later, 129,700; by 1958 the figure had climbed to 201,000, reaching 245,000 by 1962, a 306 percent increase in a quarter-century. The largest increase in the number of out-of-wedlock births occurred among nonwhite mothers, climbing 2.5 times, from 46,700 in 1938 to 130,900 in 1957.[56]

The crucial ingredient in the origins of the revolution in adoption practice was not the increase of supply factors, though these were important, but on the demand side, as childless couples besieged adoption agencies pleading for a child to add to their household. Even before the war years, the nation found itself in an adoption boom. Startled Children's Bureau officials initially attributed the unexpected demand for adopted children to the low birth rate of the Depression years and subsequent wartime prosperity, as previously economically strapped couples found they could now afford to start adoptive families. But it was the baby boom, beginning in the mid 1940s and reaching its peak in the late 1950s, with its dramatic rise in marriages and births, that exacerbated the increased demand for children to adopt and resulted in adoption agencies being inundated with requests for children.

The baby boom was both the cause and the effect of a profound change in the national political culture that tied the security of the nation and personal happiness to an ideology of domesticity and the nuclear family. Parenthood during the Cold War became a patriotic necessity. The media romanticized babies, glorified motherhood, and identified fatherhood with masculinity and good citizenship. The consequences of this celebratory pronatalist mood, as the historian Elaine Tyler May has written, "marginalized the childless in unprecedented ways." Uncomfortable with being childless and the subject of public opprobrium, many of these childless couples sought adoption in record numbers as one solution to their shame of infertility. Contributing to the unprecedented numbers of childless couples applying for children to adopt were new medical treatments—semen examination, tests for tubal patency, and endrometrial biopsies—permitting physicians to diagnose physical sterility more easily and accurately early in marriage.[57]

Wartime prosperity, a postwar pronatalist climate of opinion, and medical advances in infertility diagnosis combined to produce a remarkable increase in the number of applications to adopt a child. In 1937 child welfare officials used incomplete returns to estimate that there were between 16,000 and 17,000 adoptions annually, of which one-third to one-half were adoptions by relatives. By 1945, the Children's Bureau estimated that adoptions had increased threefold, to approximately 50,000 annually; a decade later the number of adoptions had nearly doubled again, to 93,000, and by 1965 climbed to 142,000. In less than thirty years, the number of adoptions had grown nearly ninefold.[58]

In the decade after World War II, this new interest group—white, middle-class, childless couples—overwhelmed the understaffed and underfunded adoption agencies, which had failed to anticipate the increase in adoption applicants. The demand far exceeded the number of available children. By the mid-1950s one expert estimated that of the four and a half million childless couples, fully one million were seeking the approximately 75,000 children available for adoption. By 1957, depending on what region of the nation a prospective adoptive couple inhabited, CWLA executive director Joseph P. Reid estimated that the odds were between 18 to 1 and 10 to 1 against receiving a child.[59]

## Notes

4. John F. Brosnan, "The Law of Adoption," *Columbia Law Review* 22 (1922): 333. These purposes included "preventing the extinction of a bloodline, preserving a sacred descent group, facilitating the generational transfer of a patrimony, providing for ancestral worship, or mending the ties between factious clans or tribes." Jamil S. Zainaldin, "The Emergence of a Modern American Family Law: Child Custody, Adoption, and the Courts," *Northwestern University School of Law* 73 (1979): 1041.

****

6. Jack Goody, *The Development of the Family and Marriage in Europe* (Cambridge: Cambridge University Press, 1983), pp. 71–75. Goody attributes the Church's animus toward adoption to financial advantage. Kristen Elizabeth Gager, *Blood Ties and Fictive Ties: Adoption and Family Life in Early Modern Europe* (Princeton, NJ: Princeton University Press, 1996), pp. 3–7.
7. Michael Grossberg, *Governing the Hearth: Law and the Family in Nineteenth-Century America* (Chapel Hill: University of North Carolina Press, 1985), pp. 268–269.
8. Lawrence A. Cremin, *American Education: The Colonial Experience, 1607–1783.* (New York: Harper & Row, 1970), p. 113.
9. Geraldine Youcha, *Minding the Children: Child Care in America from Colonial Times to the Present* (New York: Scribner, 1995), p. 18; Robert Frances Seybolt, *Apprenticeship and Apprenticeship Education in Colonial New England and New York* (New York: Columbia University Press, 1917). Quotation from Edmund S. Morgan, *The Puritan Family* (New York: Harper & Row, 1943), p. 77.
10. O. Jocelyn Dunlop and Richard D. Denman, *English Apprenticeship and Child Labour* (New York: Macmillan, 1902), pp. 68–71.
11. Seybolt, *Apprenticeship*, p. 34, Homer Folks, *The Care of Destitute, Neglected, and Delinquent Children* (New York: Macmillan, 1902), pp. 10–11. The 7.3 percent represented approximately 173 out of a possible pool of 3,123 children per year. See Holly Brewer, "Constructing Consent: How Children's Status in Political Theory Shaped Public Policy in Virginia, Pennsylvania, and Massachusetts before and after the Revolution" (Ph.D. diss., University of California, Los Angeles, 1994), p. 385.
12. John Demos, *A Little Commonwealth: Family Life in Plymouth Colony* (New York: Oxford University Press, 1970): p. 89; Joseph Ben-Or, "The Law of Adoption in the United States: Its Massachusetts Origins and the Statute of 1851," *New England Historical and Genealogical Register* 130 (1976): 260, 265; Yasuhide Kawashima, "Adoption in Early America," *Journal of Family Law* 20 (1981–1982); Zainaldin, "Modern American Family Law," pp. 1084–1085.
13. Quoted in Helen L. Witmer et al., *Independent Adoptions: A Follow-up Study* (New York: Russell Sage Foundation 1963), p. 29, n. 1. Zainaldin, "Modern American Family Law," p. 1043, n. 12, correctly identifies the name as "Blair," not "Bair," as Whitmer has it.
14. David M. Rothman, *The Discovery of the Asylum: Social Order and Disorder in the New Republic* (Boston: Little, Brown, 1971); William I. Trattner, *From Poor Law to Welfare State: A History of Social Welfare in America*, 5th ed. (New York: Free Press, 1994), ch. 4.
15. Susan Lynne Porter, "The Benevolent Asylum—Image and Reality: The Care and Training of Female Orphans in Boston, 1800–1840" (Ph.D. diss., Boston

University, 1984), p. 198. Statistics on orphanages from Timothy Andrew Hasci, "'A Plain and Solemn Duty': A History of Orphan Asylums in America" (Ph.D. diss., University of Pennsylvania, 1993), Appendix A1.

16. New York State Senate, "Report of the Select Committee Appointed to Visit Charitable Institutions Supported by the Senate, 1857," in Robert H. Bremner, ed. *Children and Youth in America: A Documentary History* (Cambridge: Harvard University Press, 1971), vol. 1, p. 648; Bernard Wishy, *The Child and the Republic: The Dawn of Modern American Child* (Philadelphia: University of Pennsylvania Press, 1968), ch. 2–3; Susan Tiffin, *Whose Best Interest? Child Welfare Reform in the Progressive Era* (Westport, CT: Greenwood Press, 1982), chs. 3–4.

****

22. Stephen B. Presser, "The Historical Background of the American Law of Adoption," *Journal of Family Law* 11 (1971–1972): 474; Grossberg, *Governing the Hearth*, p. 271. As early as 1808, Louisiana's legal code contained an adoption statute, but in 1825 it was abolished. Ibid., p. 270.
23. Zainaldin, "Modern American Family Law," pp. 1084–1085.
24. *Acts and Resolves Passed by the General Court of Massachusetts*, 1851, ch. 324 (Boston, 1851), p. 816; Zainaldin, "Modern American Family Law," pp. 1042–1043, 1085; Witmer et al., *Independent Adoptions*, pp. 30–31.
28. George Harrison Durand, "The Study of the Child from the Standpoint of the Home-Finding Agency," *PNCCC* (Indianapolis: William P. Burford, 1907), pp. 259–260, quotation on p. 259.
29. John Whiteclay Chambers II, *The Tyranny of Change: America in the Progressive Era, 1890–1920*, 2nd ed. (New York: St. Martin's Press, 1992), pp. 140–150, quotation on p. 140.
30. "Letter to the President of the United States Embodying the Conclusions of the Conference on the Care of Dependent Children," Proceedings of the [1909] *Conference on the Care of Dependent Children* in Robert H. Bremner, ed., *Children and Youth: A Documentary History* (Cambridge: Harvard University Press, 1971), vol. 2, p. 365; Theda Skocpol, *Protecting Soldiers and Mothers: The Political Origins of Social Policy in the United States* (Cambridge: Harvard University Press, 1992), ch. 9; Robyn Muncy, *Creating a Female Dominion in American Reform, 1890–1935* (New York: Oxford University Press, 1991), chs. 2, 4.
31. E. Wayne Carp, "Orphanages vs. Adoption: The Triumph of Biological Kinship, 1800–1933," in Donald T. Critchlow and Hal H. Parker, eds., *With Us Always A History of Private Charity and Public Welfare* (Lanham, MD: Rowman and Littlefield, 1998), pp. 125–147; E. Wayne Carp, "Professional Social Workers, Adoption, and the Problem of Illegitimacy, 1915–1945," *Journal of Policy History* 6, no. 3 (1994); Galen A. Merrill, "Some Recent Developments in Child-Saving," *PNCCC* (Boston: Geo. H. Ellis, 1900), p. 226.
32. Other historians have noticed this radical change in child-savers' strategies, but none has attributed it to Brace's child-placing practices. See, for example, Michael B. Katz, *In the Shadow of the Poorhouse: A Social History of Welfare in America* (New York: Basic Books, 1986), ch. 5; Molly Ladd-Taylor, *Mother-Work: Women, Child Welfare, and the State, 1890–1930* (Urbana· University of Illinois Press, 1994), p. 137. This doesn't mean that other factors were not at work. Katz attributes the change to "psychology, sentiment, anxiety, and male backlash" (*In the Shadow of the Poorhouse*, ch. 5, esp. p. 124).

****

38. Romanofsky, "Early History of Adoption Practices," pp. 117–123; quotation on p. 119.
39. Carp, "Problem of Illegitimacy," p. 170.
40. Ibid.; Slingerland, *Child-Placing in Families*, pp. 168–169.

****

55. Sophie van Senden Theis, *How Foster Children Turn Out* (New York: State Charities Aid Association, 1924), p. 124. Theis defined "capable" as "subjects who are law abiding, who manage their affairs with good sense and are living in accordance with good moral standards of their communities" (p. 22). James W Trent, *Inventing the Feeble Mind: A History of Mental Retardation in the United States* (Berkeley: University of California Press, 1994), pp. 181–182; Helen D. Sargent, "Is it Safe to Adopt a Child" *PM* 10 (October 1935): 26; "Adopting a Baby," *Women's Journal* 14 (July 1929): 10.
56. Clark Vincent, "Illegitimacy in the Next Decade: Trends and Implications," *CW* 43 (December 1964): 515.
57. Catherine MacKenzie, "A Boom in Adoptions," *NYTM*, Nov. 10, 1940, pp. 6–7, 29; Elaine Tyler May, *Barren in the Promised Land: Childless Americans and the Pursuit of Happiness* (New York: Basic Books, 1995), pp. 127–140, 156, quotation on p. 129; Richard Frank, "What the Adoption Worker Should Know about Infertility," *CW* 35 (February 1956): 1–5; Harvey Uhlenhopp, "Adoption in Iowa," *Iowa Law Review* 40 (Winter 1955): 228, n. 4. Media perception of the percentage of childless couples—15 to 17 percent—was inaccurate. As two scholars have recently noted: "The 1950s had an actual childlessness rate among married couples of less than 10 percent, the lowest proportion of childless Americans for nearly a century." See Margaret Marsh and Wanda Ronner, *The Empty Cradle: Infertility in America from Colonial Times to the Present* (Baltimore: John Hopkins University Press, 1996), pp. 186–187.
58. Sophie van Senden Theis, "Adoption," *Social Work Year Book* 4 (New York: Russell Sage Foundation, 1937), p. 23; I. Evelyn Smith, "Adoption," ibid. 9 (1947), p. 24.
59. Michael Schapiro, *A Study of Adoption Practice* (New York: CWLA, 1956), vol. 1, p. 10. Such statistics were reported in popular magazines. See Alice Lake, "Babies for the Brave," *Saturday Evening Post*, July 31, 1954, p. 27; Reid quoted in Dorothy Barclay, "Adoption Agencies: Pro and Con" *NYTM*, Feb. 17, 1957, p. 42.

# From Modell, Judith. "Natural Bonds, Legal Boundaries: Modes of Persuasion in Adoption Rhetoric." *Imagining Adoption: Essays on Literature and Culture*, edited by Marianne Novy, U of Michigan P, 2003, pp. 207–230.

"I'm not looking for a family. I'm looking for roots. That's so important," a young adopted woman told me. She explained: "Roots means where we came from, who looks like me. It's completing the circle to have it."[27] The importance of a notion of "roots" to adoptee searches is well documented.[28] The concept also serves a rhetorical function, raising the pursuit of one's origins to a plane higher than curiosity, interest, and even the need for family history. The 1977 presentation of Alex Haley's *Roots* on television dramatized for a vast U.S. audience the idea that ancestry is something sacred and not just secular—something above the law in that sense. After *Roots*, ethnic background was seen as essential to identity—not a package of superficial traits, but absolutely crucial to who a person is. After *Roots*, the arguments made within the adoptee search movement touched the wider American public.

In the rhetoric of the adoptee search movement, knowing one's heritage and ethnicity contributes to the formation of an integrated identity. Information about and connections with those who came before complete the circle of the self—a position that accords with American cultural theories of identity formation. Linking ancestry to identity and self-fulfillment also rearranges cultural interpretations of the bonds of kinship, and this is central to the way a search solidifies an adoptee's ties to "two families."

The theme in adoptee accounts is that a search integrates the self. A search does not disintegrate the bonds within an adoptive family. The emphasis on self formation and strengthening one's identity takes search stories away from a quest for a "new family" or a search for "other parents." The implication instead is that completing the circle means becoming newly bound to previously known relatives, or, to put it another way, attached to the several roots of one's being.

Karen's narrative about finding her birth mother stressed the good it did her and her adoptive family. Gaining more self-confidence from finding her

DOI: 10.4324/9781003203827-4

roots, she told the group, allowed her to attach more closely to her adoptive family. "I think that it [searching] was something that I had to do for me and if it was selfish, I am sorry. It has done me more good than anything else in the whole world." In an *ASG [Adoptee Support Group] Newsletter* (January 1991), she wrote: "Our adoptive mothers hold our hands and are in our hearts forever. . . . Our birth mothers are always in our hearts so all we really need is to hold their hand for just a little while. There is no competition here because each plays an important role in our lives."

As Karen's story illustrates, an emphasis on self-fulfillment removes the perceived threat that searching poses to an adoptive family. The claim that searching has to do with oneself confronts a powerful objection to releasing adoption records, that when an adoptee meets a birth family she or he will desert the adoptive family. In responding to the critique, adoptee narratives further elaborate the complex meaning that *bond* already has. A concept of roots justified the search for one's own ethnic and ancestral past and for, ultimately, the sources of one's being. What came in the next round referred more closely to heritage as biological. Not precisely defined, "biology" stood for the aspect of one's identity linked to genes and the physical traits one inherits from blood relatives. "I want to see a face that has similar genes to mine." Statements like this deny the intrusion of a search into existing kinship ties; they also connect searching with contemporary articulations of the significance of genetics to who one is and will become.

An adoptee told me she was searching for her birth mother to find out why she looked the way she did—"because of this big hole, and you have to jump over it every single day, cause there's a whole big gap in your life." Another adopted person remarked: "But it just kept eating at me, you know. Mostly all my cousins looked like their sisters and brothers." As the founder of ALMA, Florence Fisher, put it: "Blood. Yes, who you look like and walk like are more than idle curiosity. Blood."[29] Whether phrased in the symbolism of blood or in the recent vocabulary of genetics and DNA, the notion of a biological template connects adoptee search narratives to a modern discourse of identity and of rights—the right not to be denied the knowledge of who you inherently are.

But adoption is a matter of kinship, and references to roots represent the kind of kinship an adopted person uniquely experiences. Search narratives describe a double-rootedness and the enduringly dual attachments that make up an adoptee's life. Rooted to a genealogical ancestry, the adoptee is not less but more tightly bound to her adoptive family. First a botanical term, then a cultural term, *roots* captures the distinctiveness of adoptive kinship, the need continuously to bridge biology and environment, blood and contract. The intertwining was noticeable in the stories told at ASG meetings. There, search narratives presented two forms of genuine kinship, one begun by birth and the other initiated by contract. The former evokes the transcendental law of nature, viewed as mystical and often described as sacred; the latter represents the power of secular law, itself sacralized in references to "the law of the land."

Adoptee narratives effected a reinterpretation of kinship by recognizing different levels of law. If trying to locate a birth parent broke the boundaries of state law, narratives showed the quest did not violate *all* law. In the framework of search rhetoric, adoption is a "man-made" contract of kinship, not the highest law binding on a person. At the same time, adoptees recognized the value of secular law for inscribing and maintaining relationships between individuals.

****

The gist of the argument that emerged from ASG stories, the *ASG Newsletter*, Karen's letters to the editors of local newspapers, and her media appearances was a reconsideration of the meaning of contracted parent-child relationships. Assessing the meaning of the contract that establishes the relationship between an adoptee and her or his adoptive parents, adoptive discourse connects the terms *contract* and *person* to their sources in American history and tradition. Traditionally, in America a contract promises freedom of signature and freedom of revocation. On the one hand, no one ought to be bound by a contract he or she did not sign; on the other hand, a contract pledges ongoing loyalty and obligation between those who agree to its terms. In the adoption reform argument, a person (no longer the "adopted child") cannot be bound by terms to which he or she did not agree. Simultaneously, entered into freely, a contract holds persons together through ties based on trust and shared concerns.

With play on its literal and legal definitions, the term *contract* is used as a symbol in adoptee discourse. As a symbol, *contract* expands the meanings and the implications of adoptive kinship, for the individual and for the culture. With the concept of contract, adoptees argue for the preservation of personhood in adoptive arrangements and for the enduring solidarity of significant relationships.

The adoption reform movement essentially demands that the historical implications of contract be incorporated into the arrangement of adoptive kinship. This may mean opening adoption at the onset—allowing all (adult) parties freedom in drawing up a contract, a freedom that requires the exchange of information and trust.[37] In the framework of the reform movement, a recognition of the full (and fully cultural) meaning of contract logically demands an extension to postadoptive relationships. Adoptive kinship and the identity of the adopted person are ongoing processes, requiring a continual "openness" about the clauses of the contract. As much symbolic as legal, *contract* represents a form of negotiation, done with honesty and dignity and recognizing personal autonomy. Moreover, the concept of contract releases the concept of bond from the connotations of being barred or imprisoned either in a genealogical or a socially constructed relationship.

The lesson of adoption reform rhetoric extends into a critique of dominant ideologies of kinship in an American cultural context. An emphasis on bonds, rights, and privileges links a concept of the person to an interpretation of being related. This link shifts "being related" away from the assumption of one absolute, impermeable, and fixed (whether by law or by birth) connection between individuals. The language of adoption reform links kinship with self-identity and with the full status of person in an American setting, while not narrowing the meaning of adoption reform, then, reforms the cultural conceptualization of kinship.

Adoptees who search are not attacking adoption. Rather, the demand for open records and for an end to sealed documents, anonymity, and the mutual invisibility of birth and adoptive families pushes adoption to its best incarnation, where freedom of information does not alienate but attaches *persons* to one another. The demand for contact and communication is a logical extension of another. The demand for contact and communication is a logical extension of contracted kinship, exploiting the potential of a contract to be continually reviewed and negotiated. Ironically, through the force of their rhetoric and the effectiveness of their modes of persuasion, reform groups comprised of adoptees and birth parents may succeed in radically redefining American kinship even if they fail to repeal specific state laws.

## Notes

27. Quoted in Modell, *Kinship with Strangers*, 143.
28. Most recently and thoroughly by Carp, in *Family Matters*.
29. Florence Fisher, *The Search for Anna Fisher* (New York: Arthur Fields, 1973).

****

37. See Modell, "Open Adoption: Extending Families, Exchanging Information," in *New Directions in Anthropological Kinship*, ed. Linda Stone (London: Routledge, Kegan Paul, 1998).

## Works Cited

Carp, E. Wayne. *Family Matters: Secrecy and Disclosure in the History of Adoption.* Harvard UP, 1998.

Fisher, Florence. *The Search for Anna Fisher*. A. Fields, 1973.

Modell, Judith. *Kinship with Strangers: Adoption and Interpretations of Kinship in American Culture*. U of California P, 1994.

———. "Open Adoption: Extending Families, Exchanging Information." *New Directions in Anthropological Kinship*, edited by Linda Stone, Routledge, Kegan Paul, 1998, pp. 246–263.

# From Leighton, Kimberly. "Addressing the Harms of Not Knowing One's Heredity: Lessons from Genealogical Bewilderment." *Adoption & Culture*, vol. 3, 2005, pp. 63–107.

Harm is prominently conceptualized in current discussions of the ethics of anonymous gamete donation through a comparison to adoption.[3] In many arguments supporting the prohibition of AGD [anonymous gamete donation], critics contend that, analogous to adoptees who have suffered from policies of closed adoption that deny them access to their original birth certificates, people who were donor-conceived suffer from policies of anonymity that deny them access to information about the identities of the donor(s) involved.[4]

More specifically, opponents of AGD are borrowing from adoption literature the concept of genealogical bewilderment. The emotional need to know that many people who were donor-conceived (or were adopted) express is considered by critics to be evidence of the need to end anonymous gamete donation. "Genealogical bewilderment" is the means by which such opponents of AGD recognize the desire to know as entailing an important moral interest, the interest in not being harmed in the way that is believed to follow from not having knowledge of one's genetic heritage. According to Naomi Cahn, a prominent critic of anonymous gamete donation, "[l]ike adoptees, children of donated gametes may feel a sense of 'genealogical bewilderment,' a feeling that they are confused about their identity and different from other children" (*Test Tube* 256).

First developed in the 1950s and 1960s to explain what psychologists Erich Wellisch and H. J. Sants considered the maladjustment of their adopted patients, genealogical bewilderment is purportedly a condition people suffer from when they do not know their genetic parents. According to Sants's much-cited 1964 article, "Genealogical Bewilderment in Children with Substitute Parents," a "genealogically bewildered child is one who either has no knowledge of his natural parents or only uncertain knowledge of them. The resulting state of confusion and uncertainty, it will be argued, fundamentally undermines his security and thus affects his mental health" (133).[5] For Wellisch and Sants, adoptees suffer genealogical bewilderment because their lack of knowledge of their natural or hereditary parents leads

DOI: 10.4324/9781003203827-5

to their having compromised psyches. This result is not an outcome of adoptees' bad genes, as earlier skeptics of adoption might have claimed, but an effect of how adoptees do not know the genes they come from.[6] In this way, the diagnosis of genealogical bewilderment seems to displace former worries about the harmful effects of illegitimacy onto worries about the effects of adoption itself.

The fundamental claim of genealogical bewilderment, that children suffer from not knowing—and not being raised by—their "real" parents, has been accepted by many in the adoption community. Following Wellisch and Sants, later psychologists of adoption have relied on genealogical bewilderment to explain the difficult adolescences they saw their adopted patients experience (e.g., Brodzinsky, Schechter, and Henig), and adoption activists have used the term in their efforts to articulate what they believe are the harms of closed adoption (e.g., Lifton, *Lost*). Through such applications of the term, genealogical bewilderment has become incorporated into the way many within and outside of the adoption community understand adoption.

This paper is an attempt to stymie what seems to be the general and growing acceptance of the idea that children who do not know their biological or genetic parents are necessarily harmed by that lack of information. I do not doubt that some people who do not have information about the people to whom they are genetically related experience distress.[7] But I am troubled by what I see as the assumptions underlying the belief in genealogical bewilderment and the implications of the argument that supports the claim that genealogical bewilderment is a real phenomenon directly caused by not knowing one's genetic genealogy. The normative framework assumed by the diagnosis of genealogical bewilderment has not been made explicit enough for us to recognize how the concept of genealogical bewilderment and the reality ascribed to it are actually part of the cause of the distress people experience rather than a means to alleviate that distress.

A close analysis of the two classic texts on genealogical bewilderment reveals that at their heart is a foundational commitment to a particular view of what a family is and, based on this view, a judgment as to what a *good* family is. The argument behind the claim that adoptees necessarily suffer from genealogical bewilderment is that a child needs to know the genealogy of his *genetic* family because only with knowledge of heredity can a child develop into a normal adult with a healthy psyche. My primary argument here is that rather than addressing the feelings of those who are distraught over what they do not know about their genetic relatives in a way that might resolve those feelings, the diagnosis "genealogical bewilderment" is itself generative of the very conditions of such suffering. If we consider it morally important to address the harms people such as adoptees and the donor-conceived report experiencing feeling in relation to what they do not know about the people to whom they are genetically related, then we must resist using genealogical bewilderment as a way to appreciate those harms.

My analysis of Wellisch's and Sants's arguments for genealogical bewilderment reveals how the reasoning behind genealogical bewilderment produces the very phenomenon it believes itself to be explaining:

The fundamental claim of genealogical bewilderment (GB) is:

Children who do not know their genetic genealogies are necessarily dysfunctional because they lack such knowledge.

The argument for GB is:

1. Genealogy of genetic ancestry provides us with knowledge about ourselves, i.e., our heredity;
2. The knowledge about ourselves that a genealogy of genetic ancestry provides is knowledge of who we really are, i.e., our identity;
3. Normal psychological development requires knowledge of identity;
4. Normal psychological development requires knowledge of heredity.

The implicit assumption in the argument is that not just *any* knowledge of identity will satisfy the third premise; it has to be the kind of knowledge that tells us who we *really* are. But even if this is the case, how do we know that heredity provides such knowledge? The only evidence that the originators of genealogical bewilderment provide to support GB is, in fact, what they consider to be the dysfunctional behavior of those who do not know their heredity. Those who do not know their heredity can never *really* know who they *really* are; that this uncertainty impedes normal psychological development can be seen in adoptees, for adoptees exhibit confusion about their identities and a desire to know who they really are, symptoms of "genealogical bewilderment." Adoptees can never be sure of who they are because only those who know their heredity have such certainty, and such certainty defends against the pathologies that come with an uncertain heredity.

The circularity of reasoning behind the claim of genealogical bewilderment has been noted by critics of the term in relation to gamete donation. Iain Walker, Pia Broderick, and Helen Correia, for example, contend that through persistent referencing to genealogical bewilderment, "it has become an uncritically accepted 'fact' that children will be psychologically damaged by it" (273). Counter to the dominant view held by the psychology and medical establishments in Australia, the researchers hold "that couples and individuals conceiving children using donated gametes or embryos have been inadvertently misled by counsellors regarding the dangers of genetic unrelatedness, and in fact their children are unlikely to suffer the emotional disturbances described as a result of their use of donated genetic material" (273). Since parents using gamete donation receive counseling that encourages the expectation that their children will be dysfunctional because the families are not genetically related, it is difficult to determine the central cause of donor-conceived children's psychological struggles. The fact that the experts' recommendations promote the idea that the ideal family is genetically related no doubt affects how parents understand and value the family they make through assisted reproduction.

The critique of genealogical bewilderment offered by Walker, Broderick, and Correia is based on the lack of supporting data behind the diagnosis, as well as on the regulatory effects of using the concept of genealogical bewilderment in the political context of assisted reproductive technology. Their main target seems to be what Walker and Broderick refer to in another article as the "attempts to reproduce psychology" (38).[8] At the heart of their criticism of the idea of genealogical bewilderment is what they see as a conflation of two concepts, genealogy and genetics: "Wellisch uses the concepts of genetics and genealogy interchangeably, to refer to genetic relatedness. However, 'genealogy' is a socially constructed bond between people linked as a family, while 'genetic linkages' are clear consanguineal links between people who may or may not be family linked in any traditional social manner. This confusion persists in the literature, and is at the basis of therapeutic recommendations by counselors" (274–75).

I do not disagree with the criticism of genealogical bewilderment offered by Walker, Broderick, and Correia, but I think their analysis stops short in its pursuit of why Wellisch and Sants confuse their terms. As I argue here, the earlier authors' conflation of (social) genealogy and (genetic) ancestry belies their deeper anxieties about the practice of adoption as a means of family-making that places children "born to" some people into the lives and families of others. The ultimate confusion that is the origin of genealogical bewilderment belongs not to adoptees who do not know who their "real parents" are, but to theorists such as Wellisch and Sants who recognize that adoption unsettles our understanding of family (Wellisch 41). A close reading of Wellisch's brief presentation of the harm of being "without genealogy" reveals his investment in a metaphysics of race. Without knowledge of our genetic ancestry, we can know neither the race that we are nor the race of the children we might produce, effectively undermining, moreover, our natural urge to reproduce. The harm that Wellisch alleges adoptees suffer because of what *they* don't know, I contend, is a displacement of the harm he sees resulting from the spreading (acceptance) of adoption. Without clear and certain knowledge of genetic genealogy, the epistemology of race as a means of assigning categories of identity to groups of individuals, based on their heredity, falls apart.

****

The assumption here is that no matter who raises us, we still have the urge to follow the tradition of the family we were born to. The urge might be general to all human beings, but one's individual urge is specified by one's "real" family—that is, by one's membership in a tradition, a term by which Wellisch means race and ethnicity. If we don't know what our real race and ethnicity are, then, even if we reproduce and even if we think we are reproducing our tradition (e.g., in the case where an adoptee has never been told of her adoption), we will not fulfill the urge. Wellisch is claiming here that not only is there a drive to sexually reproduce, there is also in us a drive to sexually reproduce something that is born into us, i.e., to reproduce our race.

To be clear: the harm of being without genealogy, for Wellisch, is not that without it we cannot reproduce. The claim here is that without knowing our genealogy, we can't know what it is that we are reproducing. Not only should we reproduce our tradition, we should know we are reproducing our tradition. Uncertainty about our so-called real parents would not be a problem unless the racial logic of heredity Wellisch is assuming included a desire for race itself. There are two threats to the urge that not knowing one's real parents seem to pose: without knowing what my real race is, I could be passing—and so could my child—as a member of the race I think I am, even if I have a different heredity. Thus, the reproduction of race is tampered with: there is no clear correlation between the race I seem to be and the race I really am. Second, without knowing what my real race is, I could have a child with someone who is the race I think I am. Our child would then not only not be a member of the race we think we are; he would be a mixing of the races, and, by definition for Wellisch, a child has only one tradition. Thus rather than simply not knowing his true genealogy, an adoptee suffers because he cannot satisfy the desire to reproduce race. This urge to reproduce race is so strong, for Wellisch, that not knowing their real parents can cause adoptees to be bewildered such that they become maladjusted. "In light of these considerations," Wellisch writes, "it is understandable that there are cases of maladjustment in children which show that the deprivation of a child's knowledge of his genealogy can have harmful consequences" (42).

The causal claim that ignorance of one's genetic genealogy results in the harm that is genealogical bewilderment thus relies upon a specific commitment to the view that race is something that both is and should be reproduced. It is psychologically harmful not to know one's "real" parents because individuals' bodies aim toward this reproduction. The psychological literature Wellisch references and draws from might get us to the claim that our body-images are affected by not knowing the people whose gametes were used in our conception. But Wellisch's argument that we need to know our "real" parents relies on the additional normative claim that psychological health requires the reproduction of our real race.

## Notes

3. Naomi Cahn, a prominent opponent of anonymous gamete donation, makes explicit that the harm of anonymous gamete donation, like that of (closed) adoption, comes from how the practice results in a kind of genetic ignorance: "both donor-conceived children and adoptees experience the same lack of connection with at least one-half of their genetic heritages. . . . It is this lack of knowledge about their biological progenitors, and the emotional needs for this knowledge that many adoptees and donor offspring articulate, that has motivated advocates within each movement to push for disclosure, and that motivates this article's call for a national, mandatory registry" (208).

   Michelle Dennison's argument against anonymous gamete donation makes full use of genealogical bewilderment to make her claim: she references the term to describe the donor-conceived, she compares the experiences of the donor-conceived to adoptees, and she cites the "adoption research" that has been done on genealogical bewilderment, referring to Sants. In addition to relying on the claim that knowing the identity of the donor will help instrumentally with the child's medical health, Dennison brings into view the fundamental claim of genealogical bewilderment, arguing that having information about the donor will in itself be healthier for the donor-conceived: "Another compelling reason for granting donor-conceived offspring access to identifying information is the argument that information about one's biological and genetic history is considered essential to the child's mental health. A useful comparison to make when considering this argument is between donor-conceived children and adopted children. Adoption research has shown that strong feelings of insecurity can arise in adoptees because they lack information about one or more biological parent. One researcher defined adoptees as 'genealogically bewildered' and argued that 'a genealogically bewildered child is one who either has no knowledge of his natural parents or only uncertain knowledge of them. The ensuing state of confusion and uncertainty fundamentally undermines his security and affects his mental health' " (8).
4. The analogy between adoptees and people who were donor-conceived is not only coming from critics of donor-conception. Activists for adoption reform also invoke the comparison. In her preface to *Lost and Found: The Adoption Experience*, for example, Betty Jean Lifton uses a comparison between adoptees and children conceived using medical assistance to make her point that her analysis of the harms caused by closed adoption is still relevant today. "Those brave new babies conceived by reproductive technologies that bypass Mother Nature's old-fashioned recipe for creating life through the physical act of lovemaking, with or without the ingredient of love, will experience the same sense of alienation and bewilderment if the circumstances of their birth and full knowledge of their heritage are denied them" (x). She goes on to point out that the ultimate cause of the harm to such "brave new babies" comes not from being genetically unrelated to their parents—who might have used their egg and sperm for the conception, in fact. Such children are harmed because "they will be raised *as if* they were born to both in a natural way, rather through the intervention of scientific engineering" (x). Her argument against closed adoption cannot simply be based on the possible harms that come from lying to a child. The information not told has to *matter*. Lifton must understand bewilderment as a product of the very method by which a child was conceived, or else whether a child was told he was conceived inside or outside of a woman's body would be irrelevant, especially when the former method, as she herself notes, can be done "with or without the ingredient

of love" and surely without meaning to. To the contrary, like with adoption, it is impossible for any couple—of any gender mix—to go through the required steps of making a child using medically assisted reproduction to do so *un*-intentionally, and it is hard to imagine them undertaking such arduous steps to make a family without at least a modicum [of] love.

5. The origin of the term *genealogical bewilderment* is commonly misattributed to Erich Wellisch, most likely because Sants states this to be the case: "The term *genealogical bewilderment* was first used by Wellisch (1952), who became interested in the fact that an apparently large number of adopted children had been referred to the child guidance clinic at which he and the present writer were then working" (133). The letter, however, makes no mention of the phrase itself, leaving Sants as its actual originator, from what this author's research suggests.
6. For an analysis of the idea that adoptees were dangerous because they were "bad seeds," see Herman, *Kinship*.
7. For examples of people who were donor-conceived discussing the suffering they believe they have experienced due to the facts of their conception, see McWhinnie; and Hewitt.
8. The main target of Walker, Broderick, and Correia's criticism is psychology's role in the processes involved in medically assisted reproduction. In their 2011 article, "The Psychology of Assisted Reproduction—Or Psychology Assisting its Reproduction," the authors question what they see as the " 'therapeutic injunction' " of psychology whereby psychological counseling is believed to be necessary for people seeking reproductive medical assistance (38). "[P]sychology has been guilty of proceeding in the absence of sound theory and sound research. It has failed to practice its own ideal of the scientist-practitioner model. It has also failed to see, let alone question, the many assumptions it makes about fertility and infertility, about parenthood, and about families. It has assumed for itself the mantle of benevolent expert, and sometimes advocate of unborn children's rights, without ever being appointed expert or advocate, without developing the necessary knowledge to be expert, and without any challenge being made by society, psychologists, or others, to its presumed expertise or right to advocate" (42). Their article concludes, "psychology and psychologists have been attempting to reproduce psychology, perhaps at the expense of developing a better understanding of the psychology of reproduction" (38).

## Works Cited

Brodzinsky, David M., et al. *Being Adopted: The Lifelong Search for Self.* Doubleday, 1992.

Cahn, Naomi. "Necessary Subjects: The Need for a Mandatory National Donor Gamete Databank." *DePaul Journal of Health Care Law*, vol. 12, no. 1, 2009, pp. 203–223.

———. *Test Tube Families: Why the Fertility Market Needs Legal Regulation.* NYUP, 2009.

Dennison, Michelle. "Revealing Your Sources: The Case for Non-Anonymous Gamete Donation." *Cleveland State University Journal of Law and Health*, vol. 21, no. 1, 2008, pp. 1–27.

Herman, Ellen. *Kinship By Design: A History of Adoption in the Modern United States.* Chicago UP, 2008.

Hewitt, Geraldine. "Missing Links: Identity Issues of Donor-Conceived People." *Journal of Fertility Counselling*, vol. 9, no. 3, 2002, pp. 14–20.
Lifton, Betty Jean. *Lost and Found: The Adopted Experience*. Harper & Row, 1988.
McWhinnie, Alexina. "Gamete Donation and Anonymity: Should Offspring From Donated Gametes Continue to be Denied Knowledge of Their Origins and Antecedents?" *Human Reproduction*, vol. 16, 2001, pp. 807–817.
Sants, H. J. "Genealogical Bewilderment in Children with Substitute Parents." *British Journal of Medical Psychology*, vol. 37, 1964, pp. 133–141.
Walker, Iain, et al. "Conceptions and Misconceptions: Social Representations of Medically Assisted Reproduction." *Social Representations and Identity: Content, Process, and Power*, edited by G. Moloney and Iain Walker, Palgrave Macmillan, 2007, pp. 267–300.
Wellisch, Erich. "Children Without Genealogy—A Problem of Adoption." *Mental Health*, vol. 13, no. 1, 1952, pp. 41–42.

# From Roberts, Dorothy. *Torn Apart: How the Child Welfare System Destroys Black Families—and How Abolition Can Build a Safer World.* Basic, 2022.

Two decades ago, a landmark case in New York federal court seemed to signal change. In January 1999, Sharwline Nicholson, a thirty-two-year-old Black mother of two young children, waited at her Brooklyn apartment for Claude Barnett, the father of her three-year-old daughter, to arrive from South Carolina. Her daughter was asleep in a crib, and her eight-year-old son from a previous relationship was at school. Nicholson planned to tell Barnett she was breaking off their long-distance arrangement. When she delivered the news, Barnett erupted in rage and began to beat her, battering her face and fracturing her arm and ribs. Nicholson called 911 as soon as Barnett left and asked a neighbor who had babysat for her in the past to take care of her children while she was in the hospital. Three police officers came to her hospital room to inquire about the incident, and Nicholson arranged with them to take her children to stay with relatives while she recuperated. Instead, Nicholson learned the following day, while still hospitalized, that ACS had placed her children in foster care with strangers.

"When I called 911, I was bleeding so badly I knew I needed medical attention," Sharwline Nicholson would recall. "I didn't know I'd end up down that road, that calling for help would escalate and I'd end up losing my kids." ACS took her children despite the fact that they never saw Barnett assault their mother. Besides, Barnett didn't have keys to Nicholson's apartment and lived hundreds of miles away—the reason why a judge had previously denied Nicholson's application for an order of protection against him.[14]

In July 2001, federal judge Jack Weinstein heard testimony in a class action lawsuit brought by Nicholson and other survivors of domestic violence who alleged that New York City child welfare officials violated their constitutional rights by taking custody of their children. During the twenty-four-day trial, April Rodriguez told the judge that ACS had put her three children, ages seven, three, and one, in foster care when she called the police to report abuse by the father of two of the children. The agency refused to return them until Rodriguez moved into a shelter, forcing her to lose her

DOI: 10.4324/9781003203827-6

job at a Manhattan video store. Although the children spent only a week in foster care, Rodriguez testified that "they weren't the same children" when they returned. "My baby's shirt was filthy and her diaper was disgusting," she said. "My son, his face was bruised and bloody, and he had pus coming from his lip."

But it was the testimony of Nicholson's caseworker that seemed to turn the case in favor of the survivors. He admitted that the city's policy had more to do with policing the mothers than protecting their children. He didn't consider Nicholson to be neglectful, nor did he bother to file a petition in family court until three business days after he placed her children in foster care. The purpose of taking the children, he conceded, was to coerce Nicholson into compliance. "After a few days of the children being in foster care," he explained, "the mother will usually agree to ACS's conditions for their return without the matter even going to court." It was plain for everyone to see that "ACS is just like the batterers," recalled the lead attorney for the plaintiffs, Carolyn Kubitschek. Once again, child welfare agents took children hostage to assert control over their mothers—at the expense of the family's safety.[15]

Judge Weinstein responded to the testimony in March 2002 by issuing a preliminary injunction in *Nicholson v. Williams*, ordering ACS to stop its practice of removing children solely because their mothers were victims of domestic violence. In a blistering opinion, the judge castigated ACS for blaming mothers who had done nothing wrong instead of providing the means to protect themselves and their children. "As a matter of policy and practice, ACS does not merely fail to advance the best interests of children by these unnecessary separations—they harm children," Judge Weinstein wrote. He concluded, "The removals of abused mothers' children, even when summarily approved by a court based on ACS representations, infringe on mothers' substantive due process rights." The city could no longer "penalize a mother, not otherwise unfit, who is battered by her partner, by separating her from her children," he ruled, "nor may children be separated from the mother, in effect visiting upon them the sins of their mother's batterer." Two years later, a unanimous New York Court of Appeals agreed, holding that parental failure to protect a child from witnessing abuse could not be equated automatically with neglect.[16]

The *Nicholson* case was supposed to radically change New York City's approach to domestic violence and serve as a model for other jurisdictions. But the experiences of Montauban and numerous other survivors tell a different story. In 2018, 25 percent of the fifty-six thousand investigations conducted by ACS were flagged as high priority for domestic violence in the family. Between 2016 and 2018, close to ten thousand children were placed under court-ordered ACS monitoring at least partially because of an allegation of domestic violence. Although child removals based strictly on exposure to domestic violence have decreased, ACS caseworkers have continued to find reasons to monitor survivors and take their children. Even if they don't remove children automatically from mothers who report intimate partner abuse, child protection workers can easily find a related pretext for intervention. Violent partners often control mothers in ways that sabotage the mother's caregiving. They may deny the mother access to needed assets, interfere with her employment, impair her physically, and cause her emotional distress. Any of these deficiencies can become grounds for CPS to charge a mother with vague allegations of neglect, endangerment, or inadequate guardianship. Caseworkers supervising survivors can evade the *Nicholson* ruling by accusing mothers of failing to comply with CPS mandates.[17]

It is no wonder that the child welfare system's punitive treatment of domestic violence survivors endangers them and their children. A 2020 study investigating the impact of laws that mandate reporting of domestic violence found alarming implications involving the child welfare system. The study analyzed a survey of more than two thousand survivors of intimate partner violence to explore how mandatory reporting laws affected their efforts to seek help. The researchers found that reporting requirements often deterred survivors from reaching out for support and reduced their ability to receive the support they sought. When triggered, domestic violence reports made the situation worse for most of the survivors. A third of the survivors surveyed said they did not ask at least one person for help because they were afraid information about the abuse would be reported to authorities.[18]

The survivors were mainly afraid of two types of state inference in their lives: by law enforcement and by CPS. The most common fear was involvement in the criminal punishment system. Many of the women surveyed expressed worry that their partners would be arrested or jailed. Incarcerating a partner could lead to dire consequences, from the abuser's deadly retaliation to losing a critical source of income and a valued relationship. The survivors wanted to end their partners' violence against them, not necessarily their connection to their partners. This finding helps to explain why a CPS requirement that mothers obtain orders of protection and cease all contact with an abusive partner can harm the family—especially when the mother's failure to comply leads to child removal, as happened to Angeline Montauban.

The fear of police intervention also corresponds to Black feminists' opposition to relying on arrest, detention, and prosecution as solutions to interpersonal violence. Black women in the antiviolence movement have warned against participating in a regime that is eager to incarcerate large numbers of Black men but will not invest in resources like housing, education, and employment that would make Black women less vulnerable to violence. They point out that police officers often arrest, injure, and kill Black victims of domestic violence who call them for help. A study of mandatory arrest policies in New York City found that 27 percent of women who called a law enforcement hotline to report experiencing violence were arrested, even though 85 percent of them had been injured. Sixty-six percent of the women arrested were Black or Latina. A grassroots organization called Survived and Punished is devoted to freeing survivors who were imprisoned for defending themselves against a violent partner, like Marissa Alexander, a Black mother who was sentenced to twenty years in prison after she fired a warning shot at her husband who was threatening to kill her.[19]

Second only to fear of criminal legal involvement was fear of losing their children to foster care. “My children would be removed by CPS from my care,” one woman stated as the reason she refrained from seeking help. Another feared “that my children would be removed and I would be blamed for everything, or called crazy.” Other study participants explained that they dared not reach out for help because it might lead their abusers to follow through on threats to exploit CPS to punish them. Battered mothers in Florida whose children had been removed similarly told *USA Today* that they were afraid to ever call the police again. In one case, a mother lost custody of her children for failing to protect them from witnessing her husband’s beatings, yet her husband was granted custody of their daughter. “The thing I regret most is that I ever called 911,” said a mother whose children spent eight months in foster care after her boyfriend hit her and brandished a gun. “But I could also have been killed that night. Which one do you pick?” On the other side of the country, a Los Angeles mother whose three children were taken after she sought protection answered this way: “I called the police for help, but I should have just let my husband beat my ass.”[20]

The CPS response to domestic violence, often triggered by a police report, makes mothers and their children less safe from the perpetrators of violence in their homes. The child welfare system blames and punishes battered mothers for exposing their children to violence, just as it blames and punishes mothers for other family problems caused by structural inequities beyond their control. A child welfare system that relies on forcing mothers into therapeutic remedies and taking their children isn’t capable of providing safety for families. Instead, mothers are victimized twice—not only by their violent partners, but also by law enforcement and child welfare agencies that address domestic violence with a coordinated carceral approach.

****

## War on Immigrant Families

During the Trump administration, the American public became painfully aware that the federal government was deploying child removal as a weapon to deter migration to the United States. Images of migrant children ripped from their parents and detained in crowded concentration camps flooded the media, evoking widespread condemnation of the inhumane family separation policy. The public is less aware that taking children as an anti-immigration measure extends beyond the southern border. US Immigration and Customs Enforcement (ICE) collaborates with local child welfare agencies throughout the United States, not only to police parents but also to deport them. The coordinated operation of ICE and CPS is yet another way the state tears apart Black and Brown families and sucks them into a carceral machine that encompasses detention centers, jails, and prisons.

Hailing from African and Caribbean nations, many undocumented families are part of Black communities and face discrimination based on their race and immigration status. Between 2012 and 2017, migrants from Haiti were the second most likely to be denied asylum, with odds close to those from Mexico. Jamaicans and Somalians also had high rates of asylum denial. Black immigrants are also the most likely to be targeted for deportation. According to the Black Alliance for Just Immigration, although only 7 percent of noncitizens in the United States are Black, they are 20 percent of those facing deportation based on criminal charges.[26]

Like the collaboration between the child welfare system and police, immigration and CPS officials share information to use against parents. Sometimes all three punitive systems—child protection, criminal, and immigration—conspire to tear families apart. Having an open CPS investigation can be a strike against parents in immigration proceedings. When an undocumented parent is picked up in a raid, the immigration judge may view any child maltreatment allegations CPS brings against the parent as grounds for deportation—even if the criminal case is dismissed. Roshell Amezcua, a family defense immigration attorney at the Bronx Defenders, has known ACS caseworkers to inform law enforcement when they discover that a parent they are investigating is undocumented.[27]

The immigration system also converges with the child welfare system when children who are separated from parents seeking asylum at the border are held in foster care while federal authorities determine the family's fate. The US held nearly seventy thousand migrant children in government custody in 2019. Children who don't have a relative in the United States who is willing to sponsor them—often out of fear of being deported—are typically relocated to federally licensed group homes and shelters. Some are placed with foster families through arrangements with child welfare agencies. Although federal officials promised that children would be held in government custody for only a week or two, migrant children have been held for months or even years.[28]

In 2018, during the Trump administration, the *Washington Post* reported that "new statistics show the government is placing a growing number in long-term foster care, sometimes hundreds of miles from their jailed parents." Some parents are deported without their children, and the long distances between those detained in the United States and the foster care facilities make it unlikely they can be reunited with their children. The children are left in limbo, lingering in foster care indefinitely. A class action lawsuit filed against the US government in 2019 by the families of migrant children seeks hundreds of millions of dollars for harms the children experienced in government custody, including sexual and physical abuse inflicted while they were in foster care.[29]

An Associated Press investigation uncovered cases of migrant parents fighting in state courts to keep their children from being adopted by US families who were supposed to be temporary caretakers. Due process rights protected by the US Constitution apply to all "persons" within the nation's borders, and immigration status alone should not be grounds to terminate the rights of parents who haven't been ruled unfit. Both the Obama and Trump administrations pledged to return children to their parents after splitting them apart at the border. But these safeguards may prove inadequate to ensure that migrant parents can withstand the devaluation of their bonds with their children by state child welfare agencies and judges.

In 2015, during the Obama administration, Araceli Ramos fled El Salvador with her two-year-old daughter, Alexa, to escape a violent partner. In one incident, the man kicked her so forcefully he left a permanent dent in the center of her forehead. At the end of their fifteen-hundred mile journey, the mother and child crossed the Rio Grande into Texas, where they were arrested by US Customs and Border Protection. A border agent denied Ramos asylum, despite the evidence of domestic violence, when he detected criminal charges in her record from El Salvador, and snatched Alexa from her mother's arms. ICE held Ramos in a detention facility in rural Louisiana. Federal immigration authorities labeled Alexa an "unaccompanied minor"—as if she had crossed the border by herself—and placed her in the care of Bethany Christian Services, three thousand miles away from her mother. Since 2014, Bethany Christian Services, one of the nation's largest foster care and adoption agencies, has contracted with federal authorities to place children in shelters and homes in Maryland and Michigan. According to its website, the Michigan-based global nonprofit arranged for 266 foster families to provide care for 667 unaccompanied children in 2019. Bethany moved Alexa in with a local white family who had joined Bethany's evangelical crusade to address the "global refugee crisis" by fostering children.[30]

In 2016, a federal immigration judge ordered Ramos to be deported; Alexa was to be returned to her mother. But the Michigan couple refused to release the girl. Instead, they filed a petition in state court alleging that Alexa's life would be threatened if she went back to El Salvador with her mother, persuading a judge to grant them continued custody pending a full guardianship hearing. Eventually, after Ramos circulated her story on Facebook and the US Justice Department intervened on her behalf, she was reunited with Alexa in El Salvador. "If they give our children up for adoption without our permission, that isn't justice," Ramos told AP reporters. "They are our children, not theirs."[31]

## Notes

14. Somini Sengupta, "Tough Justice: Taking a Child When One Parent Is Battered," *New York Times*, July 8, 2000, www.nytimes.com/2000/07/08/nyregion/tough-justice-taking-a-child-when-one-parent-is-battered.html.
15. Kramer, *Backfire*, 3–4.
16. Nicholson v. Williams, 203 F. Supp.2d 153, 250–51 (E.D.N.Y. 2002); Nicholson v. Scoppetta, 820 N.E.2d 840 (N.Y. 2004).
17. Kramer, *Backfire*, 3–4; Lynn F. Beller, "When in Doubt, Take Them Out: Removal of Children from Victims of Domestic Violence Ten Years After Nicholson v. Williams," *Duke Journal of Gender Law and Policy* 22, no. 2 (Spring 2015): 205–239, https://scholarship.law.duke.edu/djglp/vol22/iss2/2/; Jaime Perrone, "Failing to Realize Nicholson's Vision: How New York's Child Welfare System Continues to Punish Battered Mothers," *Journal of Law and Policy* 20, no. 2 (2012): 641–675, https://brooklynworks.brooklaw.edu/cgi/viewcontent.cgi?article=1083 &context=jlp; Tina Lee, "Child Welfare Practice in Domestic Violence Cases in New York City: Problems for Poor Women of Color," *Women, Gender, and Families of Color* 3, no. 1 (Spring 2015), https://doi.org/10.5406/womgenfamcol.3.1.0058.
18. Carrie Lippy et al., "The Impact of Mandatory Reporting Laws on Survivors of Intimate Partner Violence: Intersectionality, Help-Seeking and the Need for Change," *Journal of Family Violence* 35, no. 4 (April 2020), https://doi.org/10.1007/s10896-019-00103-w.
19. *INCITE! Women of Color Against Violence, editors, Color of Violence: The Incite! Anthology* (Cambridge, MA: Duke University Press, 2016); Beth E. Richie, "A Black Feminist Reflection on the Antiviolence Movement," *Signs: Journal of Women in Culture and Society* 25, no. 4 (2000): 1136, https://doi.org/10.1086/495533; Andrea J. Ritchie, *Invisible No More: Police Violence Against Black Women and Women of Color* (Boston: Beacon Press, 2017); Beth E. Richie, *Compelled to Crime: The Gendered Entrapment of Battered Black Women* (New York: Routledge, 1996); *Survived and Punished, Criminalizing Survival* Curricula, October 2018, https://survivedandpunished.org/criminalizing-survival-curricula; Victoria Frye et al., *The Family Protection and Domestic Violence Intervention Act of 1995: Examining the Effects of Mandatory Arrest in New York City* (New York: Family Violence Project, Urban Justice Center, 2001), https://doi.org/10.13140/RG.2.2.30058.31682.
20. Hirt, "Florida Blames Mothers When Men Batter Them—Then Takes Away Their Children"; Chris Martin, "Op Ed: She Reached Out for Help and Got Her Kids Taken Away," *Witness LA*, June 16, 2021, www.witnessla.com/op-ed-she-reached-out-for-help-and-got-her-kids-taken-away/.

****

26. RAICES, "Black Immigrant Lives Are Under Attack," accessed July 9, 2021, www.raicestexas.org/2020/07/22/black-immigrant-lives-are-under-attack/; Jeremy Raff, "The 'Double Punishment' for Black Undocumented Immigrants," *The Atlantic*, December 30, 2017, www.theatlantic.com/politics/archive/2017/12/the-double-punishment-for-black-immigrants/549425/;

Black Alliance for Just Immigration webpage, accessed July 9, 2021, https://baji.org/.

27. Author's interview with the Bronx Defenders staff via Zoom, July 21, 2020.
28. Christopher Sherman, Martha Mendoza, and Garance Burke, "The US Held a Record Number of Migrant Children in Custody in 2019," *USA Today*, November 12, 2019, www.usatoday.com/story/news/nation/2019/11/12/border-crisis-us-government-held-70–000-migrant-children-2019/2572376001/.
29. Nick Miroff, "'Lost' Immigrant Children? Statistics Show the Government Is Keeping More of Them Far Longer," *Washington Post*, May 30, 2018, www.washingtonpost.com/world/national-security/theres-fury-over-lost-migrant-children-but-stats-show-trumps-government-is-holding-more-of-them-longer/2018/05/30/d179b334–6438–11e8–99d2–0d678ec08c2f_story.html; Emily Atkin, "The Uncertain Fate of Migrant Children Sent to Foster Care," *New Republic*, June 20, 2018, https://newrepublic.com/article/149161/uncertain-fate-migrant-children-sent-foster-care; Associated Press, "The U.S. Has Held a Record 69,550 Migrant Children in Government Custody in 2019," *NBC News*, November 12, 2019, www.nbcnews.com/news/latino/u-s-has-held-record-69–550-migrant-children-government-n1080486; Associated Press, "Migrant Kids Separated at Border Faced Abuse in Foster Homes," *Los Angeles Times*, August 15, 2019, www.latimes.com/world-nation/story/2019-08-16/immigration-border-separations-foster-homes.
30. Bethany Christian Services, "About Us," accessed July 10, 2021, https://bethany.org/about-us/impact.
31. Garance Burke and Martha Mendoza, "AP Investigation: Deported Parents May Lose Kids to Adoption," *AP News*, October 9, 2018, https://apnews.com/article/97b06cede0c149c492bf25a48cb6c26f.

# From Sufian, Sandra. *Familial Fitness: Disability, Adoption, and Family in Modern America.* U of Minnesota P, 2022.

### Drugs, Damage, and New Children in Foster Care

Special needs foster children awaiting adoption bore the brunt of Americans' tendency to pathologize adoptees. Americans' deep and growing fears about both the drug and AIDS crises helped shape public and professional concerns about damage and disability among waiting children. They also linked the issue of dependency with damage and disability.

Conservative attacks on the welfare state and the social safety net, and policies that criminalized poverty and increased incarceration, created economic and social instability for marginalized and vulnerable sectors of American society. These policies all had racist consequences and impacted children in devastating ways. They led to the increasing numbers of children, particularly African American children, who needed to be placed in foster care when their birth parents were left in economic distress, were imprisoned for drugs, or were homeless. Children's affiliation with these problems, and their physical and psychological ramifications, made it easy for the public to attribute damage and risk to them.

Even though Nixon spoke of a "war on drugs," Reagan's war on drugs, which started in October 1982, brought illicit drug use to the forefront of American politics and culture. The George H. W. Bush and Clinton administrations sustained and amplified the political racialized panic about drugs.[12] In the late 1980s and into the 1990s, this alarm led to draconian measures against drug users, like minimum sentencing and more funding for drug enforcement. These policies led to a cycle of increased arrests, imprisonment, and mounting foster care needs. Clinton's "tough on crime" policies intensified the drug war further, so that by 1991 the United States incarcerated its citizens at rates unprecedented in world history. This pattern of mass incarceration disproportionately affected African American communities.[13]

DOI: 10.4324/9781003203827-7

****

Conservative claims about Black pathology centered on illegitimacy and a reliance upon welfare. According to this argument, irresponsible women on welfare were allegedly producing a generation doomed to fail, posing a "menace to the future" of America.[28] Press coverage added to the focus on welfare and dependency. Reportage leveraged public fears about both disability and race by representing crack babies as having limited horizons, as having no potential of being "normal," and as having "permanent brain damage."[29] Commentators called crack babies the new "biounderclass," a term that historically underscored the distinction between the "worthy" and "unworthy" poor that so often applied to policies concerning people with disabilities of all races. The term also reinforced deeply ingrained racial and gender stereotypes about women and men of color. Conservative columnist Charles Krauthammer, for example, warned that an "exploding" crack baby crisis where a "generation of physically damaged cocaine babies whose biological inferiority is stamped at birth" was emerging, "whose future is closed from day one. Theirs will be a life of certain suffering, of probable deviance, of permanent inferiority."[30] A well-known Native American adoptive parent and author, Michael Dorris, echoed these sentiments about crack babies' damaged futures and applied them to children with fetal alcohol syndrome (FAS). He even represented his son as irredeemable. Writing about babies exposed to crack or alcohol, he wrote: "A drug-impaired baby is destined for, at best, an adult life of sorrow and deprivation, and at worst, for a fate governed by crime, victimization, and premature death."[31] His words point to how the crack baby discourse and the discourse about FAS among Native American women and children mirrored one another. One Native American professional working with children with FAS even remarked that they were never able to become humans, never being able to love or be accepted into society, and never being capable of "living even in *this* world."[32]

****

Although policy experts and social scientists of all political stripes decried dependency as bad, conservative policy makers saw social welfare programs as producers of dependency. They therefore called for dismantling the welfare state as *the* way to produce reform and to rehabilitate those on welfare, particularly Black families.[37] But for foster children with disabilities who were exposed to drugs or alcohol, the disability-dependency nexus compounded the dependencies of being a child and being poor. Within the neoconservative political climate and its assault upon the welfare state, these children evoked intense cultural fears in the American public about dependency and actual or assumed Blackness that had deep historical roots.[38] These anxieties now resurfaced through the crack crisis.

The stigma of being a poor foster child with a disability, however, exceeded the expected and acceptable form of child dependency, where a child is presumably able-bodied but socially vulnerable (because of age) and is a legal dependent. By contrast, the layered dependency of being a disabled foster child was socially unexpected because of its complex multidimensional nature. The dependent disabled foster child uniquely required either state funds and services to function in daily life or efforts to take care of her bodily and emotional needs.[39] Importantly, the status of occupying interwoven dependencies had significant implications for these children's familial fitness and citizenship.[40] They delimited which children's bodies Americans believed had worthy and contributive lives. Given the pejorative notion of dependency and its racial, class, and disability axes during this time, many Americans conceptualized these children as inherently a burden, a lack, and risky candidates for family life.[41] Instead of recognizing the "inevitable dependencies" inherent in all social relations, the ideologically charged meanings of these intertwined dependencies butt up against American historical myths about rugged individualism, personal responsibility, and independence (now framed as a matter of personality). The latter ideals not only applied to political citizenship but also translated into the norms of familial citizenship.[42]

Moreover, particularly when there was a political assault on public, and therefore private, dependency, the federal government harnessed these myths to rationalize economic retrenchment and family values. The government engendered antipathy toward crack mothers and mothers addicted to alcohol towards these same ends.[43]

****

## Questioning the Lives of Children with Disabilities

The medical and cultural themes of biological perfection, disability, and notions of futurity, seen in discussions of ART, also played out in a vigorous cultural debate in the 1980s about whether to withhold treatment from disabled infants. Physicians and ethicists focused on the cases of Baby Doe and Baby Jane Doe as the debate's centerpieces. Adoptive parent applicants and adoption workers could not have been ignorant of the debate's tenor, not only because of the public potency of the issue but also because ethicists and physicians offered adoption as a solution to birth parents' rejection of disabled infants. Prospective adoptive parents were likely also aware of the issues of assisted suicide and euthanasia of adults with disabilities featured in the news, with the stories of Larry McAfee (1988) and Terri Schiavo (1990) as key cases.

Baby Doe and Baby Jane Doe prompted bioethicists Helga Kuhse and Peter Singer to write a book titled *Should the Baby Live? The Problem of Handicapped Infants*. The book discusses euthanasia or infanticide of children with disabilities. They argued that since parents would be the ones taking care of a "severely handicapped infant," they should be key decision makers about whether that child should live or die. Invoking futurity, the authors claimed that when a family does not wish to care for their disabled child, the state should take over the responsibility of the child only when "life may be in the best interests of the person the infant will become"; that is, when the state deems the child's future life as potentially worthwhile.[86] Kuhse and Singer contended that in the latter cases, the best form of care would be the adoptive family, reasonably adding: "but we would be pleasantly surprised if there were enough families willing to adopt these children."[87]

The Baby Doe case allowed doctors to withhold routine life saving surgery to fix tracheoesophageal fistula (opening between trachea and esophagus) and esophageal atresia (esophagus ends in a pouch instead of continuing to stomach) from a baby with Down syndrome in 1982. The baby eventually starved to death. But the story was more complicated. A surrogate mother, inseminated for a couple who later separated, gave birth to Baby Doe. The alleged biological father initially accepted the child but later rejected the baby, arguing that Baby Doe was actually not his own (a blood test attested to this fact). Not only did the case involve a multimillion dollar lawsuit and allegations of fraud and baby selling, but Baby Doe's physical and intellectual disabilities intensified the case's cultural import. Media reports utilized the rhetoric of the day, describing him as inferior, disposable, and as damaged goods. They commodified him as someone who could be discarded or exchanged. As a critique of these depictions, journalist Roger Rosenblatt reminded his readers that "what is being cooked up in each instance is not a cake or a car or a mail order watch but a person, small headed or not, and any situation that suggests otherwise is not just dismaying but dangerous."[88]

Despite disparaging media representations, public outcry about the Baby Doe case led the Department of Health and Human Services (HHS) to make "medical discrimination against handicapped infants" unlawful under Section 504 of the Rehabilitation Act of 1973. The regulation made withholding nutritional, surgical, or medical treatment from a disabled infant illegal "when treatment was not contraindicated by the condition." But the final HHS regulations in 1984 invoked medical custom and "reasonable judgment" as the principles upon which physicians should rely, even though many neonatal treatments were relatively new at the time and so medical custom had not been established. Furthermore, the regulations did not clearly delineate the ability to use quality of life judgments to determine medical benefit.[89]

A year later, the Baby Jane Doe case continued the debate about whether disabled infants should be denied treatment and allowed to die. It involved a child with spina bifida whose parents refused (against physicians' recommendations) to place a ventricular shunt because of the multiple disabilities she would have after the surgery. After making its way through several layers of the court system, during which time her parents allowed some surgery, the District Court of Appeals determined that the Rehabilitation Act did *not* give HHS authority to interfere in any medical decision-making regarding the treatment of disabled infants, thus undermining the original HHS regulations.[90] The Supreme Court agreed in 1986, arguing that it was parents, not the hospitals or physicians, who had the right to decline to give consent to the infant's treatment and that only states had the power and right of enforcement in this area. The judges who dissented noted that parents did not make these decisions in a vacuum and that physicians routinely influenced the decisions. Ultimately, the Court struck down the regulations that made withdrawal or withholding treatment unlawful.[91]

Although it did not amend the Rehabilitation Act to reinstate the Baby Doe regulations, Congress turned to child abuse as a way to address whether physicians could withhold medical treatment to an infant on a state level. Concerned primarily with antiabortion politics rather than enforcing Section 504 or a concern for disabled infants, Reagan signed the Child Abuse Amendments of 1984, which made withholding or withdrawing medical treatment and nutrition from a disabled infant an act of child abuse.[92] But like the Baby Doe regulations, the law allowed physicians to withhold medical treatment on the basis of "reasonable medical judgment" when treatment would prolong dying, or when it was deemed medically futile. Medical and disability advocacy groups articulated strong principles for dealing with the medical treatment of disabled infants that same year, erring on the side of providing treatment, community support, and protecting the rights of disabled infants. The Child Abuse Amendments of CAPTA deepened this debate and intensified its already principal focus on child abuse that had started in the 1970s.[93]

As a result of the amended CAPTA, state child protection services (CPS) began to spend more time and resources on potential abuse or neglect in neonatal care. This emphasis closely tied to foster care and adoption services in that when CPS turned its attention to medical neglect, it made that kind of neglect an adjunct to general neglect as a basis for placing a child in foster care. The law also required state level programs to facilitate adoption opportunities for disabled infants with life-threatening conditions. This is one of the reasons why "chronic care" and "terminally ill" children became new constituents of the foster care and adoption populations during this time.

Even prior to the law, some pediatricians and adoption workers proposed that adoption be a solution to withholding treatment from infants with disabilities. Dr. Reba Michels Hill of St. Luke's Episcopal Hospital in Houston and Jo Ann Caldwell of Homes of St. Marks Adoption Agency, for instance, suggested that adoption be used as "an alternate method for handling cases of malformed or damaged infants who are unacceptable to biologic parents."[94] Hill and Caldwell described Susie Q, who exhibited a variety of impairments at birth. Upholding cultural notions of perfection, her parents asked "if she is not normal, why salvage her?" Susie's parents refused to see or touch her; they refused to visit her in the hospital. They decided to send her to an institution and were adamant that she would not be allowed into their home. The neonatologist requested that they consider relinquishing her for adoption. Even though they "were appalled that anyone would want to adopt an imperfect child," they eventually agreed. Luckily, Susie was adopted three days after discharge from the hospital. Various parties paid for several subsequent surgeries. According to Hill and Caldwell, Susie developed into a "vivacious 6½ year old, who has cerebral palsy but now walks independently. . . . She is living proof that a child with a handicap can flourish in a loving, concerned family in which her personality and self-worth are nourished by being loved, wanted and accepted."[95]

More optimistic than Kuhse and Singer, Hill and Caldwell continued arguing for adoption as an alternative to medical neglect and rejection by birth parents. But they neither challenged parental rejection of a child based on disability nor substantially discussed supports that parents might need to navigate childcare for these children. However, they did try to find a solution to the problem of unwanted children through adoption.[96] They explained that for those biological parents who could neither cope with nor nurture a child with physical, mental, or neurological disabilities, adoption was a better alternative than death by starvation, permanent institutionalization, or physical abuse. The children had a right to this option, rather than death. But, they claimed, because "the attitude that adoptive parents only want a perfect child has been so ingrained," doctors were unaware that there were adoptive parents who could love and accept an "imperfect" child.[97] Some physicians could not imagine that possibility. Some parents who adopted severely disabled or seriously ill children reported that their doctors had told them: "I have no time for this child. He's better off in an institution—or dead—anyway. Why do you care what happens to him? He isn't *really* yours."[98]

## Notes

12. In 1989, Bush described drug use as the "most pressing problem facing the nation," while CBS News noted that 64 percent of the American public agreed with him. Michelle Alexander, *The New Jim Crow* (New York: New Press, 2010), 54.

13. One fourth of all young African American men were behind bars in the early 1990s. Alexander, 55; Stephanie Bush-Baskette, "The War on Drugs and the Incarceration of Mothers," *Journal of Drug Issues* 30 no. 4 (Fall 2000): 919–927.

****

28. Charles Krauthammer, "Crack Babies Forming Biological Underclass," *St. Louis Post-Dispatch*, July 30, 1989, 3B. For fetal alcohol syndrome and welfare, see Michael Dorris, *The Broken Cord* (New York: Harper Collins, 1989), 160, 166.
29. Briggs, "Orphaning the Children of Welfare," 75, 77, 79; Krauthammer, 3B.
30. Krauthammer, 3B.
31. Dorris, 281; G. Thomas Couser, "Raising Adam: Ethnicity, Disability, and the Ethics of Life Writing in Michael Dorris' *The Broken Cord*," Biography 21, no. 4 (Fall 1998): 434, 438.
32. Dorris, 158, 168.

****

37. Scott, *Contempt and Pity*, 191, 200–201; Fraser and Gordon, 327–328.
38. Molly Ladd-Taylor, *Fixing the Poor: Eugenic Sterilization and Child Welfare in the Twentieth Century* (Baltimore: Johns Hopkins University Press, 2017).
39. Phillips, 851.
40. Daniel Blackie, "Disability, Dependency, and the Family in the Early United States," in *Disability Histories*, ed. Susan Burch and Michael Rembis (Urbana: University of Illinois Press, 2014), Loc. 420 (Kindle); Scott, *Contempt and Pity*, 188; Fraser and Gordon, 309.
41. Fraser and Gordon, 311, 324–325.
42. Eva Feder Kittay, Bruce Jennings, and Angela A. Wasunna, "Dependency, Difference and Global Ethic of Long-term Care," *Journal of Political Philosophy* 13, no. 4 (2005): 443–445, 466, 467, 469; Fraser and Gordon, 331–332.
43. Humphries, *Crack Mothers*, 8, 12; Dorris, 166.

****

86. Helga Kuhse and Peter Singer, *Should the Baby Live?: The Problem of Handicapped Infants* (Oxford: Oxford University Press, 1985), 189. For earlier precedent on euthanasia of unfit babies, see Martin S. Pernick, *The Black Stork: Eugenics and the Death of "Defective" Babies in American Medicine and Motion Pictures since 1915* (New York: Oxford University Press, 1996).
87. Kuhse and Singer, 191.
88. Roger Rosenblatt, "The Baby in the Factory," *Time*, February 14, 1983, 90, 94–95.
89. Elias and Annas, 170–173.
90. The hole in her spine closed naturally but she was still intellectually disabled. "Data Update: Baby Jane Doe Turns Nine This Year," *New York Times*, May 17, 1992, 44.
91. Jack Resnik, "The Baby Doe Rules (1984)," *The Embryo Encyclopedia Project*, May 12, 2011, https://embryo.asu.edu /pages/baby-doe-rules-1984.
92. Elias and Annas, 177, 181. For confrontational tactics of antiabortion groups in the 1980s, see Thompson, *American Culture in the 1980s*, 31. See also

Children's Bureau, "Child Abuse Amendments of 1984, Pub. L. No. 98–457," in *Major Federal Legislation Concerned with Child Protection, Child Welfare and Adoption* (2019), 26, www.childwelfare.gov/pubpdfs/majorfedlegis.pdf.

93. For Elias and Annas's "better off dead" standard to discern what was in the "best interests" of the child in terms of withholding treatment, see Elias and Annas, 184–185. It is within this context and debate that Kuhse and Singer put forward their stance on killing disabled infants. Elias and Annas, 185–186; American Academy of Pediatrics, "Joint Policy Statement: Principles of Treatment of Disabled Infants," *Pediatrics* 73, no. 4 (1984): 559.
94. Reba Michels Hill and Jo Ann Caldwell, "Adoption: An Option for the Imperfect Child," *Pediatrics* 71, no. 4 (April 1983): 664.
95. Hill and Caldwell, 665.
96. Without childcare supports, adoption in some ways served as a solution of relocation, one that then created a "problem" for parents who adopted disabled children. Thanks Aly Patsavas for this insight.
97. Hill and Caldwell, 665.
98. Prepared statement of Mr. and Mrs. Ashton Avegno, in *Barriers to Adoption*, (1985), 163. For similar problematic attitudes of physicians and social workers in relation to preventing children from foster care placement, see Christopher G. Petr and David D. Barney, "Reasonable Efforts for Children with Disabilities: The Parents' Perspective," *Social Work* 39, no. 3 (May 1993): 252.

## Works Cited

Alexander, Michelle. *The New Jim Crow*. New Publishing, 2010.

American Academy of Pediatrics. "Joint Policy Statement: Principles of Treatment of Disabled Infants." *Pediatrics*, vol. 73, no. 4, 1984, pp. 559–560.

Blackie, Daniel. "Disability, Dependency, and the Family in the Early United States." *Disability Histories*, edited by Susan Burch and Michael Rembis, U of Illinois P, 2014, pp. 17–34.

Briggs, Laura. "Orphaning the Children of Welfare: 'Crack Babies,' Race, and Adoption Reform." *Outsiders Within: Writing on Transracial Adoption*, edited by Jane Jeong Trenka, et al., South End, 2006, pp. 75–88.

Bush-Baskette, Stephanie. "The War on Drugs and the Incarceration of Mothers." *Journal of Drug Issues*, vol. 30, no. 4, Fall 2000, pp. 919–927.

Children's Bureau. "Child Abuse Amendments of 1984, Pub. L. No. 98–457." *Major Federal Legislation Concerned with Child Protection, Child Welfare and Adoption*, vol. 26, 2019, www.childwelfare.gov/pubpdfs/majorfedlegis.pdf.

Couser, G. Thomas. "Raising Adam: Ethnicity, Disability, and the Ethics of Life Writing in Michael Dorris' *The Broken Cord*." *Biography*, vol. 21, no. 4, Fall 1998, pp. 421–444.

"Data Update: Baby Jane Doe Turns Nine This Year." *New York Times*, 17 May 1992, p. 44.

Dorris, Michael. *The Broken Cord*. Harper Collins, 1989.

Elias, Sherman, and George Annas. *Reproductive Genetics and the Law*. Yearbook Medical, 1987.

Fraser, Nancy, and Linda Gordon. "A Genealogy of Dependency: Tracing a Keyword of the US Welfare State." *Signs*, vol. 19, no. 2, 1994, pp. 319–321.

Hill, Reba Michels, and Jo Ann Caldwell. "Adoption: An Option for the Imperfect Child." *Pediatrics*, vol. 71, no. 4, 1983, pp. 664–665.

Humphries, Drew. *Crack Mothers: Pregnancy, Drugs and the Media*. Ohio State UP, 1999.

Kittay, Eva Feder, et al. "Dependency, Difference and Global Ethic of Long-term Care." *Journal of Political Philosophy*, vol. 13, no. 4, 2005, pp. 443–469.

Krauthammer, Charles. "Crack Babies Forming Biological Underclass." *St. Louis Post-Dispatch*, 30 July 1989, p. 3B.

Kuhse, Helga, and Peter Singer. *Should the Baby Live?: The Problem of Handicapped Infants*. Oxford UP, 1985.

Ladd-Taylor, Molly. *Fixing the Poor: Eugenic Sterilization and Child Welfare in the Twentieth Century*. Johns Hopkins UP, 2017.

Petr, Christopher G., and David D. Barney. "Reasonable Efforts for Children with Disabilities: The Parents' Perspective." *Social Work*, vol. 39, no. 3, 1993, pp. 247–254.

Phillips, Marilynn J. "Damaged Goods: Oral Narratives of the Experience of Disability in American Culture." *Social Science and Medicine*, vol. 30, no. 8, 1990, pp. 849–857.

Resnik, Jack. "The Baby Doe Rules (1984)." *The Embryo Encyclopedia Project*, 12 May 2011, embryo.asu.edu /pages/baby-doe-rules-1984.

Rosenblatt, Roger. "The Baby in the Factory." *Time*, 14 Feb. 1983, pp. 90–95.

Scott, Daryl Michael. *Contempt and Pity: Social Policy and the Image of the Damaged Black Psyche, 1880–1996*. U of North Carolina P, 1997.

Thompson, Graham. *American Culture in the 1980s*. Edinburgh UP, 2007.

United States, Congress, Senate. Committee on Labor and Human Resources. *Barriers to Adoption: Hearings before the Committee on Labor and Human Resources*. 99th Congress, First Session, 25 June and 10 July 1985, US GPO, 1985.

# From Zelizer, Viviana. *Pricing the Priceless Child: The Changing Social Value of Children*. Princeton UP, 1994.

Baby farms were singled out as particularly offensive and deadly institutions. "It is time," urged a *New York Times* editorial in September of 1873, "that some active means were taken to put a stop to the practice of baby farming which in the vast majority of instances, is only another term for baby killing."[20] Unnatural parents were accused of sending children out to "nurse," with the understanding that "they are to be 'put out of the way' by means that shall elude the law."[21] Since a rapid turnover of infants meant the arrival of new clients, and an additional payment, baby farmers were allegedly anxious "to get rid of the little milk imbibers as quickly as possible."[22]

But the threat posed by this "hiring out of babies," was only partly a matter of safety. Surely, in the nineteenth century, infant mortality was not much lower in officially approved almshouses and foundling asylums than in unlicensed baby farms. And, while mothers may indeed have been eager to "get rid of children that become incumbrances," it was not necessarily with the intent of infanticide. As even the alarmist editorials of the *New York Times* acknowledged, children were often put out to board permanently or only temporarily by "poor widows who desire to go out . . . to do . . . housework, where they find it very inconvenient to be incumbered by very young children."[23]

Baby farming was therefore denounced largely as a symbol of an antiquated and mercenary approach to adoption. Much as children's life insurance, the system visibly challenged the new sacred value of children by routinely pricing their lives. The parallels between both forms of "baby traffic" did not escape the New York Society for the Prevention of Cruelty to Children; "One way of getting rid of the infant was to insure it, neglect it, and so kill it off. Now it is . . . more profitable to buy and sell, and the system has become a kind of baby slave trade."

In the 1870s, the New York Society for the Prevention of Cruelty to Children was also heavily involved in a struggle against the "padrone" system, a particularly mercenary type of indenture. For a small sum of money, padrones "bought" young Italian children from their parents and brought

DOI: 10.4324/9781003203827-8

them to the United States. It was a profitable investment; the children worked in the street, as beggars or musicians, handing padrones all their earnings. By the 1880s, the NYSPCC, with the cooperation of the Italian government, succeeded in stopping the padrones' business.[24]

Child welfare workers sought to replace mercenary foster parenting of any kind with a new approach to adoption more suitable for the economically "useless," sacred child. Institutional care for dependent children had gained great popularity in the nineteenth century. Even after the 1870s, when children were removed by law from almshouses, they were transferred to orphanages and other institutions. But by the 1890s, reformers began a forceful campaign in support of foster home care. In 1909, the White House Conference on Children officially declared foster homes the "best substitute for the natural home." As the concept of home care gained increasing recognition, it became imperative to rethink carefully children's proper place in the foster home. As Hastings Hart, another prominent social worker, explained, "We have a constant missionary work to do, to lead people to realize that they are not to take children for their own selfish gratification."[25] The *Children Home Finder*, a publication of the Children's Home Society, appealed to its readers not to take a boy "for what you can get out of him, but, rather, for what you can put into him . . . ."[26] Prospective adopters were duly warned that raising a useless child was an expensive commitment: "It costs us comparatively nothing to secure a servant—the payment of a little coin, a paltry pittance. But to secure . . . a child . . . what anxious hours and days and months and years! . . . Think of the *time* bestowed . . . and the *money* spent."[27] Yet, new intangible benefits would make it all worthwhile:

> Families . . . in need of a servant . . . have gone to . . . some "orphanage," . . . and asked for a boy or girl old enough to serve them. And what have they secured? Just what they asked for: a servant. . . . But their soul has not been enriched. . . . We . . . urge that such families make a great mistake in asking for a servant. We come to say that there is a *jewel* in that abandoned child.[28]

"When you receive a baby to raise" promised the *Children's Home Finder*, "you add to your possessions heaven's sweetest benediction." Even clergymen used their pulpits to persuade parishioners that the new accounting assured a positive balance: "Does the child pay? Yes, surely he pays—a hundred, a thousand fold. A man's children are his treasure. . . . What amount of money would buy them from us? This is . . . almost equally true of those children that come into our homes by adoption."[29]

To be sure, child welfare workers did not invent the sentimental value of an adoptive child. In fact, a significant minority of children placed by the Children's Aid Society were taken just for the sake of companionship.[30] But in nineteenth-century foster homes, the sentimental value of a child did not preclude the possibility of profitably employing that same child. Such an acceptable combination of children's economic and sentimental value was declared an illegitimate contradiction by child welfare workers. For them, the instrumental value of a child negated its sacred value. An 1869 report by the Massachusetts State Board of Charities warned that if sometimes, "the child who was taken as a servant secures a place in the affections of the family taking him, and so the connection ceases to be a mercenary one,"[31] such cases were exceptional.

****

Legal adoption, rare in the nineteenth century, became increasingly popular in the twentieth century. A judge from the Boston Probate Court remarked in 1919, "the woods are full of people eager to adopt children—the number appearing to be in the increase."[74] By 1927, the *New York Times* reported that the new problem in adoption "has become one of finding enough children for childless homes rather than that of finding enough homes for homeless children." Despite greater regulation, and more thorough screening of adoptive parents, legal adoptions increased three-fold between 1934 and 1944, finally breaking a long-standing monopoly of institutional care for dependent children.[75]

The quest for a child to love turned into a glamorous and romanticized search as a number of well-known entertainment and political figures proudly and publicly joined the rank of adoptive parents. Minnie Maddern Fiske, a respected stage actress, told about her adoption of a thirteen-month-old baby, who made his stage debut in one of her tours. Al Jolson explained to the press his decision to adopt a child: "I think it is selfish to go through life without children." In the 1930s, Gracie Allen and George Burns, Mayor La Guardia, Babe Ruth, and Eddie Rickenbacker, among others, similarly announced their decision to adopt a child.[76]

The fairy-tale dimension of adoption was further magnified by many stories of poor waifs taken into the homes of generous, wealthy foster parents. A 1905 article in *Cosmopolitan* had already noted the fantastic prospect of transforming a little "plebeian" into a "lord"; "[the] little ones go from the . . . doorsteps and sewers, to comfort always, and sometimes to luxury."[77] In 1925, Edward W. Browning, a wealthy New York real estate operator, made front-page headlines when he advertised for a "pretty, refined girl" to adopt, thus opening up "the gates of fairyland for many a poor child." Browning allegedly received over 12,000 applications from all over the country. Each girl he interviewed was sent home in Browning's automobile, "with a chauffer in livery . . . and a footman to help them in and out of the coach, just like Cinderella."

The Browning case ended in a scandal after Mary Spas, the girl he adopted thinking she was sixteen years old, confessed to being twenty-one. Mary left Browning lured by an agent's offer to write her story for publication and the promise of a movie job. Browning, who claimed to have spent $20,000 for the adoption (including forty dresses for Mary), had the adoption nullified.[78] While the incident was exceptional, the social class of adoptive parents was indeed undergoing change. A comparison by the New York State Charities Aid Association of the occupations of 100 foster fathers between 1898 and 1900 with the same number of fathers in the period between 1920 and 1921, found that nearly three-quarters of foster fathers in the first period were in skilled, semi-skilled, or unskilled labor, or in farming, while in the latter period there was a predominance of men in business and office work. Sophie Van Senden Theis, author of the report, recalled how "Many of the plainest homes were used for the first children placed, for in those days the Agency had to take what it could get in the way of foster homes."

The shift in social class, detected by Theis, was tied to the sentimentalization of adoption. A study of adoptive parents in Minnesota during the period from 1918 to 1928 found that adoptive fathers surpassed the proportion of males in the general population in the higher occupational levels (professional, semi-professional, and managerial). But adoptive fathers of older, and therefore potentially useful, children were more likely to belong to a lower occupational category, in particular farming.[79]

Sentimental adoption created an unprecedented demand for children under three, especially for infants. In 1910, the press already discussed the new appeal of babies, warning, "there are not enough babies to go around."[80] The Home-Finding Committee of the Spence Nursery, an agency organized for the placement of infants, was surprised to discover that, "instead of our having to seek these homes, they have sought us, and so great is the demand for babies that we cannot begin to meet it." In 1914, Judd Mortimer Lewis, a Texas poet and humorist, achieved national notoriety by working as a one-man baby bureau, using his column in the Houston *Post* to find infants for "baby-hungry" parents. Babies, observed the *New York Tribune* in 1923, "are being taken into homes in numbers and for reasons that mark a new era in the huge task of caring for parentless children." By 1937, infant adoption was being touted as the latest American fad: "The baby market is booming. . . . The clamor is for babies, more babies. . . . . We behold an amazing phenomenon: a country-wide scramble on the part of childless couples to adopt a child." Ironically, while the economically "useless" nineteenth-century baby had to be protected because it was unwanted, the priceless twentieth-century baby, "needs protection as never before . . . [because] too many hands are snatching it."[81]

The priceless child was judged by new criteria; its physical appeal and personality replaced earlier economic yardsticks. After talking to several directors of orphan asylums, the *New York Times* concluded that "every baby who expects to be adopted . . . ought to make it a point to be born with blue eyes. . . . The brown-eyed, black-eyed, or grey-eyed girl or boy may be just as pretty . . . but it is hard to make benevolent auxiliaries of the stork believe so."[82] But the greatest demand was for little girls. Soon after launching its popular Child-Rescue Campaign in 1907, promoting foster home care, the *Delineator* commented that requests for boys were half that for girls; "a two-year old, blue-eyed, golden haired little girl with curls, that is the order that everybody leaves. It cannot be filled fast enough."[83] Similarly, in its first thirty years of work, the New York State Charities Aid Association received 8,000 applications for girls, out of a total of 13,000. While working homes sought older girls for their domestic labor value, adoptive homes wanted little girls for their domestic sentimental value: "a doll on which they could tie pink sashes." In the 1920s, wealthy Americans even imported their "English-rose" golden haired baby girls from London. Jews were apparently an exception. According to an interview with the assistant superintendent of the Hebrew Sheltering Guardian Asylum in 1910, three-year-old boys were in much greater demand among Jewish adoptive parents than little girls.[84]

Considering the widespread parental preference for a male first-born child, the popularity of adopted daughters was puzzling. As Hastings Hart observed in 1902, "When people pray for a child of their own, they are apt to pray for a boy; when they want it for adoption, they want a girl. It is an unexplainable fact that every one who is engaged in placing out children is familiar with."[85] Parents, suggested one adoption agency in 1916, "seem to feel that a girl is easier to understand and to rear, and they are afraid of a boy. . . ."[86] Twenty years later, the *Canadian Magazine* linked the persistent preference for girls to parents' fear of a lonely old age: "Girls do not break the home ties so early as boys and outside interests do not play so large a part in their lives." Why do "pretty little picture-book girls, go like hot cakes," speculated rhetorically a writer in the *Saturday Evening Post*, because they are "grand little self advertisers and they know instinctively how to strut their stuff. . . . They stretch out their dimpled arms, gurgle some secret baby joke, smile a divine toothless smile . . . and women and strong men go mad, become besotted with adoration. . . ." Boys, on the other hand were promotional failures, "slower, more serious and aloof."[87]

The sex and age preferences of twentieth-century adoptive parents were clearly linked to the cultural revolution in fostering. While the earlier need for a useful child put a premium on strong, older children, preferably male, the later search for a priceless child led to babies and particularly, pretty little girls. It was not the innate smiling expertise of females, but established cultural assumptions of women's superior emotional talents which made girls so uniquely attractive for sentimental adoption. The new appeal of babies was further enhanced by the increasing acceptance, in the 1920s, of environmental theories of development. Couples considering adoption were now reassured that "heredity has little or nothing to do with our characters. It is the environment that counts. . . ."[88] Intelligence tests and improved methods of determining children's physical health, reduced the "old prejudice against thrusting one's hand in a grab-bag, eugenically speaking, and breeding by proxy."[89] Even the stigma of illegitimacy was turned into an asset by suggestions that "love babies" were particularly attractive and desirable.[90]

Ironically, as the priceless child displaced the useful child, the dangers of adoption shifted from economic to emotional hazards; the previously exploited little laborer risked becoming a "pretty toy." Prospective adopters were warned: "If you are planning to have a plaything to cuddle and pet and dress prettily, don't do it!"[91] Parents were also advised against seeking an emotionally or psychologically "useful" child. Experts now wrote about the dangers of "seeking compensation in children for frustrated affections," or unfulfilled ambitions.[92] If child placing agencies were less often confronted by requests for a sturdy working child, they now faced new expectations, as the couple who applied to the New York State Charities Association for a three-month-old baby, "who could eventually go to Princeton."[93]

## Notes

20. *New York Times*, Sept. 6, 1873, p. 4. "Baby Butchery," the first Times editorial on baby farming, appeared on Aug. 29, 1872.
21. "Slaughter of the Innocents," *New York Times*, Aug. 6, 1874, p. 4.
22. New York Society for the Prevention of Cruelty to Children, 15th Annual Report, 1890, p. 31.
23. "Baby-Farming Practices," *New York Times*, July 22, 1880, p. 5. Day nurseries, established in the 1880s and 1890s, for the care of young children whose mothers worked, were not popular among working mothers. Sheila M. Rothman, *Woman's Proper Place* (New York: Basic Books, 1978), pp. 89–90.
24. Robert H. Bremner, "The Children with the Organ Man," *American Quarterly* 8(1956):277–82. See NYSPCC, 15th Annual Report, 1890, p. 31. For an excellent analysis of the campaign against baby farming in England, see George K. Behlmer, *Child Abuse and Moral Reform in England, 1870–1908*, (Stanford, CA: Stanford University Press, 1982), chapter 2.
25. *Proceedings of the 29th National Conference of Charities and Correction*, 1902, p. 404. Institutions, however, were difficult to displace. A 1923 U.S. Bureau of the Census report of child placing found that 64.2 percent of dependent and neglected children under care remained in asylums. On the turn-of-the-century debate between supporters of institutions and advocates of foster home care, see Martin Wolins and Irving Piliavin, *Institution or Foster Family—A Century of Debate* (New York: Child Welfare League of America, 1964).
26. Children's Home Finder 5(Apr.-May, 1897):21.
27. Rev. M.T. Lamb, *The Child and God*, (Philadelphia, PA: American Baptist Public Society, 1905), p. 66.
28. Ibid.

29. *Children's Home Finder* 10(Feb. 1902)7; *Delineator* 73(Mar. 1909):508.
30. Bellingham, "Little Wanderers," p. 68.
31. Cited in Abbot, *The Child and the State* II, p. 39.

****

74. Robert Grant, "Domestic Relations and the Child," *Scribner's Magazine* 65(May 1919): 527. Legal adoption did not exist in common law. The first adoption statute in the United States was passed by Massachusetts in 1851 and it became the model for other states. See Jamil S. Zainaldin, "The Emergence of a Modern Adoption Law: Child Custody, Adoption and the Courts, 1796–1851," 73 *Northwestern University Law Review* 1038–89 (1979) and Stephen B. Presser, "The Historical Background of the American Law of Adoption," 11 *Journal of Family Law* 443–556 (1971).
75. *New York Times*, May 8, 1927, VII, p. 14. See "Moppets on the Market: The Problem of Unregulated Adoptions," 59 *Yale Law Journal* 716 (1950). The increase was not only in adoptions by unrelated persons but also in adoptions by relatives, particularly step-parents. By 1962, the 1923 statistics on the substitute care of dependent children were reversed; 69 percent of these children were in family care (adoptive and boarding homes), and only 31 percent in institutions. Wolins and Piliavin, *Institution or Foster Family*, pp. 36–37.
76. *New York Times*, Mar. 17, 1923, p. 9; Jan. 20, 1925, p. 19; Dorothy Dunbar Bromley, "Demand for Babies Outruns the Supply," *New York Times Magazine*, Mar. 3, 1935. P- 9 –
77. Ada Patterson, "Giving Babies Away," *Cosmopolitan* 39(Aug. 1905)411.
78. *New York Times*, July 7, 1925, p. 1; Aug. 5, 1925, p. 1; Aug. 10, 1925, p. 1.
79. Alice M. Leahy, "Some Characteristics of Adoptive Parents," *American Journal of Sociology* 38 (Jan. 1933): 561–62; Sophie Van Senden Theis, *How Foster Children Turn Out* (New York: State Charities Aid Association, 1924), pp. 60–63. On the increase of upper-class adoptive parents in England between the 1920s and 1940s, see Nigel Middleton, *When Family Failed* (London: Victor Gollancz, 1971), p. 240.
80. Arno Dosch, "Not Enough Babies To Go Around," *Cosmopolitan* 49 (Sept. 19 10):4 3 1-
81. Spence Alumnae Society, *Annual Report*, 1916, p. 37; Judd M. Lewis, "Dealing in Babies," *Good Housekeeping* 58 (Feb. 1914): 196; *New York Tribune*, cited in "Cradles Instead of Divorces," *Literary Digest* 77 (Apr. 14, 1923), p. 36; Vera Connolly, "Bargain-Counter Babies," *Pictorial Review* 38 (Mar. 1937), p. 17. The Spence Nursery, as well as the Alice Chapin Adoption Nursery, organized respectively in 1909 and 1910 in New York, became leading agencies for the placement of infants.
82. "Blue-Eyed Babies," *New York Times*, Jan. 17, 1909, VI, p. 7.
83. Mabel P. Daggett, "The Child Without a Home," *Delineator* 70(Oct. 1907): 510.
84. Dosch, "Not Enough Babies to Go Around," p. 434; Carolyn C. Van Blarcom, "Our Child-Helping Service," *Delineator* 95 (Nov. 1919)34; *New York Times*, Mar. 12, 1927, p. 3.
85. Hastings H. Hart, *Proceedings of the 29th National Conference of Charities and Correction*, 1902, p. 403.
86. Spence Alumnae Society, *Annual Report*, 1916, p. 38.

87. Frederick A. Given, "Bargains in Babies," *Canadian Magazine* 83(Apr. 1935): 30; Frazer, "The Baby Market," pp. 25, 86. For an analysis of daughter preference in adoption, see H. David Kirk, "Differential Sex Preference in Family Formation," *Canadian Review of Sociology and Anthropology* I(Feb. 1964)31–48, and Nancy E. Williamson, *Sons or Daughters* (Beverly Hills, CA: Sage, 1976), pp. 111–15.
88. Josephine Baker, "Choosing a Child," *Ladies'Home Journal*, 41(Feb. 1924)36
89. Grant, "Domestic Relations," p. 527. See Tiffin, *In Whose Best Interest?*, pp. 269–70. >
90. Gatlin, "Adopting a Baby," p. 84; Ida Parker, *"Fit and Proper"? A Study of Legal Adoption in Massachusetts* (Boston, MA: Church Home Society, 1927), p. 18. A more lenient view of illegitimate children was consequential, since most adoptable children were born out of wedlock.
91. Honore Willsie, "When Is a Child Adoptable?," *Delineator* 95(Dec. 1919):35; Honore Willsie, "Not a Boy, Please!," ibid., (July 1919): 33.
92. Mary Buell Sayles, *Substitute Parents* (New York: Commonwealth Fund, 1936), p. 17.93. *New York Times*, May 8, 1927, VII, p. 14.

# From Park Nelson, Kim. *Invisible Asians: Korean American Adoptees, Asian American Experiences, and Racial Exceptionalism*. Rutgers UP, 2016.

## Racial Roles of Korean Adoptees

The model minority phenomenon is well described in Asian American studies research and is succinctly summarized by Tuan, who states that Asian Americans "remain 'model minorities,' the best of the 'other' bunch but not 'real' Americans."[40] Because the insidious nature of the model minority myth has yet to be well understood within mainstream and adoption circles, it is sometimes embraced as a form of acceptance into dominant society.[41] Some published Asian adoptee research even takes a celebratory view of this position of racialization for Asian adoptees. Chinese adoption scholars Richard C. Tessler and Gail Gamache write that the Asian American model minority image, "sets a positive example for socially responsible and achieving behavior. . . . It is possible that children adopted from China will gain from these positive images. On the other hand, they may suffer if negative images predominate."[42] The research of transnational adoption scholars Sara Dorow, Heather Jacobson, and Kristi Brian show the perception of Asians as the "model minority" is one reason adoptive parents choose Asian children over other children of color.[43]

Currently, Korean American adoptees constitute a little less than one percent of the Asian American population (approximately 7 percent of Korean Americans, who are themselves approximately 10 percent of the Asian American population).[44] In addition, most Korean adoptees have been or are being raised in non-Asian homes, largely in isolation from Korean American or other Asian American cultural influences. Because of their acculturation separate from other Asian Americans, and the general racial segregation still common in the United States, they might not be considered or might not consider themselves a part of Asian American communities. So, in many ways, Korean adoptees cannot be considered representative of Asian Americans numerically or culturally. However, despite their minority status within Asian America, Korean adoptees epitomize what it means to be Asian American, in several different ways. These include Korean adoptees' positions as

DOI: 10.4324/9781003203827-9

colonial subjects, created by acts of war in the quest for imperial domination; as Asian Americans acculturated to embody the ideals of colorblindness; as examples of a hybrid Asian American identity, Asian by birth and American by acculturation; and as persons subject to model minority expectations to assimilate willingly and quickly into dominant society.

Korean adoptees experience many of the same issues of identity and positionality at an individual scale that other Asian Americans experience at a familial or community scale, though the personal histories of Korean adoptees are often different from those of other Asian American populations. In their American families and communities, Korean adoptees are subject to a Whitened racialization. Other second- and third-generation Asian Americans experience a similar Whitening through acculturation, where Whiteness is seen as analogous to American-ness,[45] but for adoptees this process is accelerated. The Whitening of adoptees, technically first-generation immigrants, is achieved through assimilative processes in (usually) predominantly White families, processes that include colorblindness as a common parenting strategy.[46]

Korean adoptees are generally accepted as "culturally White" and often assume roles as racial and cultural bridge-makers that are remarkably similar to the social roles of Asian Americans described by Henry Yu in *Thinking Orientals*. Yu explains how early sociological research of the Chicago School produced scholarship that cast Asian Americans in roles that they still occupy today. Themes of the Asian American "caught between two worlds" and the role of the "marginal man"[47] are reproduced among Korean adoptees in my research, even though they are largely isolated from much of the rest of Asian America. Adoptees are imagined by adoptive parents as providing the adoptive family with an entrée into communities of color, and positioned as ambassadors by the Korean government; though I recognize these roles as disempowering for Asian Americans, my own research indicates that they still obtain. The racialized position of Asian Americans in general, and of Korean adoptees in particular, between Black and White (or at least between White and non-White), with responsibilities to act as racial and cultural mediators, is certainly problematic, perhaps especially because of how fully many adoptees have embraced this role.

## "Passing" for White: Korean Adoptees in Colorblind America—White Family, White Community

In her essay "Brown-Skinned White Girls," about women of African descent who self-identify as White, France Winddance Twine summarizes four necessary conditions for the construction of a White identity among a population visibly coded as non-White: 1) isolation from other non-Whites;[48] 2) "racially neutral" environments that enforce colorblind interpretations of family and community; 3) an ethic that privileges individualism; and 4) high priority placed on the material achievements of a middle-class existence.[49] In many ways, Twine's theories can be applied to Korean adoptees as well; most are in family and social environments that fulfill Twine's conditions. In their White American families, the Korean adoptees I interviewed tended to be "raised White,"[50] possibly because the adoptive parents were not interested in the birth culture of the adoptee, certainly because of the lack of availability of parenting models that privileged the modeling of another culture over the parents' own.

Korean adoptees' assimilation into the family is followed by assimilation into racial and cultural identities of Whiteness. Many adoptees remarked that the only people they saw, growing up, were White. Because of acculturation to Whiteness through rearing, many Korean adoptees find easy access to White privileges and life options, because of both a general support for White identities and a lack of support for non-White ones.

The practice of transracial adoption both highlights and erases race in adoptees. While most adoptees can never escape the reality and the heightened racial visibility that they are one of the few persons—if not the only person—of color in their adoptive families (and often in their communities), White parents and even entire communities often work to lower adoptee racial visibility and erase racial differences using a number of strategies, including instilling the values of a "weak" multiculturalism (which, as noted in chapter 4, celebrates difference but does not address a history of racism and imperial injustice), downplaying racial incidents, and enacting racially homogenizing ideologies.

For Korean adoptees, the ambiguity of Asian American racialization is compounded by racial ambiguity within adoptive families that use colorblindness to smooth over racial differences and conform to a normative construct of family that includes blood ties and physical resemblance between parents and children.[51] Twila L. Perry calls this tendency "colorblind individualism," and argues that it includes a belief that transracial adoption "constitutes a positive step towards a more integrated, nonracist society."[52] Paradoxically, although a colorblind ideology seems to have become a norm for adoptive parents in raising their transracially and transnationally adopted children, that the process of searching for a child to adopt is, recent research reveals, typically highly racialized and full of race-based selection preferences.[53] Most adoptive families continue to acknowledge racial differences, but these differences can be wiped away by the claiming of a single culture and national identity (usually White-dominated American culture). Recent studies of the tendency to conflate culture and race in mainstream American society have illuminated this privileging of cultural sameness over racial difference in adoptive families.[54]

Individualism is highly valued in mainstream American society, and especially, perhaps, in adoptive families, in which parents have approached child acquisition with much decision-making and deliberation.[55] It is the experience of choosing, described by transnational adoption scholar Sara Dorow as "the discursive power of the 'chosen child,'"[56] that is deployed to compensate for the lack of normativity in family building by adoption. Many adoptive parents tell their adopted children, "I chose *you*!" in order to make adopted children feel special despite their lack of biological relation to the family, a practice Kristi Brian attributes to the emphasis on choice for prospective adoptive parents in the transnational adoption industry.[57] Although there are surely good intentions in this particular parenting strategy, unbeknownst to parents, this can be construed by adoptees as a very one-sided choice; most adoptees understand very well that they had absolutely no choice in their family placement, certainly no more than biological children have in being born into a family.

The conditions identified by Twine for the creation of a White identity regardless of phenotype—racial isolation, a racially neutral environment, and emphasis on individualism and material attainment—are in place for most Korean adoptees. That they would develop White identities while in White families could be seen as predictable, even unavoidable. Vincent Cheng notes that, for better or for worse, interracial and intercultural "adoptions make a radical mockery of any notions of an authentic identity. Children adopted as infants . . . have almost no experience of their birth parents and of the culture of their birth parents."[58]

****

## Adoptee Identity between Races

Recent studies of Korean American adoptee identity corroborate this work in their complication of racial binaries among adoptees. Grace Kim, Karen Suyemoto, and Castellano Turner identify "Korean adoptee" as an important identifier among some adoptees, as well as the recognition of separate racial (Asian) and cultural (American) identities among their Korean adoptee subjects.[78] Jiannbin Shiao and Mia Tuan, in their study of sixty adult Korean adoptees, separated their subjects into four groups, rating them according to their degree of self-identification with either Asian American or White American identity.[79] However, the life histories of Korean adoptees in this research suggest that these classification schemes are not entirely adequate to describe Korean adoptee-identified individuals. First, identity formation for many of the participants in this work has been fluid throughout the lives of the adoptees; many reported that their racial identities had changed over the course of their lives. Similarly, Dani Meier found that most of the Korean adoptees in his study "opted out of Korean cultural experiences" as children.[80] So how have adoptees who exhibit strong Korean adoptee identity developed this identity over time? Most of the participants in this research who elected to express a Korean adoptee identity reported that the decision to do so grew out of experiences of marginalization that were difficult to reconcile in White or nonadopted circles, or out of meeting other adoptees with whom they felt a meaningful connection. Through these common experiences, an adoptee identity is formulated.

****

The accounts noted reflect a range of experiences around Korean adoptee identity, and many also reflect changes in identity that take place over adoptees' lifetimes. In her work on mixed-race identities, Maria Root finds that many mixed-race individuals change their self-identity over their lifetimes.[84] Researchers Cookie White Stephan and Walter G. Stephan make similar findings in their research on mixed-race Japanese Americans: identity is often based on the particular social context each person is in, and the social pressure for mixed-race persons to only have a single ethnic identity is psychologically harmful.[85] Although most of the Korean adoptee informants with whom I spoke were not of mixed race, transracial adoptees are in many ways culturally mixed in their cultural identities of White, Asian, American, Korean, and/or adopted, and many identified as White earlier in life, while living with parents, and had an epiphany of sorts sometime during adulthood where their racial designation changed from White.

In their study of Korean adoptee college students, Joy Hoffman and Edlun Vallejo Peña note that "adoptees assumed two identities—one being Asian and/or Korean, and one of being White."[86] Some experienced this as adolescents, some as young adults, some not until they were in their thirties. Not surprisingly, I found ambivalence in adoptees as they were transitioning and questioning their racial and cultural identities. For many, the price of changing racial and cultural identities (from White to Korean or Asian) was high. Most eventually chose identities as Asian or Asian American. However, many remarked that even this identity did not entirely fit their life experiences. One subject said that "as an adoptee, you're always going to be in between; you're not Asian enough and you're not White enough."[87] In a more complicated rendering of this idea, Gail remarked on the stark contrasts between her White and Korean identities, "Minnesota is profoundly White; it doesn't get any Whiter than this, except North Dakota, and I'm from a town near the North Dakota border. The population and the ignorance and the White privilege that comes with that. But then I think what is the alternative. I can move to California or Hawaii. . . . but . . . I can't even make it to the grocery store . . . I can't even make it to King's [a local Korean restaurant], because then I have to be profoundly Korean."[88]

* * * *

Gratitude has always been a prerequisite for people of color to be admitted into White American society; non-Whites accepted and loved by Whites are expected to be grateful for this privilege. Embedded in the demand for gratitude is the strong maintenance of White as hierarchically superior to all other races. Using this logic, any non-White person elevated to a position of Whiteness should be grateful.[101] The accusation of ingratitude is both common and disturbing when launched at Korean adoptees. This charge almost always refers to adoptees' failure to appreciate the benefits afforded them through adoption. Inferred here is the ethnocentric assumption that any person adopted from Korea (or any poor country that sends its children to rich White countries for adoption) should be grateful for their adoption, since the quality of life as an American is obviously higher than that of a Korean. Those who accuse adoptees of ingratitude are attempting to enforce the colorblind racial etiquette of transracial adoption by accusing the adoptees of breaking the rules of etiquette. Any adoptee who is ungrateful, especially if racial difference is seen as the basis for personal problems experienced by individual adoptees, is disrupting the more harmonious norm of colorblindness—a norm that denies racialization as potentially divisive and threatening for people of color in America.

Ingratitude among Korean adoptees potentially threatens adoptive family systems and relationships, the multimillion-dollar transnational adoption industry, and paternalistic relations between the United States and the nations that supply adoptable children. So, for grateful Korean adoptees, becoming and remaining White (equated with becoming and remaining American) fulfills an important nation-building function of transnational adoption. With the stakes so high, there is little tolerance for adoptees who express interest in Asian, Korean, or in-between identities.

Despite efforts to regulate Korean adoptee identity by setting up a dichotomy of angry Asian or grateful White, many Korean adoptees respond to being placed in the either/or position by staking a claim to the in-between space. Although adoptees do express frustration at being neither here nor there, neither American nor Korean, neither White nor Asian, Korean adoptee identity occupies any and all of these identities as well as any number of hybridized identities between and outside them.

## Notes

40. Tuan, *Forever Foreigners*, 161.
41. Heather Jacobson, *Culture Keeping: White Mothers, International Adoption, and the Negotiation of Family Difference* (Nashville: Vanderbilt University Press, 2008).

42. Richard C. Tessler, Gail Gamache, and Liming Liu, *West Meets East: Americans Adopt Chinese Children* (Westport, CT: Bergin & Garvey, 1999), 20.
43. Sara Dorow, *Transnational Adoption: A Cultural Economy of Race, Gender, and Kinship* (New York: New York University Press, 2006); Jacobson, *Culture Keeping*; Kristi Brian, *Reframing Transnational Adoption: Adopted Koreans, White Parents, and the Politics of Kinship* (Philadelphia: Temple University Press, 2012).
44. "The Asian Population: 2010. 2010 Census Briefs." Bureau of the Census. March 2012. www.census.gov/prod/cen2010/briefs/c2010br-11.pdf
45. Zhou, "Are Asian Americans Becoming 'White'?"
46. Oh Myo Kim, Reed Reichwald, and Richard Lee, "Cultural Socialization in Families with Adopted Adolescents: A Mixed-Method, Multi-Informant Study," *Journal of Adolescent Research* 28: 1 (2013): 69–95.
47. Henry Yu, *Thinking Orientals* (New York: Oxford University Press, 2002), 101, 109.
48. This is debatable in her example, since a number of her subjects were living with their non-White mothers.
49. France Winddance Twine, "Brown- Skinned White Girls," in *Displacing Whiteness: Essays in Social and Cultural Criticism*, ed. Ruth Frankenburg (Durham, NC: Duke University Press, 1997), 214–243.
50. Phrase borrowed from Twine, "Brown- Skinned White Girls," 218.
51. Hawley Fogg-Davis, *The Ethics of Transracial Adoption*, (Ithaca, NY: Cornell University Press, 2002).
52. Twila L. Perry, "The Transracial Adoption Controversy: An Analysis of Discourse and Subordination," *New York University Review of Law & Social Change*, 21:1 (1993–1994): 33–108.
53. Quiroz, *Adoption in a Color-Blind Society* and Jacobson, *Culture Keeping*.
54. Song, *Choosing Ethnic Identity*, 18. Song discusses the politically correct tendency to emphasize culture over race in contemporary British society, and I would argue that the substitution of culture for race operates similarly in American society.
55. Interestingly, the practice of colorblindness can also be individuated within adoptive families; in *Choosing Ethnicity, Negotiating Race*, Tuan and Shiao document White adoptive families who judge their Korean adopted children not to have color, while asserting highly racialized attitudes toward people of color outside the family.
56. Dorow, *Transnational Adoption*, 181.
57. Brian, *Reframing Transnational Adoption*.
58. Cheng, *Inauthentic*, 70.

****

71. Richard M. Lee, "The Transracial Adoption Paradox: History, Research, and Counseling Implications of Cultural Socialization," *The Counseling Psychologist* 31:6 (2003): 711–744.
72. Oral History 4.
73. Sara Docan-Morgan, "Korean Adoptees' Retrospective Reports of Intrusive Interactions: Exploring Boundary Management in Adoptive Families," *Journal of Family Communications* 10 (2010): 137–157.
74. Christopher Bagley and Loretta Young. "The Identity, Adjustment and Achievement of Transracially Adopted Children: A Report and Empirical

Report," in *Race, Education, and Identity*, ed. Gajendra K. Verma and Christopher Bagley (New York: St. Martin's Press, 1979), 192–219. William Feigelman, "Adjustments of Transracially and Inracially Adopted Young Adults," *Child and Adolescent Social Work Journal* 17:3 (2000): 165–183. Madelyn Freundlich and Joy Kim Lieberthal, "The Gathering of the First Generation of Adult Korean Adoptees: Adoptees' Perceptions of International Adoption" (Adoption Institute, 2000), paper published online, available from www.adoptioninstitute.org/proed/korfindings.html. Leslie D. Hollingsworth, "Effect of Transracial/Transethnic Adoption on Children's Racial and Ethnic Identity and Self-Esteem: A Meta-Analytic Review," *Marriage & Family Review* 25:1–2 (1997): 99–130. H. J. M. Versluis-den Bieman and F. C. Verhulst, "Self- Reported and Parent Reported Problems in Adolescent International Adoptees," *Journal of Child Psychology & Psychiatry & Allied Disciplines* 36:8 (1995): 1411–1428.

75. Oral History 7.
76. Oral History 39.
77. Oral History 59.
78. Grace Kim, Karen L. Suyemoto, and Castellano B. Turner, "Sense of Belonging, Sense of Exclusion, and Racial Ethnic Identities in Korean Transracial Adoptees," *Cultural Diversity and Ethnic Minority Psychology* 16:2 (2010): 179–190.
79. Jiannbin Shiao and Mia Tuan, "A Sociological Approach to Race, Identity, and Asian Adoption," in *International Korean Adoption: A Fifty- Year History of Policy and Practice*, ed. M. Elizabeth Vonk, Kathleen Bergquist, Dong Soo Kim, and Marvin Feit (New York: Routledge, 2007), 155–170.
80. Dani I. Meier, "Loss and Reclaimed Lives: Cultural Identity and Place in Korean-American Intercountry Adoptees" (PhD diss., University of Minnesota, 1998).

****

84. Root, "Rethinking Racial Identity Development."
85. Cookie White Stephan and Walter G. Stephan, "What Are the Functions of Ethnic Identity?" in *We Are a People: Narrative and Multiplicity in Constructing Ethnic Identity*, ed. Jeffery W. Burroughs and Paul Spickard (Philadelphia: Temple University Press, 2000): 229–243.
86. Joy Hoffman and Edlun Vallejo Peña, "Too Korean to be White and Too White to Be Korean: Ethnic Identity Development among Transracial Korean Adoptees," *Journal of Student Affairs Research and Practice* 50:2 (2013): 152–170.
87. Oral History 8.
88. Oral History 11.
101. Twila Perry articulates a similar critique, focusing on the transfer from a devalued mother to a valued mother, and how children who experience this transfer are considered by society at large to be lucky, in "Transracial and International Adoption: Mothers, Hierarchy, and Feminist Legal Theory," *Yale Journal of Law and Feminism* 10 (1998): 101–164.

# From Strathern, Marilyn. *After Nature: English Kinship in the Late Twentieth Century.* Cambridge UP, 1992.

For a decade now, considerable publicity has been given to artificial parenthood, and particularly to the figure of the surrogate mother. In the image of the surrogate mother appears the possibility of splitting apart functions that in nature are contained in the one body, ovulation and gestation. The English reaction to the new reproductive technologies in general has predictably ranged from wonder to fear. For they appear to make within human reach other dreams/nightmares, such as cloning—the possibility of individuals reproducing themselves many times over—and genetic determination—that parents may be able to screen out or preselect certain attributes of the child for whom they wish.

The divergence of views can be summarised in the two positions stated during the Parliamentary debate on Enoch Powell's *The Unborn Children (Protection) Bill* in 1985. The debate raised general questions about medical research into human fertilisation; I quote from Naomi Pfeffer's 1987 essay.

One Member of Parliament stated the case as follows: 'The object of our interest in medical research into embryology and human fertilisation is to help humanity. It is to help those who are infertile and to help control infertility[.] . . . The researchers are not monsters, but scientists. They are medical scientists working in response to a great human need. We should be proud of them. The infertile parents who have been helped are grateful to them' (House of Commons Debates, 1984–5, 73, column 654). Opposing this view, Pfeffer adds (1987: 81), 'are those who see these means of treating infertility as misguided and unethical because they see them as meddling with the secrets of life itself. This technology, they argue, "promises benefits perhaps, but [it] could end by destroying the essential humanity of man[.] . . . The technology that promised a paradise now shows signs of delivering a hell" *(ibid.*, column 649)'.

Technology can also be understood as 'too much' culture; nonetheless as a source of anxiety in this field it seems a relatively new target. Anxieties over artificial insemination, for instance, have taken interestingly different forms over the last fifty years. I continue Pfeffer's account.

DOI: 10.4324/9781003203827-10

Artificial insemination (using donor semen) has been clinical practice as an infertility treatment in England since the late 1930s.[11] However, not until case details were later published in the *British Medical Journal* was it widely known. It then became a matter of public outcry, likened to 'human stud farming', a reference to the introduction of agricultural centres for cattle insemination in the early 1940s.

> An article published in the *Sunday Despatch* in November 1945 articulated many of the contemporary concerns about artificial insemination using donor semen. It warned that 'a super-race of test-tube babies will become the guardians of atom bomb secrets[.] . . . Fathers will be chosen by eugenic experts of the United Nations'.
>
> (1987: 93)

Different concerns surfaced during the 1950s. A divorce court had been asked whether artificial insemination by donor constituted adultery if a wife went ahead without her husband's consent. A committee of enquiry was set up in 1959.

> The social issue . . . was the question of legitimacy. As Lord Brabazon of Tara put it, 'When we come down to brass tacks, the whole thing revolves on whether the child should be a bastard or not'. Bastardy was perceived as a growing threat; since the Second World War the number of illegitimate births had been rising steadily[.] . . . To many it appeared that the institution of the family, which they believed underpinned Western civilisation, was under threat. Children conceived through donor semen represented a conscious effort to bring forth an illegitimate child within marriage . . . artificial insemination would be used by the greedy and unscrupulous to defeat claims to titles and estates not rightly theirs. And not only was patrimony threatened; paternity itself was in jeopardy[.] . . . 'knowledge that there is uncertainty about the fatherhood of some is a potential threat to the security of air.[12]
>
> (1987: 94, references omitted)

In the 1980s, however, the debates are less about the animality of the procedures than about the intrusion of technology into biological process, less about the lawfulness of a union than about the kind of contract the parties should make with each other, and less about the property claims to bastards than about rights to the products of one's body. Finally, they are less about the ownership and disposal of whole persons than about the ownership and disposal of reproductive cells.

Long established as procedures for artificial insemination might be, they find a new context in the 1982 committee chaired by Mary Warnock.

> Handling human gametes [eggs and sperm] and embryos outside of the body raised the problem of moral responsibility and legal ownership. It is not surprising therefore to find that very many of the recommendations of the Warnock Report are about their ownership. supply and disposal. In many ways the Warnock Report recapitulates the anxieties about adoption of children current in the 1920s. Then adoption was not regulated by the law; it could be and was exploited as a source of cheap child labour [.] . . . Instead of a traffic in children, we have [today] a trade in human gametes and embryos. and in place of white-slave traders, in the public imagination are desperate infertile men and women and unscrupulous doctors and scientists. In this context. the reasons for the inclusion of artificial insemination using donor semen and surrogacy for consideration by the Committee chaired by Mary Warnock become clear; in both gametes are purchased either by doctors or through commercial agencies.
>
> (Pfeffer 1987; 95–6, emphasis removed)

The public mind, as reflected through the Warnock Committee, links artificial insemination to commercialism, to market manipulation and consumer choice.[13] And where those earlier anxieties touched on the implications for people's legal and social standing, the present anxiety concerns interference with natural relations. Civilisation is not so much under threat; Nature very much is.

Natural process is also about future potential. Hence clinically established procedures such as artificial insemination, and newer ones such as in vitro fertilisation, come to be put aside 'technologies' such as ectogenesis and parthenogenesis which are little more than imaginative extrapolations into the future. The Warnock Report (1985: 4) claims they all have in common 'the anxiety they [have] generated in the public mind'; the question is the kind of future one can expect. Hilary Rose expands the point.

> Certainly beyond IVF and the actual or potential gene therapies lies a scientific and technological horizon along which are ranged other possible reproductive interventions: would it be possible to rear a foetus from fertilization to independent 'birth' entirely in vitro (ectogenesis)? To clone identikit copies of individuals from single cells or 'gene libraries'? To rear a human embryo in the uterus of a non-human creature or even make human-non-human hybrids? Or to provide a technique that would enable women to give birth without the need for sperm to fertilize their eggs (parthenogenesis, a form of cloning)?

> Could men have babies? These prospects and others form the stuff of science-fantasy dreams.
>
> (Rose 1987: 158)

Here the hybrid is no metaphor drawn from another domain (plant breeding), and does not describe cultivated characteristics. It refers to the literal possibility of producing human beings by graft.

Crossing human gametes with those of other species is at present technically impossible (Ferguson 1990: 24), and in any case unlikely to be developed for therapeutic purposes when transpecies genetic implants hold instead a realistic promise of development. Much of this thinking must remain in its science-fiction form, but it still remains thinking about the future. And the future has always been imagined as a matter of infinite possibilities. Thus Ferguson notes it is a possibility that the embryo may be manipulated so as to engineer into it additional genes which, for example, may not naturally occur in the human species' (1990: 14). Perhaps some of the apparently irrational fears such writers seek to allay are fears for the future of possibility itself.

If technological mastery were indeed gained over genetic makeup, the expressed fear is that the way would be open for eugenic programmes that would inevitably lead to preferences for particular types of persons. As the English are used to telling themselves, it is less the technology that is in doubt than how it will be used. Perhaps the prominence of the clone image in people's vision of the future encapsulates the anticipation that the exercise of choice in this regard would take away choice. The very idea of selecting for clones obviates the idea of selection itself. Choice would thus be shown up for something other than it seemed. More technology does not seem to compenesate [sic] for less nature.

Technology, for those who are afraid of it, is a kind of culture without people. Meanwhile one is at the mercy of people. The reduction of naturally produced genetic material, like reduction in the diversity of the world's species, is symbolised in the fantasy that if those with the power in fact get their hands on the appropriate technology, they would produce versions of themselves over and again and/or counter versions such as drones and slaves. A particular individual would be reproduced—but its multiplication would be the very opposite of individuation. Diversity without individuality; individuality without diversity.

## Notes

11. According to Rivière (1985: 2), artificial insemination by the husband was first recorded in 1776. I note that the former acronym for artificial insemination by donor (AID) has been replaced by DI (donor insemination).

12. '[The Committee] concluded that whilst it could not condone the practice of artificial insemination using donor semen because clearly it was immoral, it could not prevent it from taking place between consenting adults. Thus the wives of infertile men who were inseminated with donor semen became stigmatized because . . . *they were indulging in an unnatural act* in order to conceive a bastard within the institution of marriage' (Pfeffer 1987: 95, my emphasis).
13. See the discussion in Wolfram (1987: 210f). Pfeffer (1987: 97) adds that the 'mercenary image of the infertile, their alleged commodification of parenting, is reinforced by the ways in which the cash nexus has infiltrated the alleviation of infertility. Not only are there now commercial agencies arranging surrogacy [but] . . . cuts in funding in the NHS have led many District Health Authorities to cut back on [free] services for the treatment of infertility which they see as an expensive luxury'.

## Works Cited

Ferguson, Mark. "Contemporary and Future Possibilities for Human Embryonic Manipulation." *Experiments on Embryos*, edited by A. Dyson and J. Harris, Routledge, 1990, pp. 5–22.

Pfeffer, Naomi. "Artificial Insemination, In-vitro Fertilization and the Stigma of Infertility." *Reproductive Technologies: Gender, Motherhood and Medicine*, edited by Michelle Stanworth, Polity, 1987, pp. 81–97.

Riviere, Peter. "Unscrambling Parenthood: The Warnock Report." *Anthropology Today*, vol. 4, 1988, pp. 2–7.

Rose, Hilary. "Victorian Values in the Test-Tube: The Politics of Reproductive Science and Technology." *Reproductive Technologies: Gender, Motherhood and Medicine*, edited by Michelle Stanworth, Polity, 1987, pp. 151–173.

Warnock, Mary. *A Question of Life: The Warnock Report on Human Fertilisation and Embryology*. Basil Blackwell, 1985.

Wolfram, Sybil. *In-Laws and Out-Laws. Kinship and Marriage in England.* Croom Helm, 1987.

# From Singley, Carol. "Teaching American Literature: The Centrality of Adoption." *Modern Language Studies*, vol. 34, iss. 1/2, 2004, pp. 76–83.

## American Adoption

Adoption, a widely acknowledged, routinely practiced way to form families, appears in Western cultural mythologies and privileged literary texts dating from the biblical story of Moses and the Greek tragedy *Oedipus*. Yet adoption is often missing in literary discourse about constructions of American individual, family, and national identity. The omission occurs in part because theories of identity are often predicated, implicitly or explicitly, on genealogically-based models and in part because adoption, kinship, and genealogy are less likely to be employed as critical tools for examining literature than are other identifying marks of difference. However, from John Winthrop's declaration in 1637 that "A family is a little commonwealth, and a commonwealth is a great family" (166) onward, notions of American kinship and nationality have been understood as mutually reinforcing. Viewing the family as microcosm [sic] of the republic, American writers and their critics have used the social and moral pulse of the family to predict as well as to assess the health of the nation.

Once we help students see how family structures are central to understanding American literature and culture, they become attentive to the kinship patterns that adoption both displaces and replicates. They also become aware of the various American literary forms and themes that adoption engenders. Adoption, for example, can illuminate the tensions between American concepts of dependence and independence, of separation and affiliation, of origins and fresh starts. Adoption practices, as well as the religious, economic, political, and psychological forces that shape them, provide a window through which we view a wide American literary and cultural landscape. One way to appreciate adoption's signifying power is to realize that at many points in history adoption has been marginalized, stigmatized, and even made secret by custom and law (Carp 2–3, Melosh 108–09). It has not, to use Priscilla Wald's phrase, been part of the "[o]fficial stories [that] constitute Americans" (2). At the heart of discussions about adoption, then,

DOI: 10.4324/9781003203827-11

lies ambivalence, a feeling that students often report when they begin to address this topic. In Western culture and American society, in particular, this ambivalence stems from the tension between a deeply rooted, historical definition of identity as derived only through bloodline, and an equally strong belief in self-improvement and the power of individuals to define and shape their own lives.

These competing, archetypal sensibilities gain special potency in an American context, in which the genesis and development of the republic is predicated on genealogical rupture and fusion. I begin most discussions of American adoption by helping students see that the story of adoption is embedded in that of the nation itself. The republic was founded on the concept of breaking away from a "birth parent" country, England, and adopting, or being adopted by, a new land. The nation was initially "imagined," to borrow Benedict Anderson's term, not as continuous genealogy, but as community constructed by a consensual process of disaffiliation and re-affiliation. Students easily identify with the hybridity of American culture but they may not automatically make connections between familial and national ideologies. Indeed, the United States remains today a nation of immigrants drawn together by geography and common purpose rather than by blood—a nation as dependent on creation as on generation. Often intercultural as well as interfamilial, adoption speaks to this American experience. Yet even as they embrace newness as a hallmark of national identity, Americans remain fascinated by genealogy. Researching family trees, after gardening, is the favorite national hobby (Beizer 245, citing Seabrook 58). Ambivalence toward adoption derives from this preoccupation with origins, located in the inheritance of a hegemonic Anglo European culture and an ideological commitment to severing all genealogical ties, starting over, and creating oneself and one's nation anew. Alexis de Tocqueville described this tension, or doubleness, in American society as early as 1835, when he visited the new nation and recorded his impressions in *Democracy in America*. On a small scale, adoption narratives dramatize the struggle of individuals and families to draw and redraw lines of bonds and affection; on a larger scale, they portray a nation wrestling in multiple ways with conflicting notions of citizenship in which belonging and entitlement are bestowed either by birthright or by ideology.

## Orphancy and Homelessness

After establishing a theoretical foundation for linking adoption and American literary experience, I turn to early American texts. I focus on adoption motifs in the seventeenth century, for example, on the accounts of hopeful but estranged settlers aboard Winthrop's Arabella. Feeling bereft and homeless, they longed for the protective embrace of the old world, sought adoptive shelter in the new one, and developed a Calvinist theology consistent with those feelings. Poet Anne Bradstreet, for example, writes about her revulsion to unfamiliar surroundings in a spiritual autobiography addressed to her children: "[I] came into this country, where I found a new world and new manners, at which my heart rose. But after I was convinced it was the way of God, I submitted to it" (241). In her poem, "A Dialogue Between Old England and New," Bradstreet uses the maternal imagery that typifies her literary style to address her native England as "dear Mother, fairest queen and best" (l. 1), to whom she promises allegiance: "You are my mother nurse, and I your flesh" (l. 216). William Bradford writes that upon landing at Plymouth Rock, the Pilgrims "fell upon their knees and blessed the God of Heaven who had brought them over the vast and furious ocean" (56). However, the land appeared as threatening and inhospitable as the sea: "they had now no friends to welcome them nor inns to entertain or refresh their weatherbeaten bodies; no houses or much less towns to repair to, to seek for succour" (57). I consider Calvinist sermons, especially one by Cotton Mather entitled "Orphanatrophium" (1711), which exhorts congregants to open their homes to orphaned children and models the rescue of needy children on the desire for heavenly adoption by God. Mather's Calvinist theology, applied domestically, erected the frame on which future narratives of adoption as salvation would be positioned. A study of early American adoption also includes Indian captivity narratives—for example, those by Mary Rowlandson or Mary Jemison—in which the relocation of adults and children into non-blood related kinship structures is charged with political and religious ideology. In the seventeenth century, equating Indians with savages and with the devil itself, threatened settlers termed their inscription into Indian society "captivity," despite the fact some individuals chose to remain with Indians.

I then analyze nineteenth-century historical romances such as *Hope Leslie* (1827), by Catharine Maria Sedgwick, in which the white protagonist's sister is adopted into Indian society and an Indian girl becomes a captive servant in a Puritan household. *Hobomok* (1824) by Lydia Maria Child, radical in its depiction of miscegenation, describes the eventual adoption and anglicization of the child of an Indian-white marriage. James Fenimore Cooper in the *Leatherstocking Tales* tells the stories of many orphans, including Alice Munro, Cora Munro, and Uncas in *The Last of the Mohicans* (1826) and the Hutter sisters in *The Deerslayer* (1841). These narratives of ethnic cross-adoptions suggest various meanings attached to the practice and demonstrate the various ways that adoption serves—across a broad spectrum—to save, integrate, enfranchise, commodify, appropriate, or even enslave others. Later in the nineteenth century, when the U.S. government removed Indian children from their homes and boarded them at federally supported schools, the term "captivity" was not used; neither, however, was adoption, which signifies legal as well as emotional bonds and responsibilities between the adopter and the adopted. Zitkala-Ša's *American Indian Legends* (1921) narrates the profound sense of dislocation that this forced assimilation into white society produced in her. A look at cross-adoptions of Indians and whites reveals that the transfer of children across families and cultures, as well as the power to name these transactions, rests with the adopter.

A study of American adoption literature might also include Benjamin Franklin's *Autobiography* (1791–1798). Although he was not adopted, Franklin's writings reflect a struggle between adoptive and genealogical impulses as he reconciles loyalties toward England with growing commitments to American independence. Franklin's autobiography is commonly read as a blueprint for the "get ahead, go ahead" American success story. Yet his narrative reveals fundamental ambivalence about the political project with which he is so identified. Franklin's role as founding father depends upon his willingness to rebel against the restrictive parental authority of England and lead the nation toward liberty and self-adoption. But by addressing his letter to his son—who responds to questions of loyalty by becoming a Tory, not a rebel—Franklin reveals his own attachment to blood. The opening pages of the autobiography underline this point by describing the significance Franklin attached to a genealogical search conducted in England. However, although Franklin's return to the mother country confirms his identity and validates roots, the narrative also tells students that knowing blood origins, while important, cannot fully tell us who we are. In Franklin's case—and that of many adoptees writing about their experiences—the drive to discover roots fuels a process of self-discovery and self-construction based, but not necessarily dependent, on origins. A static past, then, propels a dynamic process of identity-making.

* * * *

In portraying families that were made, not born, writers retold the American story of upward mobility and limitless opportunity, helping to define the terms upon which the nation's development would continue. The process of adoption, confirming inclusion at the same time that it acknowledges genealogical rupture, contributed to the nation's sense of itself as cohesive yet flexible, capable of extending its boundaries and absorbing new ideas and individuals.

Adoption is not simplistically optimistic. On the one hand, the inscription of the child in a loving home affirms a national desire for well-being and progress. On the other hand, the disruption attendant upon adoption inscribes the worries of a new republic facing such challenges as an influx of immigrants; increased mobility and loosened patriarchal family authority; and broken family bonds caused by slavery. Stories of adoption celebrate the nurturing elasticity of the nation through the microcosm of the family, asserting the expansion of its borders but also recording the restrictions of those possibilities for certain groups, such as Indians and African Americans. Writers also present adoption as distinctly gendered, practiced more by female characters than male characters. In much literature of the mid-nineteenth century, girls who demonstrate piety, obedience, and faithful service to others are rewarded with adoption and eventual marriage, while boys are likely to avail them selves of temporary adoptions or mentoring and then move on to make their individual fortunes. In sum, studying adoption narratives and their parallel issues of American nationhood reveal a generation of writers and readers embracing inclusion but equally uneasy about its social effects.

Although adoption meets practical needs by providing homes to orphans and offspring to the childless, throughout most of the nineteenth century adoption also carries the symbolic meaning of rescue or salvation, replicating a Christian doctrine in which taking in a destitute or parentless child mirrors God's salvation of humankind. Students who study domestic fiction may come to see how adoption as child-saving represents on a small scale a national preoccupation with reform on a larger scale. Sentimentality, a preferred fictional mode for these dramas of salvation, carries a sense of fulfillment or completion and affirms a fundamental assumption behind social reform: that people can be recovered or restored.

* * * *

That the American family functions in politics and literature as a microcosm of the nation is now a critical commonplace. What these wide-ranging representations of adoption offer, however, is a lens through which to examine contested spaces in this productive conflation of family and nation. Juxtaposing biological kinship ties with adoptive ones, these narratives of adoption raise the larger questions of which they are a part: questions of allegiance to individual and community; tensions between independence and affiliation and between roots and fresh starts; and lines demarcating social exclusion and inclusion. Narrating experiences of home lost and found, these texts demonstrate the various ways that adoption serves—across a broad spectrum—to negotiate the sense of belonging obtained by entitlement and by birthright. In short, students come to see how adoption performs "cultural work," to use Jane Tompkins' term. Multi-cultural and multi-familial, adoption appears not only as an isolated literary feature but as a complex expression of ambivalent, sometimes contradictory, notions about the child, family, community, and nation. Teaching adoption as a part of American literature makes the present visible in ways that fulfill the goals of literary study, helping students become more sensitive, perceptive readers of texts and able to make personal and public sense of the world.

## Works Cited

Anderson, Benedict. *Imagined Communities: Reflections on the Origin and Spread of Nationalism.* Revised edition, Verso, 1991.

Beizer, Janet. "One's Own Reflections on Motherhood, Owning, and Adoption." *The Adoption Issue*, special issue of *Tulsa Studies in Women's Literature*, vol. 21, no. 2, Fall 2002, pp. 237–255.

Bradstreet, Anne. "A Dialogue Between Old England and New," and "To My Dear Children." *The Works of Anne Bradstreet*, edited by Jeannine Hensley, Harvard UP, 1967, pp. 179–188; 240–245.

Carp, E. Wayne. *Family Matters: Secrecy and Disclosure in the History of Adoption.* Harvard UP, 1998.

Melosh, Barbara. *Strangers and Kin: The American Way of Adoption.* Harvard UP, 2002.

Seabrook, John. "The Tree of Me." *The New Yorker*, 26 Mar. 2001, pp. 58–71.

Tocqueville, Alexis de. *Democracy in America.* 2 vols., Vintage, 1945.

Tompkins, Jane. *Sensational Designs: The Cultural Work of American Fiction, 1790–1860.* Oxford UP, 1985.

Wald, Priscilla. *Constituting Americans: Cultural Anxiety and Narrative Form.* Duke UP, 1995.

Winthrop, John. "A Defense of an Order of Court." *The Puritans in America: A Narrative Anthology*, edited by Alan Heimert and Andrew Delbanco, Harvard UP, 1985, pp. 164–168.

# From Callahan, Cynthia. *Kin of Another Kind: Transracial Adoption on American Literature.* U of Michigan P, 2010.

Before discussing adoption specifically, it makes sense to briefly outline a few of the significant cultural and historical contexts for American Indian adoption. Adoption, as such, was not always the threat to tribes that it became in the mid-twentieth century and had long been practiced in ways that enriched tribal communities and differed starkly from European/American kinship practices. During first contact between tribes and colonists, prisoners of war were often incorporated into tribal communities, and captives replaced lost members of the tribe (Askeland, "Informal" 4–7). Adoption sometimes involved people with living parents who joined another family either in a ceremony or simply as a matter of fact (Holt 23). Just as tribal adoption practices have differed from European/American ones, so do kinship patterns, which, for tribes, often extend beyond the nuclear family to include extended families and sometimes members of the community. As historian Marilyn Holt explains, the traditional extended family in tribal communities raised children collectively, which means that the untimely death of parents did not result in orphancy in the same way that it did in American society; rather, other family or tribal members would care for children without parents. These extended family relationships also served an important socializing function, instructing all children in their cultural practices and ensuring the vibrancy of the tribe (Holt 20). Because of the centrality of the extended family to tribal life, any initiatives that weakened the family also undermined the community. One of the most significant of these initiatives, a precursor to the mass adoptions of the mid-twentieth century, was the boarding school movement, established by the federal government in the late nineteenth century with the goal of mainstreaming American Indian children by sending them to boarding schools far from their reservations. The boarding schools were part of a larger assimilationist strategy that included, in particular, the division of collectively held tribal lands into individual allotments on reservations. While in boarding schools, children were forbidden from using their native languages or practicing their customs. Intended to "civilize" Indians (Stark and Stark 127), the boarding school

DOI: 10.4324/9781003203827-12

movement had far-reaching consequences—not only for the children, who returned to their reservations unable to speak to their families and unfamiliar with traditional practices, but for the communities that relied on each individual's active participation in the culture (Holt 15–16).

Within this longer history of family disruption, the outplacement of Indian children for fostering and adoption remains particularly problematic, the consequence of U.S.-tribal relations and shifting attitudes toward adoption in the nation as a whole. The Indian Adoption Project (1958–67), initiated by the Bureau of Indian Affairs and the Child Welfare League of America, was held up by its administrators as a success (Herman 240), yet the placement rates tell a different story of the damage done by this and other policies that privileged foster care and adoption over solutions that kept children with their tribes. As many as 25 to 35 percent of children were removed from their tribes and placed in non-Indian homes by the early 1970s (Herman 241). Individual placement rates were sometimes much higher, as in Wisconsin, where "Indian children ran the risk of being separated from their parents at a rate nearly 1600 percent greater than non-Indian children" (Stark and Stark 131). Social services agents who viewed Indian families through the lens of white, middle-class nuclear family models often encouraged adoptions and deemed Indian childcare practices inadequate (Unger; Byler).

Beyond the cultural disconnect between social workers and tribal families and the general disregard for the integrity of tribal communities, the adoption of American Indian children in the middle of the twentieth century was driven by the changing culture of American adoption. Native adoptions out of the tribe were remarkable because they departed from the "matching" policies of the midcentury, which placed children with families on the basis of similar physical characteristics, intellect, religion, and race. As adoption demand grew, those who could not adopt "blue-ribbon" white infants because of eligibility limitations—age or already having biological children—turned to Native children as a viable alternative. Adopters did not necessarily prefer American Indians as such, though some did profess an affinity for tribal culture (Fanshel 82).

Instead, the practice reflected the relativity of American racial hierarchies, with difference measured within and against the poles of black and white. As Ellen Herman puts it, "White adopters of Native American children in the 1950s and 1960s were far less willing to consider adopting African American mixed-race children (even in cases where the child's appearance did not testify to his or her racial background) than 'Oriental' children, children older than eight, children with mental retardation, or even children with serious, uncorrectable physical disabilities" (198). American Indians were more desirable candidates for adoption because they were deemed less racially "other" in the view of some whites.

The federal Indian Child Welfare Act of 1978 addressed objections—voiced in congressional hearings, tribal resolutions, and the media—to the large number of adoption and fostering placements in white homes. It prohibits the adoption of American Indian children outside of the reservation without the permission of the tribe and lays out a series of priorities to help govern child placement ("Indian"). In the public discussion preceding the ICWA, tribal leaders and their supporters framed their concerns in terms of cultural impact. Critics of the practice often cited cultural loss and damage to the tribes, linking adoption to larger projects of assimilation and encroachments on tribal sovereignty. For instance, William Byler, executive director of the Association on American Indian Affairs, testified before the Senate Subcommittee on Indian Affairs in 1974, "I think it's a copout when people say it's poverty that's causing family breakdown. I think perhaps the chief thing is the detribalization and the deculturalization, Federal and State and local efforts to make Indians white. It hasn't worked and it will never work and one of the most vicious forms of trying to do this is to take their children. Those are the great emotional risks to Indian families" (Byler). Eschewing much of the language of race common in the African American debate, Byler articulates these practices in terms of culture and identifies them as an attack on tribal cultures, which are comprised of and sustained by Indian families and their children. Like Byler, tribal chief Calvin Isaac, of the Mississippi Band of Choctaw Indians, focuses on adoption's long-term consequences, and he uses similar language. Isaac testified,

> Culturally, the chances of Indian survival are significantly reduced if our children, the only real means for the transmission of the tribal heritage, are to be raised in non-Indian homes and denied exposure to the ways of their People. Furthermore, these practices seriously undercut the tribes' ability to continue as self-governing communities. Probably in no area is it more important that tribal sovereignty be respected than in an area as socially and culturally determinative as family relationships.
>
> (Quoted in "History")

Isaac establishes the interconnection of issues, designating children as a crucial component of ensuring tribal heritage: adoption outside of the tribe does a disservice to the children by denying them their culture; further, it undermines the community itself; and finally, but not least, it violates tribal self-government.

The issue of tribal sovereignty raised by Chief Isaac helps to explain why opposition to the adoption of American Indian children was often voiced in terms of culture and tribal environment rather than race or other concepts that signal innate differences, language that appeared frequently in debates over the adoption of African American children and would arise again, in more muted form, around the adoption of children from Asian countries. Not only were tribes that lost significant numbers of children potentially unable to maintain communities and at risk of eradication, but the intervention of social workers from outside meant that tribes themselves were not granted the right to determine the well-being of their own members in accordance with their own values. Thus, despite the fact that American Indian extra-tribal adoptions most frequently get grouped under the category of "transracial" placements, the primary concern for tribes was not racial integrity as such but national sovereignty, an issue that went hand in hand with the cultural health of a vibrant, populous tribe. This observation is not to say that advocacy for the ICWA was articulated exclusively in terms of culture or tribal sovereignty.[13] In fact, as Stark and Stark point out, these implicit appeals to tribal sovereignty may not have been as persuasive to many legislators as another central theme in the hearings, the effects of adoption on the psychological development of individual children (134). With the debates over African American transracial adoption fresh in the public consciousness, the argument based on psychological impact would have been familiar and persuasive; moreover, it fits with the "best interest" mandate of American child welfare, which privileges the individual child over other, more holistic concerns. Responding to the welfare of individual children and their psychological needs is much less "political" than explicitly affirming the rights of American Indian tribes as distinct cultural entities and, furthermore, as sovereign nations. These concerns intersect in the adoption novels of Dallas Chief Eagle, Barbara Kingsolver, Leslie Marmon Silko, and Sherman Alexie, discussed in chapter 5. They attempt to navigate the competing concerns about individual and cultural identities raised by extra-tribal adoption, at the same time that the authors speak through adoption to address tribal sovereignty, cross-racial relations, and individual self-definition.

## Note

13. For instance, one exception to the tendency to argue in terms of culture is the Oglala Sioux, which used explicitly racial language in a resolution protesting adoption and foster care outside the tribe ("Oglala Sioux" 88).

## Works Cited

Askeland, Lori. "Informal Adoption, Apprenticeship, and Indentured Children in the Colonial Era and the New Republic, 1605–1850." *Children and Youth in Adoption, Orphanages, and Foster Care*, Greenwood, 2006, pp. 3–16.

Byler, William. "Indian Child Welfare Program." *U. S. Senate Subcommittee on Indian Affairs*, 3 Jan. 2010. Liftingtheveil.org/byler.htm.

Fanshel, David. *Far from the Reservation: The Transracial Adoption of American Indian Children*. Scarecrow, 1972.

Herman, Ellen. *Kinship by Design: A History of Adoption in the Modern United States.* U Chicago P, 2008.

"History Behind the Enactment of the Indian Child Welfare Act." *Indian Child Welfare Act Law Center*, 3 Jan. 2010, lcwlc.org.

Holt, Marilyn Irvin. *Indian Orphanages.* U of Kansas P, 2001.

"Indian Child Welfare Act of 1978." *Children and Youth in Adoption, Orphanages, and Foster Care*, Greenwood, 2006, pp. 134–35.

"Oglala Sioux." *The Destruction of American Indian Families*, edited by Steven Unger, Association on American Indian Affairs, 1977, p. 88.

Stark, Heidi Kiiwetinepinesiik, and Kekek Jason Todd Stark. "Flying the Coop: ICWA and the Welfare of Indian Children." *Outsiders Within: Writing on Transracial Adoption*, edited by Jane Jeong Trenka, et al., South End, 2006, pp. 125–138.

Unger, Steven, editor. *The Destruction of American Indian Families.* Association on American Indian Affairs, 1977.

# From Potter, Sarah. *Everybody Else: Adoption and the Politics of Domestic Diversity in Postwar America.* U of Georgia P, 2014.

Chicago, like many northern cities, was the destination of many black southerners who migrated north in search of jobs and greater opportunity in the twentieth century. During the first wave of the Great Migration, in the years around World War I, Chicago's black community grew 148 percent from 1910 to 1920, with an influx of 65,355 migrants. A second, even larger wave of migrants headed north during and after World War II. Although this wave caused a smaller percentage increase in black population in Chicago than the first, in absolute numbers it dwarfed the earlier one, with over five hundred thousand African Americans coming to the city between 1940 and 1960.[16]

For many black Chicagoans, the experience of migration from South to North proved important to their priorities and values, and served as a frequent touchstone in the communication between black applicants and their (often black) social workers. Applicants suggested that the harsh conditions in the Jim Crow South made the black family a locus of support and security prior to migration, and the uncertainties involved in moving so far from home tended to further strengthen family bonds. In addition, the records described the move north as central to applicants' hopes and dreams for their family lives, since many longed to provide their children with more opportunities than they themselves had had growing up in the South.

Scholars have offered a range of interpretations as to the impact of migration on the black family. In a 1930 study of black household patterns in Chicago based on census data from 1920, researchers from the University of Chicago considered the crowded conditions and general poverty of many of the city's black families as the first wave of migration north was coming to a close. They argued that residential patterns suggested "family solidarity," noting that "the presence of so many related individuals and families in these Negro households, especially married sons and daughters, is another indication of tendency to help one another out, and for kin to stick together." Likewise, black mothers often worked, leaving their children unsupervised or in the care of other family members and friends. The

DOI: 10.4324/9781003203827-13

researchers suggested that "all the evidence points to the fact that these mothers work with the principal object of keeping the home together, and not because they prefer the greater independence of a wage earner to the duties of home making."[17] They concluded that a reliance on family unity was crucial to coping with conditions in the urban North.

Several prominent researchers working later in the decade found contrary patterns. They suggested that migration weakened black family life, particularly among the lower classes. In his 1939 *The Negro Family in the United States*, E. Franklin Frazier suggested that as men and women left the confines of rural life, many also abandoned all sense of sexual respectability and personal responsibility. Frazier argued that individuals who migrated without the company of family members were often pulled into lives of impropriety and crime. Unschooled in city ways, they found themselves baffled by the complexity of the urban North and vulnerable to exploitation. Frazier described both northern and southern black urban communities as plagued by single mothers, deserting fathers, and intractable children and youths. Likewise, in their groundbreaking study, *Black Metropolis: A Study of Negro Life in a Northern City*, St. Clair Drake and Horace Cayton portrayed Chicago's Black Belt during the 1930s and early 1940s as troubled by the disorganized family lives and lax morals of the black lower class. Although all of these scholars contended that most middle-class and elite black families were in fact models of family devotion, they suggested that lower-class family patterns were a significant problem for the black community—and that migration was primarily to blame.[18]

Recent historical scholarship has overturned many of these conclusions. It has shown that the experience of migration tended to intensify black Chicagoans' ties to family and close friends. For instance, historian James Grossman suggests that the Great Migration was deeply connected to family and institutional networks that reached black communities on both sides of the Mason-Dixon Line. Job advertisements and editorials in Chicago's chief African American newspaper the *Defender*, correspondence from family and friends, and even relocations of entire church congregations all shaped southern blacks' decisions to migrate northward and their experiences when they got there. Many found housing and work upon arrival in Chicago with the help of hometown family and friends, and they relied on these individuals for assistance. The centrality of personal and family connections to relocation meant that many aspects of southern values and culture—and even entire communities—survived in the urban North.[19]

Black applicants described migration as crucial to their conception of family life. For those whose entire families had migrated, parents and adult siblings often lived near one another and visited back and forth frequently. Relatives who had made the journey together were described as a primary source of support and friendship. Likewise, crowded housing conditions in the Black Belt usually made nuclear family privacy impossible, which tended to encourage more intense (though sometimes more volatile) relationships with in-laws and other kin living in the household. For those who had left parents and siblings in the South in order to come to Chicago, the experience of migration could foster close relationships with other relatives living in the city and family friends who had migrated first.[20]

Further, many couples maintained strong relationships with their families despite the distances involved. For instance, Henry and Virginia Franklin, a young pharmacist and his wife, left Virginia's family, who owned a restaurant, in Texas. When the couple was unable to visit them one Thanksgiving, her family sent a whole turkey for the couple to enjoy and throughout the year sent cookies and cakes.[21] For others with relatives still in the South, a yearly visit back home was a priority, and southern relatives also tended to come to the city every year or two for a stay of at least a month.

Families' closeness in the North built upon already strong family relationships developed in the Jim Crow South. African American applicants with southern roots frequently described long histories of helping to support their families, noting that educational opportunities were fewer and the need for family labor more persistent in the South. Even before the Depression, those from poor black communities frequently relied on each other for support. For example, Charles Clark explained that in his large family in Georgia in the 1910s and 1920s, "as was the custom, the older children assumed responsibility for the younger ones as soon as they were able to help in any way. None of them ever resented having to work as his parents taught them early that it was the duty of each member of the household to share whatever he had or could offer to the other. . . . When he grew older his clothing was shared with the other siblings without question." His experiences growing up were considered by applicant and worker alike as evidence of his sincere commitment to his family.[22]

Applicants had often left the South in order to pursue better jobs and to escape the confines of Jim Crow. These goals were believed to particularly benefit one's children, and parents' dreams of offering a better life to their children often justified the move. Applicants placed special emphasis on giving their children both the emotional and educational opportunities they had missed growing up in segregated communities and often in grinding poverty. For instance, Florence Reed had grown up at a boarding school because her single mother had had to work as a live-in domestic in the South and had not been able to keep her daughter with her. Although Florence appreciated that she had been able to stay in school and receive an education, she also regretted that she had missed building a close relationship with her mother. Further, the family's poverty meant that while all of the other students at the boarding school received care packages and frequent visits, her mother was unable to provide these things. Florence vowed to provide more for her own daughter after moving North. She told her social worker that "if . . . [her adolescent daughter] hadn't been such 'a good child' she thinks she might have spoiled her because she tried so hard to give her everything she didn't have from her own mother."[23]

Raising a child outside of the South also allowed for better educational and social opportunities. Leon Nelson wanted his son to "be able to do some of the things he had not done" when he was growing up in the South. His social worker recorded that he had come "from a poor family in a small town with poor schools. The school was [open] for six months out of the year for Negro children. He seemed to feel bitter because white people control[led] the town and arranged for their children to go to school for nine months a year. The Negro children had to stop in order to work on the farm." Leon believed that his son would receive better and more equitable schooling in Chicago.[24]

Yet Chicago was an intensely segregated city, and black migrants did not always find the welcoming opportunities they had anticipated. Chicago's black neighborhoods were physically and culturally separate from the white neighborhoods surrounding them, and any expansion of the Black Belt faced fierce resistance. Further, the city's Black Belt had been integrated into the city's Democratic political machine through a strong black submachine in the 1930s, which meant that the community's fortunes rose and fell based on the whims of the local Democratic Party. Though African Americans made some gains under the relatively friendly administration of Mayor Edward Kelly, who was in office between 1933 and 1947, Kelly's successors felt less compelled to cater to the black vote in the city. While Kelly had pushed for housing integration, Martin Kennelly, who took office in 1947, and Richard J. Daley, who succeeded Kennelly in 1955, frequently ignored the black community's demands even as they relied on their votes. Though life in Chicago was for many preferable to the Jim Crow South, poverty, discrimination, and inferior housing and education continued to plague Chicago's black families.[25]

Despite these ongoing hardships, many black Chicagoans focused on the positives the city offered for their children. The story of the McKays, a poor black family who lived on Chicago's West Side, demonstrates the importance of children to migrants' feelings about their decision to leave the South—even when conditions remained difficult in the North. The McKays were studied extensively as part of a research project under the purview of the University of Chicago's Allison Davis, an African American anthropologist and education professor. Known as the Washington family in Davis's published work about them, the family struggled to support their children in the North, but they still believed that they were better off than they would have been in the South.[26]

The McKays faced a number of hardships in Chicago. In 1945, the family had eleven children, ranging in age from newborn to twenty-four years old. The parents, Claude and May Della McKay, were in their forties and had moved to Chicago in approximately 1922 after marrying several years before in Kentucky. The couple believed that the older children in the family had benefited from the move north. These children had music lessons, a piano, and the chance to go to school rather than pick cotton.[27] The situation of the younger children was less hopeful, however. The family had fallen on hard times during the Depression, and they called the children born after 1930 "rats" or "panic children." The family usually had ample (though monotonous) food during the Depression, but they struggled to keep the children clothed well enough to attend school. They had difficulty keeping all of the children in shoes and warm winter coats, and even the loss of a comb would lead to days of unkempt hair because they could not afford to replace it. The couple's furnishings were poor, there was minimal plumbing, and the family could rarely afford soap, but family members did what they could to get along. Claude worked long hours at his job, and the older children also contributed to the household income. May Della worked outside the home for pay occasionally and was often busy at home running a numbers game that brought in extra income.[28]

The couple believed that Chicago was a hard place to raise a large family but that the deprivations were worth it to escape southern racism. Even during the comparatively flush war year of 1943, Claude complained of the difficulty of supporting such a large family in the city. A researcher quoted him as saying, "Children in a city is too hard on one man. Back in Kentucky in the country kids any size can get out and chop cotton and pick cotton and help out some, but here in town a kid ain't got nothing to do but eat and sleep and go to school and they don't even want to do that." Yet Claude himself had never returned to the South—even to visit—after having left twenty-four years before, and he suspected that his children would not fare well there: "I know if my boys was in the South, they'd get lynched, cause I'd get lynched myself. White folks down South will lynch a man for nothing, just the least little thing."[29] He later explained, "Sometimes I wish I was back on the farm with this big family I got. That's where I need to be with all these children. It's too hard to raise children in a big city like this. But I wouldn't go back there now. Them white people don't treat colored people right."[30] Even though their lives were not terribly comfortable in the North and their children no longer had the kinds of opportunities Claude and May Della had hoped to provide, the move from South to North was still justified as good for the family because it spared the children southern racism—if not northern poverty.

Black men and women highlighted the journey from South to North as crucial to the African American experience in Chicago, and they suggested that the experience was intimately related to their commitment to their family lives. They described migration as strengthening family bonds and improving children's educational and social opportunities. Although ongoing racial inequality in the North was never far from parents' minds, conditions in the South were never distant either. Building on a long tradition of placing the family at the heart of African American culture, black Chicagoans pointed to experiences of racism in both locations, and the family as a site of resistance and support, as integral to their commitment to their families during the postwar era.

## Notes

16. Arnold R. Hirsch, *Making the Second Ghetto*, 16–17. See also Grossman, *Land of Hope*; Lemann, *The Promised Land*; and Gregory, *The Southern Diaspora*.
17. Graham, "The Negro Family in a Northern City," 49, 51.
18. Frazier, *The Negro Family the United States*; Drake and Cayton, *Black Metropolis*, especially 526–715. See also Frazier, *Black Bourgeoisie*.
19. Grossman, *Land of Hope*. See also Phillips, *AlabamaNorth*; Wilkerson, *The Warmth of Other Suns*.
20. There are too many instances of these kinds of relationships and living arrangements in the records to list here, but for a few examples, see files 50198, 51164, 52336, 54349, 56050, 56262, 60071, 68298, ICH&A Adoption Program Applications (Children's Home + Aid, Chicago). Housing will be discussed in more detail in chapter 6.
21. File 61279, 1959, ICH&A Adoption Program Applications (Children's Home + Aid, Chicago).
22. File 50312, p. 12, 1948; see also files 51267, 52316, ICH&A Adoption Program Applications (Children's Home + Aid, Chicago). See also Jones, *Labor of Love, Labor of Sorrow*.
23. File 53320, p. 5, 1951, ICH&A Adoption Program Applications (Children's Home +Aid, Chicago).
24. File 58062, "adoption application" yellow sheet, 1956, ICH&A Adoption Program Applications (Children's Home + Aid, Chicago).
25. For more on the black community's relationship with the Chicago Democratic machine during these years, see Biles, *Richard J. Daley*, chaps. 1–4; Cohen and Taylor, *American Pharaoh*, chaps. 1–8.
26. For Davis's published work on this family, see Allison Davis, *Father of the Man*.
27. Washington Family, December 1, 1943, Allison Davis Papers, box 38, folder 12, Special Collections Research Center, University of Chicago Library; Claudette and Ruth-Topeka, Allison Davis Papers, box 38, folder 17, Special Collections Research Center, University of Chicago Library; T. S. Downs, notes, March 3, 1943, Allison Davis Papers, box 38, folder 19, Special Collections Research Center, University of Chicago Library; J. L. Neely, notes, July 26, 1943, Allison Davis Papers, box 38, folder 20, Special Collections Research Center, University of Chicago Library.
28. Claudette and Ruth-Topeka, Allison Davis Papers, box 38, folder 17, Special Collections Research Center, University of Chicago Library; T. S. Downs, notes, March 29, 1943, Allison Davis Papers, box 39, folder 2, Special Collections Research Center, University of Chicago Library.
29. T. S. Downs, notes, March 3, 1943, Allison Davis Papers, box 38, folder 19, Special Collections Research Center, University of Chicago Library.
30. J. L. Neely, notes, July 26, 1943, Allison Davis Papers, box 38, folder 20, Special Collections Research Center, University of Chicago Library.

# Part 2

# Embodiment and Adoption

## Introduction: What We Do With Bodies

In this section, readers will encounter one of CAS scholars' areas of serious attention: that is, the body in adoption as a location for unsettling gender, race, sex, class, and nation: medicalized, imagined, metaphoricalized, instrumentalized, interpreted, and silenced, bodies figure significantly in all our conversations. We begin with Shelley Park's discussion of queer adoptive motherhood: "[A]doptive maternal bodies," she writes, "are not . . . natural bodies. We are bodies marked as 'damaged.' . . . And yet bodies [are] chosen [by adoption professionals] for motherhood on the basis of being marked as 'desirable by gatekeepers.' . . . [W]e know how to pass as a real mother." Park's observation shows us the way in which adoption can reveal conflicts of interpretation, here around motherhood, that focus on the body—that can sit uncomfortably in opposing narratives of "the natural/unnatural" and "the desirable/undesirable," can "pass" if the body behaves and appears "real." Here, too, is the idea, significant for CAS scholars, of the body in adoption as surveilled, scrutinized, read to be judged, and existing differently in social spaces. For Park, "it makes little sense to consider biological maternal bodies as natural objects outside of social contexts. . . . [I]t makes sense to speak of motherhood as a status [earlier, she calls it "an *identity*"] that may be conferred or withheld in processes involving the potential intervention of strangers." Sometimes "strange" bodies are appropriated for projects such as nation-building or genocide, or when their difference is deemed threatening. Margaret D. Jacobs addresses Indigenous childhood and US attempts to reform the bodies of native children through assimilation and re-racing, which required

> state and church authorities [to] intentionally weaken . . . Indigenous families and communities, making it difficult for them to sustain

DOI: 10.4324/9781003203827-14

> Indigenous ways of caring for and raising children. . . . Such policies [as forced removal of children to institutions] had undermined some Indigenous families to such an extent by the second half of the twentieth century that it became difficult [for them] to care for their own children."

The goal in that removal was to make such children "indistinguishable from the rest of the population," to cause, as an act of genocide, Indigeneity to disappear. It didn't work, however, given individual and tribal resistance to assimilation and public outcry, but the attempt left marks: "rates of child removal and fostering are still elevated. . . . Indigenous child welfare crises persist because Indigenous people lack full self-determination and true justice." In this case, as Jacobs notes, what happens to the child happens to the community and the nation.

In Elizabeth Bartholet's work, one can see the common-sense objection to restrictions on child removal from communities in crisis: that is, that children might be physically and emotionally harmed if left in dire circumstances. Bartholet acknowledges but sets aside the causes for those circumstances to point out that stigmatizing adoption, whatever harms adoption itself might create, can endanger the lives of real children by removing options for their care. For her, adoption can be a positive good, capable of saving lives however they were threatened; it "should be recognized as a positive form of family." That is, for Bartholet, "Adoption stigma helps shape reality in problematic ways" since it not only makes it difficult to help where help is needed, but also over-privileges the body in discussions of children's futures. "I would like," she writes, "to put biology in its place and give appropriate value to nurturing and other social aspects of the parenting relationship"—in paying too much attention to heredity, genetic connection, and blood ties, she asserts, we pay too little to the possibilities arising from family care. In this sense, Bartholet and Judith Butler address a similar set of questions about the purposes of kinship in that for both writers, adoption can be life preserving and life affirming as care. Butler's claim is that (to echo David Schneider), "kinship is a kind of *doing*, one that does not reflect a prior structure but which can only be understood as an enacted practice. [It] would help us," she continues, to privilege communal, active relations over a less involved and potentially more passive kinship-by-blood, an abstraction that "lurks behind" and makes lesser the operations—I think of these as the quotidian tasks of kinning, including nurture, care, and education—of enfamilying. One concern for Butler is how (she is speaking of France, but her logic is extendable) "as-if"-seeming families are underpinned by "the law" so that they can, or as they, perform the reproduction of (raced) culture, which is itself in the service of building and shoring up "a fantasy of the nation that is already, and irreversibly, under siege." In essence, kinship through bodies can undo and certainly de-emphasizes the need for active social and familial engagement and caring—real human nurturance—while simultaneously providing cover for nationalist narratives that themselves disguise the flimsiness of national coherence. In Jacqueline Stevens's writing, the body is gendered through political apparatus ("statutes" and "courts") that hide the fact that reproduction and kinship are not absolutely linked: "Any kinship system exists in relation to an otherwise unregulated process of reproduction. That is, kinship suggests the possibility of species reproduction absent kinship," a statement of the obvious but nonetheless destabilizing, given how tied, as reproduction generally is, to gendered kinship roles such as "mother" and "father." (Stevens calls these roles "state creations.") She further notes, quoting Kingsley Davis, "the structure of the human family is rooted not in biology but in folkways and mores" and, in her own voice, that "it is true that reproduction is necessary for the species to survive. It is not true that reproduction must be gendered"—that bodies have to be gendered and kinned to reproduce. In essence, naturalized gender tied to reproducing bodies reproduces the state in the form of blood kin. Stevens shows us that this has been made to look simply natural when it's not.

It is the bodies of children, particularly Black and Indigenous children, that Laura Briggs attends to in her writing here. It is a kind of reframing of the question others ask—what about children really at risk? Should they not be saved, and isn't saving them by adopting them what we should do? Briggs turns our attention back to the conditions that create crisis: "The history of child separation," she writes, "follows these broad contours, where an overt racial definition of the state allows for the genocidal separation of children, and a civic nationalism often demands a fig leaf to cover its racism, and so requires that child separation *look* humanitarian" (emphasis added). She argues that family separation was (and, by implication, is still) a way in which to punish especially Black and Native communities for political activism—"particularly at a time [in the mid-twentieth century] when political rebellion was quickly tied to communism." Because they agitated for change, racialized natal families lost children to foster care and adoption, and systems of "assistance" such as the ADC-Foster Care Program were used not just to support them but to determine the precarity of these children so as to mark them for removal. The 1972 National Association of Black Social Workers Statement condemning transracial adoption of Black children was, in Briggs's words, "a fight about what became of children who were taken, sometimes maliciously, by Welfare officials" to punish their parents in the name of helping the child.

Marianne Novy's writing turns us back to literature to think about how bodies work to make family through resemblance, and here she looks in particular at Shakespeare, for whom "recognition scenes . . . emphasize bodily connections in the family." She notes that "it is part of a still dominant ideology that babies are supposed to look like someone else in the family, and if that resemblance is not obvious, it will be imagined": that is, yet again, CAS scholars are marking and then questioning typical ways of noticing or even forming kinship bonds through the body. Here, in Shakespeare's plays, the resembling (family) body is the recognized (family) body, though Novy notices a secondary valence. "In spite," she says, "of all the blood-and-birth imagery, much of the play's presentation of heredity could be seen as a construction mediated by a good foster parent." Shakespeare provides the accepted narrative of kinship through bodily similarity: in other words, while undermining it by providing parenting from adults who don't resemble those they care for, we are asked to wonder how much resemblance is imagined or important. And it's the role of imagination in kinning that Sara Dorow examines when she looks at "adoption image culture," at referral photographs of children waiting to be matched, or being matched, to adoptive parents. Here, too, is the one-two punch of acknowledging adoptive difference and fantasizing it's otherwise, that adoptive kinship is natural, embodied, not different from blood ties. "Bureaucratic processes can, and perhaps must be constructed [by all involved in adoption] as a conduit for fate," she notices: children must be believed to have come to the parents they were destined for regardless of the machinery that moves them into adoptive homes. This has to be the way adoptive parents and, indeed, all the parties facilitating adoption regard it. And yet "the referral photo equally, and paradoxically, grounds the parents in the reality of their adoption and magnifies the fantasy of connected fate." Through an image of the waiting child, parents are given both a way to cathect the potential adopted person ("their child") and a reminder of difference and strangeness, since the photograph "invites comparison of the child's past and future."

For Sarah Franklin, popular representations in narrative of these parents' bodies—narratives of infertility, usually—place them in the uncomfortable position of alienation and strangeness. The narratives frame the infertile body as unnatural and diseased or broken, given the (false but valuable) narrative of natural fertility as a cultural commonplace. Franklin writes,

> Reproduction is, of course, a hugely naturalized activity in the Euro-American cultural tradition. Into this highly naturalised domain, then, enters medical science, on behalf of the "desperate" infertile couples for

> whom "life's progression" has been held hostage to the random injustice of nature's lottery in making them unable to conceive.

It is only through the comparatively unnatural process of artificial reproduction technologies that parental bodies can be naturalized, an irony Franklin notes as "significant":

> "[H]appy couples" stories present both a continuity and a commensurability between biological science and the biological family. The achieved route of conception stands in for conjugality and family as a *social* achievement, "after nature," though in this context, "after technology" as well.

The profoundest irony in this play of narratives, however, is as Franklin notes, that in resorting to technology to produce fertile bodies (and children), "hope is the important flip-side of the fact that assisted conception usually does not work." In this way, we can see the dysfunction and dystopia Marina Fedosik describes in her analysis of the *Blade Runner* film franchise. It is in "narratives of the future [that] trouble familiar reproductive scenarios" that we can see how the promise of bodily reparation through technology might have a wildly different outcome than expected. Such narratives, Fedosik writes, "bend towards the apocalyptic or at least imagine nonheterocoital forms of reproduction [reproduction outside heterosexual coitus] as a threat to humanity." This threat is both to systems based on reproduction through the fertile body—nation, corporation, the family itself—and to the individual who will be cut off from their humanity in losing connection to their biological roots—to, in essence, their own body as reproductive and a reproduction of the bodies that came before it:

> [H]eterocoital biological origins . . . remain a necessary condition for individuation, and this frame of reference is considered by most Western cultures necessary for the cultural (self) recognition of the person who deserves inclusion into the system of human relatedness as a legible and legitimate human subject.

It is harmful narratives of colorblindness, as a feature of an American liberalism that informs transracial adoption, to which David Eng calls our attention. The embodied differences of race matter and don't or can't matter, simultaneously. In examining the films of Deann Borshay Liem, Eng attends to the tension between the idea that the racialized child needs to be rescued and the idea that adoption, taking in and making family, makes familial race consistent and unified. "Public histories of colonialism, civil war, social conflict, and abject poverty in Korea cannot sit easily under the sign of anti-racism," he writes, "whose stuttering logic goes something like this: *we are all different, but we are all the same, too . . . but it really doesn't matter.*" This irresolvable conflict between bodies raced differently but familied the same creates "a psychic state of suspension between 'over there' and 'over here,'" a site, for Eng, where colorblindness becomes a kind of law no one can live with.

# From Park, Shelly M. *Mothering Queerly, Queering Motherhood: Resisting Monomaternalism in Adoptive, Lesbian, Blended, and Polygamous Families.* SUNYP, 2014.

As noted in earlier discussions of maternal profiling, good families and the good mothers who inhabit them are typically middle or upper class. They have spacious, clean homes. Good families include heterosexual, married parents. These parents care about education and know how to discipline children without resorting to corporal punishment. They have strong and healthy relationships with their own families of origin. Ideally, they are Christian or, perhaps, Jewish. If not affiliated with a mainstream Western religious denomination, the prospective parents will at least subscribe to mainstream Western religious values, including a strong work ethic. They will drink in moderation only, if at all. They will not have an arrest record for drugs, nor will they have committed other infractions of the law—or of good taste. They will practice good personal hygiene and wear fresh, unrumpled clothing.

Good families afford their children race and class privilege. They live in suburban neighborhoods featuring good schools and allegedly safe streets. They enroll their children in piano and ballet lessons. They do not let their children watch too much TV or hang out with the "wrong" crowd. They take their children on vacations. They have college funds for their children. They feature stay-at-home mothers or, failing this, hire full-time nannies to care for their children.

Good families enjoy heterosexual privilege. They do not embarrass or "damage" their children by participating in sexual or affectional relationships that depart from the norm. They provide both male and female role models for their sons and daughters. As this suggests, good families also exemplify traditional gendered divisions of labor. Good fathers are good breadwinners. Good mothers are good homemakers. Good fathers are stable and dependable and know how to enforce discipline. They coach little league and mow lawns. Good mothers are emotionally available and know how to develop self-esteem in their child. They make cookies for bake sales and arrange playdates for their children.

Few families fit this profile in all of its dimensions. However, families (such as my own) who are successful at adopting a child typically fit several

DOI: 10.4324/9781003203827-15

aspects of this profile—or, at any rate, are knowledgeable enough about this profile to provide answers to questions and dress and act in ways that make us appear desirable as parents. Adoptive maternal bodies are not, thus, natural bodies. We are bodies simultaneously marked as "damaged" (i.e., infertile, whether or not this is true) and yet bodies chosen for motherhood on the basis of being marked as "desirable" by gatekeepers. We are bodies who know how to announce ourselves as normal, even as we are marked as "abnormal." We know the dominant social script for mothering and thus know how to pass as a real mother. In this respect, adoptive mothers share certain affinities with light-skinned persons of color who know how to perform the script for whiteness and with closeted lesbians or gays who know how to perform the script for heterosexuality.[3]

Biological maternal bodies may escape the closet, but do not escape surveillance, as often is thought. Berg (1995), for example, explaining why women use reproductive technologies, claims that biological parenting is meaningful because it allows women to participate in a "remarkably natural process." She contrasts this "natural" process of gestation and birth giving to the process of adoption wherein "parents receive their child from a stranger in a process regulated by lawyers, adoption agencies and the courts" (83). Yet, the notion that biological parenting is natural requires critique in the social context of contemporary Western medicine. Here doctors play the role of gatekeepers, determining how the good mother will act (e.g., she will eat only healthy foods, get adequate rest, take prenatal vitamins, refrain from smoking and drinking, avoid strenuous exercise, and abstain from certain sexual practices). The physician also determines who will have access to medical services. This is the case especially when reproductive technologies are used, but it is also the case in so-called "normal" cases of conception, gestation, and childbirth.

I discover this in my third trimester of pregnancy: Having discovered on a sonogram that my placenta is displaced, my obstetrician orders me to bed rest. When I resist her suggestion, indicating that I am our family's primary breadwinner and we require my summer teaching salary (something that I hope another professional woman might understand), she looks at me disapprovingly, noting that my refusal to follow her instructions will put my pregnancy and baby at risk. She also cautions me that I have gained too much weight and need to more carefully monitor my caloric intake. Later, as I successfully reach my due date (despite a lack of full-time bed rest), she indicates that my labor will need to be artificially induced if I have not given birth within the next ten days. I am not altogether certain I wish to follow these instructions, but do not argue with her at this moment, as I have another issue I wish to discuss with her. "Will you tie my tubes after I have given birth?" I ask, noting that it is my understanding that this is a relatively simple procedure if done at the time of birthing. She responds that this is unadvisable, as I might want another child. When I remind her that I am thirty-three years old, already have another child, and explain that my husband and I will be happy to adopt another child should we consider more children a necessary addition to our life, she conjectures that I "might feel differently" after I have a child of "my own." Too tired to address the presumptions included in this nonmedical advice, I depart and prepare to tell my husband that he will need to have a vasectomy.

As Laura Woliver (1995) indicates, "the medical profession's gatekeeping role," including "its monopoly over birth control information and services" displays a tendency to "control and medicalization" that precedes its involvement in designing and implementing new reproductive technologies (347). The bodies of birth mothers, like those of adoptive mothers, are created by disciplinary discourses (e.g., the languages of medicine, sociology, and psychiatry) operating in conjunction with social institutions (e.g., hospitals and social service agencies). The medical language of "fertility" and "infertility," for example, produces subjects who are viewed as—and who, thus, come to view themselves as—beings defined in terms of their procreative capacity. Taken in conjunction with theories of social psychology (and, notably, Freudian psychoanalytic theory) that deem a woman's fulfillment to reside in procreation, these discourses serve to define an "abnormality" in particular women that is to be resolved by the practices and technologies of modern medicine.

As Foucault (1978) indicates, persons who engaged in particular sex acts came to be seen as a type of person (homosexuals) during the eighteenth century. The marking of homosexuality as a deviant identity (comprising much more than a sex act) simultaneously produced compulsory heterosexuality as the norm (125). Similarly, we see in the late twentieth century the emergence of a *type* of person who is "fertile" or "infertile." The marking of infertility as an abnormal identity produces procreative sexuality as the norm, reinforcing compulsory motherhood and heteronormativity. Compulsory (heterosexual) motherhood preceded medical discourses concerning fertility, but now take a particular form that marks biological motherhood as the essential form of mothering. Practices of adoption—like homosexual behavior—have long existed, but adoptive motherhood as an *identity*—like homosexual identity—only emerges at a particular historical juncture. Moreover, the deviance of the adoptive maternal body serves to mark out biological motherhood as natural. Neither adoptive mothers, nor biological mothers have an *a priori* essential nature, however. Indeed, throughout much of history—and still within many indigenous cultures—the distinction between adoptive mothers and natural (or real) mothers would not be a salient distinction (Carp 1998; Novy 2001).

Foucault (1978, 1979, 1980) observes that surveillance is a disciplinary mechanism that constitutes and regulates subjects into oppositional relations. At the same time, power also essentializes the oppositional categories it has constructed, making them henceforth appear both natural and immutable. In order to interrogate the categories that pose as "natural" in the oppositions thus created (e.g., heterosexual/homosexual, fertile/infertile, biological/adoptive, normal/queer), it is useful to view them through the lens of their allegedly opposing construction. If, for example, we look at mothering through the lens of adoption, the social regulation of "having" children is made explicit and the social rules and discourses governing motherhood obscured in cases of biological motherhood are rendered visible. Gatekeepers may sometimes differ (with social workers, courts and, in the case of transnational adoption, consulates and immigration authorities, mediating maternity for adoptive mothers and nurses, physicians, pharmacists, and drug companies mediating maternity for biological mothers), but the gates are still kept. Moreover, the gatekeepers do not always differ, as women deemed "unfit" for parenting know all too well. Physicians act in concert with the courts that mandate birth control for mothers convicted of drug offenses. Social service agencies regulate the activities of poor mothers receiving welfare. Social workers enlist the help of the legal system to remove children from mothers identified as unfit. Children thus removed are returned, if at all, only if their mother follows court-ordered rules governing her conduct. Lesbian mothers risk having their fitness queried by ex-husbands and the custody of their children revoked by the courts. Teen mothers and mothers with cognitive disabilities are routinely assumed unfit and encouraged by their own family members as well as social service agencies to relinquish their children.[4]

In light of these issues, it makes little sense to consider biological maternal bodies as natural objects outside of social contexts. Biological maternal bodies, like adoptive maternal bodies, are always embodied in social, cultural, economic, and political contexts—contexts marked by racism, classism, sexism, heterosexism, ageism, and ablism. In both cases, therefore, it makes sense to speak of motherhood as a status that may be conferred or withheld in processes involving the potential intervention of strangers—as well as the potential intervention of friends, neighbors, and family members. Those for whom motherhood is experienced as natural are precisely those who have—like the adoptive mother—successfully embodied what Nancy Miller (1995) terms "the dominant social script" about mothering. The difference between biological mothers and adoptive mothers is an epistemological one: adoptive mothers know that their status as mothers depends on mastery of the social script for good mothering; the contingency of their status as mothers is largely invisible to biological mothers who embody the norms regulating their status as mothers—unless and/or until such time as they inadvertently deviate from that script.

****

Infertile maternal bodies, although frequently portrayed as "damaged," "inferior" or even "desperate" bodies (see, e.g., Berg 1995), can also be interpreted as healthy and resistant bodies. Adoptive mothers do not have to adjust to the rapid changes in embodiment that accompany pregnancy and post-partum; we are less physically exhausted and/or traumatized from childbirth than biological mothers of infants and thus have more energy; we do not suffer the tenderness of breasts laden with milk; we are thus better able to retain some degree of independence from our children, and so forth. Adoptive mothers do not, moreover, risk the short and long term health consequences of the prolonged hormone regimens that are a part of fertility treatments and we avoid the cost and invasiveness of expensive, complicated medical procedures. Many infertile maternal bodies are bodies who, like Miller and myself, delayed childbearing until after the completion of their education and the establishment of their careers. As such, we are female bodies who have established an identity and meaningful relationships for ourselves outside of the norms of compulsory motherhood. We are also bodies who have resisted procreation during our most fertile years. We are bodies who, for years or decades, have uncoupled sexuality and procreation. And in discovering our infertility and choosing to pursue adoption over fertility treatments, we are bodies who continue to resist making sex into a procreative ritual.

The personal and political reasons for which women may choose adoption over procreation as a means of creating a family are varied. For some fertile women—like infertile women who refuse fertility treatments—adoption represents a conscious personal choice to maintain a nonprocreative sexual body. For others, such as those who adopt "special needs" children, adoption may represent a way of sharing resources with children in need and/or of creating families that embody diversity. For at least some of those who pursue transnational adoption, this route to motherhood may represent the ability to avoid U.S. norms mandating two-parent, heterosexual, nuclear families. For yet other women, adoption represents an environmental choice related to concerns about global overpopulation.

None of these motives are uncomplicated. Some women who choose not to become pregnant may do so for reasons linked to questionable beauty ideals. Some white women who adopt children of color or disabled children may do so, consciously or unconsciously, for reasons linked to self-aggrandizement, religious principles or even humanitarian motives (such as I address in the next chapter) that are questionable from a queer, feminist, anti-racist and/or anti-ablist, point of view. Single women and lesbian women who adopt transnationally may turn a blind eye to issues related to the western appropriation of global resources. Similarly, some Western women who choose adoption to resist contributing to global overpopulation may remain oblivious to the ways in which Western consumption of global resources damages environmental stability. Nonetheless, these maternal bodies also can be read as resisting romanticized versions of the gestational maternal body, as refusing to define family in terms of genetic inheritance and ownership, and as rejecting notions of motherhood and of two-parent, heterosexual families as "natural." In this sense, adoptive maternal bodies are a close relation to the "nonprocreative adult" bodies of Sedgwick and Miller. Our bodies mark social difference in a way that enables a cultural critique of the dominant social script governing motherhood.

This is so whether or not we consciously resist social norms governing motherhood. In fact, however, adoptive mothers will typically be conscious of their resistances. The myriad questions that we answer in applying to become an adoptive parent are not merely invasions of privacy; they are also cause for self-reflection about one's maternal desires and capabilities. In completing the application for adoption, one is forced to think about whether and why one wants to become a mother and about one's own capacities for mothering. One must also think about why one views adoption as preferable to other alternatives. One thus formulates a story that is both about desire (what one wants) and about repulsion (what one doesn't want). In circulating these stories, we authorize ourselves "to have the decisive role in deciphering [the] meaning [of our bodies] and adjudicating their circulation in the world" (N. Miller 1995, 9).[6] This is especially prevalent in cases of transracial adoption and open adoption. Here no sustained secrecy or pretense of being a mother within a "normal" biological family is possible.

## Notes

3. In light of this, it is not surprising that persons of color who know how to perform the script for whiteness and lesbians and gays who know how to perform the script for heterosexuality are among those marginalized folk most likely to be approved for adoption.

****

4. For discussions of the surveillance and regulation of black, Latina, indigenous, lesbian, teen, and poor mothers, as well as those who have neglected or abused their children, see Fineman and Karpin (1995).
6. Miller (1995) comments on the Boston Women's Health Collective's now classic text *Our Bodies, Our Selves*, but the point holds for the circulation of adoption narratives as well.

## Works Cited

Berg, Barbara. "Listening to the Voices of the Infertile." *Reproduction, Ethics, and the Law: Feminist Perspectives*, edited by Joan C. Callahan, Indiana UP, 1995, pp. 80–108.

Carp, Wayne E. *Family Matters: Secrecy and Disclosure in the History of Adoption.* Harvard UP, 1998.

Fineman, Martha A., and Isabel Karpin, editors. *Mothers in Law: Feminist Theory and the Legal Regulation of Motherhood.* Columbia UP, 1995.

Foucault, Michel. *Discipline and Punish: The Birth of the Prison.* Translated by Alan Sheridan, Vintage, 1979.

———. *Power/Knowledge: Selected Interviews and Other Writings, 1972–1977.* Translated and edited by Colin Gordon, Pantheon, 1980.

———. *The History of Sexuality, Vol. 1, An Introduction.* Translated by Robert Hurley, Vintage, 1978.

Miller, Nancy. "Mothers, Daughters, and Autobiography: Maternal Legacies and Cultural Criticism." *Mothers in Law: Feminist Theory and the Legal Regulation of Motherhood*, edited by Martha A. Fineman and Isabel Karpin, Columbia UP, 1995, pp. 3–26.

Novy, Marianne. "Introduction: Imagining Adoption." *Imagining Adoption: Essays on Literature and Culture*, edited by Marianne Novy, U of Michigan P, 2001, pp. 1–16.

Woliver, Laura. "Reproductive Technologies, Surrogacy Arrangements, and the Politics of Motherhood." *Mothers in Law: Feminist Theory and the Legal Regulation of Motherhood*, edited by Martha A. Fineman and Isabel Karpin, Columbia UP, 1995, pp. 346–360.

# From Jacobs, Margaret D. *A Generation Removed: The Fostering and Adoption of Indigenous Children.* U of Nebraska P, 2010.

A comparative and transnational approach to studying the Indigenous child welfare crises of the late twentieth century leads to a valuable perspective. When we examine the removal of one Indigenous child in a particular place and at a specific time, it is easy to get caught up in clashing notions of what constitutes proper care and what is in the best interests of one individual child. When we zoom out and take a global view, we see parallel Indigenous child welfare crises as part of a pattern among settler colonial nations. The ubiquity of Indigenous child removal, fostering, and adoption in the United States, Canada, and Australia in the post-World War II era profoundly challenges the pronouncements of many local authorities who claimed they were simply acting in the best interests of Indigenous children.

The Indigenous child welfare crises of the late twentieth century represented both a legacy of earlier settler colonial policies and the latest manifestation of them. Australia, the United States, and Canada had all originated as distinctive British settler colonial projects that rested on the displacement of Indigenous peoples from their lands and their replacement with a settler population through what Patrick Wolfe so evocatively calls "the logic of elimination."[15] Once the United States gained its independence and Australia and Canada became nations in their own right, they continued to act on settler colonial logic. Yet none of these settler colonial ventures ever resulted in the complete elimination of Indigenous people or the transfer of all their lands into settler hands, despite the use of brute violence, legal maneuvers, and sometimes treaty making. British humanitarianism and homegrown reform movements gained ascendance in the mid to late nineteenth century, and outright massacres of Indigenous people or blatant land grabs became increasingly indefensible. Instead, all three settler colonial societies turned to assimilation efforts by the late nineteenth century, to eviscerate cultural differences and undermine vestiges of communal landholding. Officials focused these assimilation efforts on Indigenous children. Authorities claimed to be intervening in Indigenous families as a gesture

DOI: 10.4324/9781003203827-16

of benevolence, but their policies served the same settler colonial aims and continued to inflict great trauma on Indigenous peoples.

Through the forcible removal of children to institutions from the late nineteenth century onward, state and church authorities intentionally weakened Indigenous families and communities, making it difficult for them to sustain Indigenous ways of caring for and raising children. At the same time, paternalistic policies and the ongoing dispossession of Indigenous people of their lands undermined Indigenous livelihoods and impoverished generations of Indigenous people.[16] Such policies had undermined some Indigenous families to such an extent by the second half of the twentieth century that it became difficult to care for their own children. This was a bitter legacy of earlier settler colonial policies.

The Indigenous child welfare crises of the late twentieth century cannot be attributed merely to past policies and their disastrous consequences for Indigenous families, however. Authorities in the post-World War II era often removed Indigenous children from their families without good reason. Indigenous child welfare crises also derived from specific postwar policies based on a relentless drive to eliminate Indigenous peoples' distinctive status and their claims to land and sovereignty. Each of these settler colonial nations continued to wrestle with their Indigenous "problem," as officials referred to the persistence of Indigenous people, and the removal, fostering, and adoption of Indigenous children constituted a primary means of managing Indigenous populations in the post-World War II era. New bureaucratic imperatives to rid federal governments in the United States and Canada and state governments in Australia of their longstanding obligations to Indigenous peoples dovetailed with purportedly color-blind liberalism in all three of these nations to make the adoption of Indigenous children a particularly appealing solution to the Indigenous problem.

Authorities claimed to be acting on the laudable notion of extending universal human rights to Indigenous minorities, but their policies and practices actually divested Indigenous people of their sovereignty and group rights. They required that Indigenous people assimilate or integrate into the larger population and cease to affiliate with their prior group identity. As in earlier eras, authorities deemed children the best hope for enacting their vision. Indigenous children would become indistinguishable from the rest of the population if they could be separated from their communities and raised in modern white families, and Indigeneity would eventually disappear. Authorities in all three nations were hell bent on assimilating Indigenous people rather than providing for their real needs. They failed to muster the resources—adequate jobs, sufficient public assistance, useful social services—that would truly have helped Indigenous families, and they undermined Indigenous people's efforts to take control of their own destinies. Instead government authorities demonized and then penalized poor Indian families. Claiming to have the best interest of their children at heart, they robbed Indigenous people again, this time of their most precious resource.

These postwar policies had many unanticipated results. Proponents of Indigenous adoption, who claimed to be blind to color, did not foresee the troubles that many Indigenous adoptees would face as they grew up in decidedly color-aware societies. Most adoptees lived in predominantly white communities with few Indigenous people, and they often suffered from a sense of alienation. Donna Micklos, of Edmonton, Alberta, remembers that when she walked anywhere, people would stare and gawk at her and her family.[17] School proved particularly painful. Joanne Nimik, of the Swan Lake First Nation in Manitoba, was the only Indian in her class, and she felt singled out and embarrassed because her textbook depicted the Indian way of life as degraded. Similarly, Denise Roulette remembered, "When questioned by the teacher in front of the class to explain my family history, all I knew was I was a dirty, lazy Indian."[18]

James Savage experienced a similar sense of dislocation as well as blatant racism. According to his adoptive sister Glenise, the communities of Starke and Salem, Florida, "were the worst places the family lived in terms of the way Savage was treated," especially at church, where the other children, including his siblings, sought to exclude him from activities. Florida may have been a particularly difficult environment for Savage as de facto segregation still prevailed. When Reverend Savage sought to integrate the board of the small Bible college where he was president, his family "suffered incredible persecution" and received death threats.[19] Although treated as a black by whites, Savage did not fit in with the black community either, and thus he endured "absolute cultural isolation" in Florida. As Aboriginal activists put it, "To be a minority of one is to be the object of perpetual discrimination." Unlike Aboriginal adoptees in Australia, "shorn from his cultural heritage, Russell Moore had nobody there when he encountered harassment from people who viewed him as 'different.'"[20]

* * * *

Adoption schemes did not lead, as expected, to the seamless assimilation of Indigenous adoptees into mainstream life. Instead they created a defining feature of modern Indigenous life in all three of these nations: removal and displacement. In the worst-case scenario this led to a profound sense of alienation from both Indigenous and non-Indigenous communities, as in Russell Moore's case. It would be a mistake, however, to assume that Russell Moore's case epitomizes the adoptee experience, or to characterize all Indigenous adoptees and fostered children as tragic victims. In some circumstances their experiences could lead to what one adoptee, "John," characterized as living in the best of both worlds. John told me that through his adoptive family, he had a "world of prospect" opened to him, while his extended Indian family offered him the place that "became home." Many adoptees experienced great trauma, but as the scholar Raven Sinclair puts it, "There are those who persevere and extract the best they can from their experiences." She concluded that the participants in her study were "resilient and insightful."[34] My own experience of meeting many adoptees and former foster children, as well as reading countless accounts, confirms this portrait of adaptive survivors.

Authorities did not envision that many adoptees would seek to reunite with their communities (84 percent in Harness's study of twenty-five American Indian adoptees). Many have embarked on recovery and healing through reconnecting with their Indigenous families and communities. Sandy Whitehawk, who followed a trajectory of self-hate and self-abuse, eventually reclaimed her life through reuniting with family members from the Rosebud Sioux reservation. Since then she has established the First Nations Orphans Association and the First Nations Repatriation Institute and has developed a powerful welcoming home ceremony to help adoptees or those who have been in foster care. The ceremony includes an honor song for adoptees and family members who have lost children and a Lakota ceremony known as "wiping away the tears" or Wanblecheya.[35] Sinclair remarks that repatriation of adoptees to their Indigenous communities and cultures is often "concurrent with a sense of healing."[36] Although the promotion of fostering and adoption did rupture many Indigenous families and led to serious trauma for many Indigenous children, it did not result in the hoped-for disappearance of Indigeneity. In yet another way authorities failed to foresee the consequences of Indigenous child removal in the late twentieth century. They never imagined the strength of the resistance that would form among Indigenous people to government schemes. While policy and practice followed similar patterns in all three nations, opposition among Indigenous people also developed along parallel lines. Women took leading roles in the Indigenous child welfare movement in all three countries. Their efforts to organize themselves as Indigenous women coalesced with their campaign to address the Indigenous child welfare crisis. Indigenous women's movements made family and child welfare a centerpiece. They asserted that their traditional caring roles had been highly valued in Indigenous societies, and they articulated a distinctive type of Indigenous feminism that was at odds with both the mainstream feminist and some of the Indigenous self-determination movements of the time.

By the late 1970s and early 1980s, Indigenous struggles to reclaim the care of children had paid off in the 1978 Indian Child Welfare Act in the United States, the ascendancy of the Aboriginal Child Placement Principle among state governments in Australia, and with myriad tripartite agreements in Canada. Tribes and Indigenous groups also formed independent child welfare agencies to care for children within their own communities. Attempts by authorities to obliterate Indigeneity through removing children thus backfired, leading instead to greater self-determination among Indigenous communities.

Resistance to Indigenous child removal eventually built into social movements that questioned the very foundations of settler colonial society, at least in Australia and Canada. The James Savage/Russell Moore case played an important role in exposing the experience of the Stolen Generations and leading to a government inquiry in Australia. As Russell's aunt Nellie Moore explained, "For the first time the white Australian people are getting to know what really happened to our kids. This has really happened and this is the end result. Some people can survive their experiences and some can't." Rather than giving in to despair over Russell's fate, the Moore family hoped Australians would take steps to ensure that his experience would not be repeated. As Nellie Moore put it, "Our hearts are broken but our spirits will never give in. My heart aches for Russell. . . . He was a young Aboriginal man brought up in another country, unsure of what or who he was. Whatever happened to him happened to hundreds of our children who, as teenagers began to return back to us to live with their own families, unsure, because they had lost their years of belonging."[37]

****

Despite these important developments, by and large, the American nation as a whole has ignored the issue. The Stolen Generations and the Indian residential schools garnered headlines and engendered public debate in Australia and Canada, but the American federal government and most American media are virtually silent about American Indian child removal. The Supreme Court issued a landmark ruling on the *Adoptive Couple v. Baby Girl* case in 2013 that weakened ICWA, but the media focused primarily on the court's rulings on the Defense of Marriage Act and provisions of the Voting Rights Act. American Indians are a small minority who have little impact in national elections, so they are at pains to make their grievances known and have them taken seriously. It is doubtful, however, that American Indian communities can achieve full self-determination as well as economic and social equality within American society, or that the United States can transcend its settler colonial past and present, without a full historical reckoning of the devastation wrought by Indigenous child removal policies and practices.

Indigenous people have gained a greater voice in deciding the destinies of their children, but rates of child removal and fostering are still elevated within their communities. According to attorney Robert McEwen, in 2013 American Indian children "represent[ed]. 9 percent of all children but represent[ed] 2 percent of the total number of children in the foster care system in the United States . . . They are twice as likely to be investigated, as compared to the general population, by the child welfare system. They are twice as likely to be substantiated, as compared to the general population. And they are three times as likely to be placed outside of their home, as compared with the general population." Some states have a higher overrepresentation of Indian children. Native American youth comprised 1.8 percent of that population but made up 7.1 percent of out-of-home placements in Nebraska in 2013.[54] Aboriginal and Torres Strait Islander children comprised 4.6 percent of Australian children in 2011–12 but 34 percent of all children living in out-of-home care. Indigenous children in Australia are ten times more likely than non-Indigenous children to be removed from their homes. Due to the Aboriginal Child Placement Principle, however, 68.8 percent of all Indigenous children were placed within their extended families, with other Indigenous carers, or in Indigenous residential care.[55] In Canada the rate of investigations for child maltreatment was 4.2 times higher for Aboriginal children than non-Aboriginal children in 2008.[56] Indigenous child welfare crises have proven much more intractable than Indigenous activists foresaw in the heady days of the late 1970s and early 1980s when ICWA gave Indigenous communities so much hope in the United States and abroad.

This persistence of Indigenous child welfare problems has many causes. Governments did not follow through with promises to provide adequate financial support to make Indigenous-run preventative and rehabilitative services a reality. The U.S. Congress, for example, did not consistently appropriate adequate funds for the implementation of ICWA, especially for the preventative social services called for in Title II of the act.[57] Efforts to slash budgets for *all* welfare and public assistance programs among these three nations throughout the last several decades have also made it difficult for Indigenous communities to develop and sustain viable programs.[58] The crises persist, too, because Indigenous child removal has been a multigenerational, cyclical phenomenon that is difficult to reverse. Authorities had been carrying out Indigenous child removal for about a century when Congress passed ICWA in 1978. By then multiple generations had been affected by this damaging practice. It may take longer than a few decades to repair the damage. Justice Murray Sinclair, head of Canada's TRC, explained in a presentation in November 2013 that seven generations went through the residential schools in Canada. "Families were lost through disruption and breakdown. Communities lost leaders. Tribes lost status and authority," Sinclair points out. He believes that it may take seven generations to fix the damaged relationships within families and between Indigenous people and other Canadians.[59]

At base, the Indigenous child welfare crises persist because Indigenous people lack full self-determination and true justice. Justice will prove elusive until non-Indigenous people become fully aware of and properly acknowledge just what transpired. It will remain out of reach until the citizens in each nation make a genuine reckoning with past policies and practices of Indigenous child removal.

## Notes

15. Wolfe, "Land, Labor, Difference"
16. Jacobs, *White Mother*
17. *Book of Voices*, 140.
18. *Book of Voices*, 157, 171.
19. State of Florida, "Answer Brief of Appellee," 21, 30.
20. National Aboriginal and Islander Legal Services Secretariat, "Amicus Curaie," 9

****

34. Sinclair, "All My Relations," 29.
35. Kreisher, "Coming Home"; *Book of Voices*, 260–61; "To Dry the Eyes of Indian Adoptees," originally published in *Daily Yonder*, March 16, 2010, reprinted in DeMeyer and Cotter-Busbee, *Two Worlds*, 247–253.
36. Sinclair, "All My Relations," 239.
37. "Nellie Moore's Story," *Koorier* 3 (June 1990): 25.

****

54. State of Nebraska, Senate, Transcript, Health and Human Services Committee Meeting on Nebraska Indian Child Welfare Act, 9–10; see also testimony of Liz Neeley, member of the Foster Care Review Office, 35. Thank you to attorney Robert McEwen for sharing this document with me.
55. Australian Institute of Family Studies "Child Protection" fact sheet. A majority of Indigenous removed from their families in the Northern Territory and Tasmania are living in non-Indigenous families.
56. Sinha, et al. *Kiskisik Awasisak: Remember the Children*, x-xii.
57. Blanchard, "To Prevent the Breakup," 307.
58. Strong-Boag, *Finding Families, Finding Ourselves*, 46; Briggs, *Somebody's Children*, 9.
59. Sinclair, "Indian Residential School System in Canada."

## Works Cited

Australian Institute of Family Studies. "Child Protection and Aboriginal and Torres Strait Islander Children." *Fact Sheet*, June 2013. www.aifs.gov.au/cfca/pubs/factsheets/a142117/.

Blanchard, Evelyn. "To Prevent the Breakup of the Indian Family: The Development of the Indian Child Welfare Act of 1978." PhD diss., U of New Mexico, 2010.

*Book of Voices: Voices of Aboriginal Adoptees and Foster Children*. Stolen Generations, 2000.

Briggs, Laura. *Somebody's Children: The Politics of Transracial and Transnational Adoption*. Duke UP, 2012.

Jacobs, Margaret D. *White Mother to a Dark Race: Settler Colonialism, Maternalism, and the Removal of Indigenous Children in the American West and Australia, 1880–1940.* U of Nebraska P, 2009.

National Aboriginal, and Islander Legal Services Secretariat Inc. "Brief of Amicus Curiae, in Support of the Appellant." James Hudson Savage, Appellant vs. State of Florida, Appellee, Case No. 75–494, in the Supreme Court of Florida. Filed October 12, 1990.

"Nellie Moore's Story." *Koorier*, vol. 3, 1990, p. 25.

Sinha, Vandha, et al. *Kiskisik Awasisak: Remember the Children—Understanding the Overrepresentation of First Nations Children in the Child Welfare System.* Assembly of First Nations, 2011.

State of Nebraska, Senate. Transcript, Health and Human Services Committee Meeting on Nebraska Indian Child Welfare Act. 25 Sept. 2012.

Strong-Boag, Veronica. *Finding Families, Finding Ourselves: English Canada Encounters Adoption from the Nineteenth Century to the 1990s.* Oxford UP, 2006.

"To Dry the Eyes of Indian Adoptees." *Daily Yonder*, 16 Mar. 2010. Rpt. in *Two Worlds: Lost Children of the Indian Adoption Projects*, edited by Trace A. DeMeyer and Patricia Cotter-Busbee, CreateSpace, 2012, pp. 247–253.

# From Bartholet, Elizabeth. *Family Bonds: Adoption and the Politics of Parenthood.* Beacon, 1993.

Although some progress was made in the earlier part of this century in upgrading the status of adoptive parenting, powerful forces at work in recent years have revitalized the traditional stigma associated with parenting that is not biologically linked. The search movement, consisting of birth mothers and adoptees, the various advocacy and support groups they have formed, and professionals associated with their cause, represents one such force. The movement has grown apace in the past two decades and exerts a powerful influence. Its basic message is that children "belong" in some primal sense with their family of origin.

The immediate focus of the search movement's efforts is the sealed record system. Movement members advocate opening records so that birth parents and adoptees can identify and connect with each other. The underlying rationale is that biologic links are of fundamental importance.

The long-term goal for many members of the search movement is to eliminate adoption altogether, or at least to limit it to situations of absolute necessity. A recent statement by two search movement leaders argues that the time has come to move beyond the demand for openness to address the "basic issues." It condemns adoption as a "flawed institution," one that "causes pain and lifelong suffering to all the parties involved," and calls for its transformation to a form of guardianship that would permit birth parents to retain some rights over their children even in those "last resort" situations in which it would be necessary physically to remove a child from the birth family.[10]

Search movement activists paint an overwhelmingly negative picture of the impact of adoptive arrangements on all the key parties. They describe a tragic triangle involving the birth parents, the adoptive parents, and the adoptees, with each set of characters doomed to a lifetime of grieving. The birth parents must forever suffer the pain associated with the loss of their child and, if they bear no other children, the loss of genetic continuity into the future. Adoptive parents who are infertile, as is commonly the case, must forever suffer the pain associated with their loss of genetic continuity

DOI: 10.4324/9781003203827-17

into the future and of the genetic child of their dreams. Adoptees must forever suffer the loss of their birth parents and the related loss of genetic continuity with the past. In addition, they will suffer the pain of rejection as they become aware of the "original abandonment" involved in their birth parents' decision to give them up, and will struggle with the resulting injury to their sense of self. They will be prone to "genealogical bewilderment" as they struggle to live a life cut off from their genetic origins, in family structures characterized as inherently abusive.[11]

The movement has generated a significant body of literature in recent years whose fundamental message is that the institution of adoption is sick to its core and destructive of the human beings it affects. A news column by Betty Jean Lifton, a leading figure in the movement, gives a sense of the message that is being promoted. She writes about a fourteen-year-old child who killed his adoptive parents by setting fire to their home, allegedly so that he could search for his birth mother, and describes his actions as related to the so-called adopted child syndrome: "The syndrome includes conflict with authority, preoccupation with excessive fantasy, setting fires, pathological lying, stealing, running away from home, learning difficulties, lack of impulse control." Lifton claims that while most adoptees "adjust" to their unfortunate condition, others "cannot control the inchoate rage caused by their feelings of powerlessness and of rejection by the birth parents."[12] Elsewhere she writes that the adoptee, "by being excluded from his own biological clan, forced out of the natural flow of generational continuity, feels as if he or she has been forced out of nature itself. He feels an alien, an outsider, . . . outside the natural realm of being."[13]

Other forces at work in the society at large have helped to make adoption newly suspect in today's world. There has been a new emphasis in recent decades on the importance of "roots" and of group identity. People are supposed to go back to their roots and derive strength from their racial, ethnic, and national communities of origin. This thinking provides fertile ground for theories that children belong with their birth families and that they will suffer a grievous loss if cut off from their prebirth history and their genetic group. And, of course, it helps make transracial and international adoption particularly problematic.

Egalitarian politics have also contributed to the new stigmatization, with critics attacking adoption as one of the ultimate forms of exploitation of the poor by the rich, the black by the white, the Third World by the capitalist West, the struggling single mother by the economically privileged couple. The fact that adoption functions to improve the economic situation of birth mother and child is ignored.

Finally, the current emphasis on the importance of genetic heritage has revived certain classic fears about the viability of adoption—fears rooted in an assumption that parent-child relationships are likely to work only to the degree that parent and child are significantly alike. In the ongoing nature-nurture debate, the voices of genetics theorists have prevailed lately.[14] Their new studies do not show that environment is an unimportant influence. They simply show that biologic heritage is also important and that children do not start life as blank slates on which adoptive parents can write what they will.[15] But those who think that parent-child relationships are threatened by differences in intellect and personality will find it troubling to think that genetic heritage plays a significant part in the child's development. And those who believe that children belong with their birth parents will find confirmation in the evidence of genetic influence.

The last couple of decades have been bad ones for adoption. Its advocates can easily get the sense that they are fighting the tide of history.

* * * *

My point is not that adoption is the same as biologic parenting but that it should be recognized as a positive form of family, not ranked as a poor imitation of the real thing on some parenting hierarchy. My attack on the adoption stigma should be understood as an argument for adoption but not against biology. I do not think we should jettison the biologic model of parenting and insist on a universal baby swap at the moment of birth. But I would like to put biology in its place and give appropriate value to nurturing and other social aspects of the parenting relationship.

In my view, there are many good reasons for having some presumption in favor of biologically linked parenthood. Birth parents no doubt do generally feel significant pain at the prospect of severing their relationship to the child they have created and in some sense "known" during pregnancy, and in my view they should; our world would be sadly diminished if relinquishment were a nonevent. I am prepared to think that there are other good things to be said for biologic parenting, and even that there may be some risks inherent in adoptive parenting. The sense that a child is your genetic product, the experience of pregnancy and childbirth, the experience of parenting and nursing a child during its first moments of life—all these things may help create a healthy bond between parent and child, and their absence may create a greater potential for problems. Genetic heritage is an important influence on intellect and personality, and it may be that for many parents some level of likeness is important and too much difference is problematic. Adoption may require parents who are more open to difference, more flexible, and more imaginative than the norm. For these among other reasons, the rule giving biologic parents presumptive parenting rights and the rule forbidding payments to induce birth parents to surrender their children seem to me good rules.

But we can recognize the validity of the biology-based family without denigrating adoption.

The adoption stigma helps shape reality in problematic ways. Saying that adoption is a bad thing helps make it a bad thing. In a world in which adoptive status is degraded, it will not feel good to be adopted. While it might feel perfectly all right in some world we can imagine, it will feel problematic in a world in which you and all those around you are conditioned to think that good mothers don't "abandon" their children for others to raise, a world in which others react to the nature of your family situation by saying, "I'm sorry." Thus the adoption stigma necessarily shapes the experience of birth parents who surrender children, of adoptive parents, and of adoptees. Birth parents are conditioned to think that they should feel lifelong pain as the result of their "unnatural" act of giving up their "own" child for another to raise. The infertile are conditioned to think that they should forever grieve over their inability to reproduce biologically.[38] Adoptive parents and children are conditioned to think that their family relationships are significantly inferior to those enjoyed by "real" families.[39] In fact, they are instructed by the new adoption dogma that they should experience and "acknowledge" the problematic differences between their families and normal families. Claims to normalcy are often treated as evidence of pathology.[40]

The stigma also affects the vision of those doing research on adoption. Conditioned to believe that children "belong" in some essential sense with their birth parents, they are predisposed to look for problems in adoptive parenting situations and to see in such situations the explanation for problematic behavior.[41] It is worth speculating about what they would see if they thought more positively about adoption and designed studies to look for the positive. What if they started with the assumption that the norm and the ideal was the adoptive family, and the question was whether biologic parents should be allowed to raise the children they produce? What might the studies "find" if their starting assumption was that biologic parenting had inherent risks?

Stigma shapes reality in another way, helping to form the policies that in turn help to define the adoption experience. Social regulators translate their suspicion of adoption into screening rules that make the process of becoming an adoptive parent seriously frustrating and unpleasant, so that the infertile have all the more reason to see adoption as a last resort. And the policies designed to protect the biologic tie create the foster care limbo, which in turn produces the damaged children who may well have adjustment difficulties in adoption.

Given the predictable impact of the negative myths about adoption, it is a wonder that the evidence about the actual experience of those involved looks so positive. Given the power of those myths, it is hard to imagine thinking differently. But we should try to free ourselves from the forces that condition us to equate procreation with parenting. We should try to imagine living in a society in which adoption is revered rather than denigrated. We should focus on what might be the unique benefits of parenting relationships built entirely on social rather than genetic ties. We should come to understand adoption as a uniquely positive form of family—not necessarily better than the biologic family, but not inherently inferior, either. We should make this imaginative leap because adoption is quite obviously a good solution for existing human beings in this world, most particularly the millions of children in need of nurturing homes. But we should also do it because we have a lot to learn about parenting and family and community from adoptive relationships.

Adoption involves the provision of homes to children in need, and thinking well of adoption should involve placing a higher value than we now do on the nurturing aspects of parenting and a lower value on the self-perpetuating and proprietary aspects. Adoption also involves the exercise of conscious choice in matters related to parenting. Thinking well of adoption should be liberating for birth parents and the infertile, giving them far more choice and control over their lives.

The fact that conscious choice is a defining feature of this form of parenting is unnerving for those conditioned to think of biologic inevitability as a part of what parenting is all about, but it can be seen as an enormously positive feature of this form of family. Adoption critics scorn the tradition of referring to the adoptee as a "chosen child," but adoptees are chosen children. Adoptive parents may initially have wanted to produce a biologic child, and they are of course limited in the choice of which particular child they will adopt. But all of them consciously choose to become parents, and most of them devote a great deal of effort to becoming adoptive parents. By contrast, it is doubtful that as many as half of all biologic parents initially conceive out of a conscious desire to parent. Many conceive by accident, and many consider abortion or adoptive placement and reject these options not because they actually want to parent but because keeping their child seems the least bad of the various bad options available. The fact that a person has consciously chosen to parent seems as important an indicator of the likely success of the parenting relationship as any factor could be.[42] And indeed, controlled studies comparing wanted with unwanted children have shown a stark contrast; the unwanted do very badly.[43]

Virtually all the aspects of adoptive parenting that are generally understood to be "risk factors" can as easily be understood as opportunities for the development of a particularly good parenting relationship. They can also give us insight into possible problems in our current biologic parenting models. We could view the absence of a genetic connection as liberating. Adoptive parents might, for example, be more able to avoid neurotic forms of overidentification with their children, be more able to let their children develop their own personalities and interests, and feel less driven to relive their own lives through their children. Because of the existence of another set of parents, adoptive parents might have a lessened sense of entitlement to complete control and possession, and this could empower children in healthy ways.

Parents and children could experience a range of special satisfactions in family relationships that cross the various lines of difference involved in adoption. As a parent, I revel in the brown skin and thick black hair and dark eyes and Peruvian features that I could not have produced. I have also felt the shock of seeing myself—my intensity, my gestures, my expressions—as I watch these children. I am enchanted by the tempestuous moods of one child and the laid-back good nature of the other. I am intrigued by the mystery of who they are and will be and what part I will play in this. I am ever conscious of the miracle that these children who possess me to the core of my being are mine and also not mine. I am aware of myriad ways in which my consciousness has been expanded and my life enhanced by these adoptions, and I think of people who have known only biologic parenting as people who are missing a special experience. It is likely that adoptive parents and their children would testify to a wide range of special qualities in their family life if there was an audience for such evidence.

Adoptive parenting may produce parents and children who are unusually open to and tolerant of a wide variety of differences. There is evidence that children raised in transracial adoptive families or by gay or lesbian adoptive parents exhibit these traits. There is also evidence that parents who are initially interested only in adopting a healthy same-race infant, and who in fact adopt such a child are significantly more open at the time of their second adoption to considering an older, handicapped child of a different race.

Adoption creates a family that in important ways is not "nuclear." It creates a family that is connected to another family, the birth family, and often to different cultures and to different racial, ethnic, and national groups as well. Adoptive families might teach us something about the value for families of connection with the larger community.

## Notes

10. Baran and Pannor, "It's Time for a Sweeping Change," p. 5.
11. See also Carole Anderson, "Child Abuse and Adoption," unpublished ms. for Concerned United Birthparents, Inc., Des Moines, Iowa, 1991. This paper by the president of the leading birthparent or organization argues that Issues of infertility and the lack of a genetic connection between parent and child contribute to a great risk for child abuse in adoptive families. See generally ch. 4, note 4.
12. "How the Adoption System Ignites a Fire," *New York Times*, March 1, 1986, p. 27.

13. Betty J. Lifton, "Brave New Baby in the Brave New World," *Woman and Health Magazine* 13, no. 1–2 (November 1987): 149–53.
14. See Remi J. Cadoret, "Biologic Perspectives on Adoptee Adjustment," in David M. Brodzinsky and Marshall D. Schechter, *The Psychology of Adoption* (New York: Oxford University Press, 1990), pp. 25–41.
15. See John C. Loehlin, Lee Willerman, and Joseph M. Horn, "Personality Resemblances Between Unwed Mothers and Their Adopted-Away Offspring," *Journal of Personality and Social Psychology* 42 (1982): 1089.

****

38. See Eaton, "Adoption v. Reproductive Technologies"; Sartor, "The Biological Link," pp. 24–27.
39. See Charlene E. Miall, "The Stigma of Adoptive Parent Status: Perceptions of Community Attitudes Toward Adoption and the Experience of Informal Social Sanctioning," *Family Relations* 36 (1987): 34, 37; Bohman and Sigvardsson, "Outcome Adoption," p. 94, which states that adoptive families' "minority status" and "special existential situation" may create considerable stress; Kaye, "Acknowledgment or Rejection of Differences?" p. 140, which asserts that the fundamental differences between early-adopted and nonadopted children, apart from the disappearance of significant figures from their lives, are the "hurts and embarrassments caused by a social stigma and by people's cruelty"; Kirk, *Shared Fate*, a classic work describing adoptive families as constituting a minority group that lacks the' support of social and historical traditions common to biologic kinship relations. Stein and Hoopes, *Identity Formation*, asked their group of adopted adolescents how it felt to be adopted. Most indicated that it produced no ill effects and was not that different from being raised by birth parents as far as they could tell. One commented, "It's not adoption that is the problem but what other people think of adopted kids" (pp. 60–61).
40. Compare Kaye, "Acknowledgment or Rejection of Differences?" pp. 140–41, which finds that families of early-adopted adolescents tend to emphasize the normalcy of their situations rather than the differences, and concludes that this emphasis should be understood as healthy rather than pathological.
41. By contrast, Kaye (ibid.) emphasizes that both adopted and biologic children develop self-esteem problems if they do not experience a sense of "belonging" in their environment, and that the adoptee is different primarily in that he "has a real historical loss of ties to which to attribute the problem or in which to see hope of rectifying it" (p. 142).
42. See Marquis and Detweiler, "Does Adopted Mean Different?" pp. 1063–64, which speculates that positive findings about the adoptive parenting relationship may be related to the adoptive parents' particularly strong motivation to become parents; David M. Brodzinsky and Loreen Huffman, "Transition to Adoptive Parenthood," *Marriage and Family Review* 12 (1988): 267, 276, which discusses other apparent benefits associated with adoptive parenting. Laraine M. Glidden's work reveals that the choice to adopt a child with developmental disabilities is associated with greater parental well-being than being the birth parent of such a child. See Glidden, "Adopted Children with Developmental Disabilities: Post-Placement Family Functioning," *Children and Youth Services Review* 13 (1991): 363–77; Glidden, "The Wanted Ones: Families Adopting Children with Mental Retardation," *Journal of Children in Contemporary Society* 21 (1990): 177–205. See also Katherine A. Kowal and Karen M.

Schilling, "Adoption through the Eyes of Adult Adoptees," *American Journal of Orthopsychiatry* 55 (1985): 354–65, which finds that adoptees report feeling chosen or special twice as often as they report feeling uncomfortable with the fact of their adoption.

43. Mothers who are denied abortions are described as feeling an extremely high level of anger and resentment toward their children, who are in turn described as "much likelier to be troubled and depressed, to drop out of school, to commit crimes, to suffer from serious illnesses and to express dissatisfaction with life than are the offspring of willing parents"; "Study Says Anger Troubles Women," *New York Times*, May 21, 1991, p. C-10.

# From Butler, Judith. "Is Kinship Always Heterosexual?" *differences: A Journal of Feminist Cultural Studies*, vol. 13, no. 1, 2002, pp. 14–44.

So why would the structuralist account of sexual difference, conceived according to the exchange of women, make a "comeback" in the context of the present debates in France? Why would various intellectuals, some of them feminist, proclaim that sexual difference is not only fundamental to culture, but to its transmissibility, and that reproduction must remain the prerogative of heterosexual marriage and that limits must be set on viable and recognizable forms of nonheterosexual parenting arrangements?

To understand the resurgence of a largely anachronistic structuralism in this context, it is important to consider that the incest taboo functions in Lévi-Strauss not only to secure the exogamous reproduction of children but also to maintain a unity to the "clan" through compulsory exogamy as it is articulated through compulsory heterosexuality. The woman from elsewhere makes sure that the men from here will reproduce their own kind. She secures the reproduction of cultural identity in this way. The ambiguous "clan" designates a "primitive" group for Lévi-Strauss in 1949 but comes to function ideologically for the cultural unity of the nation in 1999–2000 in the context of a Europe beset by opening borders and new immigrants. The incest taboo thus comes to function in tandem with a racialist project to reproduce culture and, in the French context, to reproduce the implicit identification of French culture with universality. It is a "law" that works in the service of the "as if," securing a fantasy of the nation that is already, and irreversibly, under siege. In this sense, the invocation of the symbolic law defends against the threat to French cultural purity that has taken place, and is taking place, through new patterns of immigration, increased instances of miscegenation, and the blurring of national boundaries. Indeed, even in Lévi-Strauss, whose earlier theory of clan formation is redescribed in his short text, *Race and History*, we see that the reproducibility of racial identity is linked to the reproduction of culture.[16] Is there a link between the account of the reproduction of culture in Lévi-Strauss's early work and his later reflections on cultural identity and the reproduction of race? Is there a connection between these texts that might help us read the cultural link that

DOI: 10.4324/9781003203827-18

takes place in France now between fears about immigration and desires to regulate nonheterosexual kinship? The incest taboo might be seen as working in conjunction with the taboo against miscegenation, especially in the contemporary French context, insofar as the defense of culture that takes place through mandating the family as heterosexual is at once an extension of new forms of European racism. And we see something of this link prefigured in Lévi-Strauss, which explains in part why we see the resurrection of his theory in the context of the present debate. When Lévi-Strauss makes the argument that the incest taboo is the basis of culture and that it mandates exogamy, or marriage outside the clan, is "the clan" being read in terms of race or, more specifically, in terms of a racial presupposition of culture that maintains its purity through regulating its transmissibility? Marriage must take place outside the clan. There must be exogamy. But there must also be a limit to exogamy; that is, marriage must be outside the clan but not outside a certain racial self-understanding or racial commonality. So the incest taboo mandates exogamy, but the taboo against miscegenation limits the exogamy that the incest taboo mandates. Cornered, then, between a compulsory heterosexuality and a prohibited miscegenation, something called culture, saturated with the anxiety and identity of dominant European whiteness, reproduces itself in and as universality itself.

There are, of course, many other ways of contesting the Lévi-Straussian model that have emerged in recent years, and its strange resurgence in the recent political debate will no doubt strike anthropologists as the spectral appearance of an anachronism. Arguments have been made, for instance, that other kinds of kinship arrangements are possible within a culture and that there are other ways of explaining the ordering practices that kinship sometimes exemplified. These debates, however, remain internal to a study of kinship that assumes the primary place of kinship within a culture and assumes for the most part that a culture is a unitary and discrete totality. Pierre Clastres made this point most polemically several years ago in the French context, arguing that it is not possible to treat the rules of kinship as supplying the rules of intelligibility for any society and that culture is not a self-standing notion but must be regarded as fundamentally imbued by power relations, power relations that are not reducible to rules.[17] But if we begin to understand that cultures are not self-standing entities or unities, that the exchanges between them, their very modes of delimiting themselves in distinction, constitute their provisional ontology and are, as a result, fraught with power, then we are compelled to rethink the problem of exchange altogether, no longer as the gift of women, which assumes and produces the self-identity of the patrilineal clan, but as a set of potentially unpredictable and contested practices of self-definition that are not reducible to a primary and culture-founding heterosexuality. Indeed, if one were to elaborate on this point, the task would be to take up David Schneider's suggestion that kinship is a kind of *doing*, one that does not reflect a prior structure but which can only be understood as an enacted practice. This would help us, I believe, move away from the situation in which a hypostatized structure of relations lurks behind any actual social arrangement and permit us to consider how modes of patterned and performative doing bring kinship categories into operation and become the means by which they undergo transformation and displacement.

The hypostatized heterosexuality, construed by some to be symbolic rather than social and so to operate as a structure that founds the field of kinship itself—and that informs social arrangements no matter how they appear, no matter what they do—has been the basis of the claim that kinship is always already heterosexual. According to its precept, those who enter kinship terms as nonheterosexual will only make sense if they assume the position of Mother or Father. The social variability of kinship has little or no efficacy in rewriting the founding and pervasive symbolic law. The postulate of a founding heterosexuality must also be read as part of the operation of power—and I would add fantasy—such that we can begin to ask how the invocation of such a foundation works in the building of a certain fantasy of state and nation. The relations of exchange that constitute culture as a series of transactions or translations are not only or primarily sexual, but they do take sexuality as their issue, as it were, when the question of cultural transmission and reproduction is at stake. And I do not mean to say that cultural reproduction takes place solely or exclusively or fundamentally through the child. I mean only to suggest that the figure of the child is one eroticized site in the reproduction of culture, one that implicitly raises the question of whether there will be a sure transmission of culture through heterosexual procreation, whether heterosexuality will serve not only the purposes of transmitting culture faithfully, but whether culture will be defined, in part, as the prerogative of heterosexuality itself.

****

One can see how quickly kinship loses its specificity in terms of the global economy, for instance, when one considers the politics of international adoption and donor insemination. For new "families," in which relations of filiation are not based on biology, are sometimes conditioned by innovations in biotechnology or international commodity relations and the trade in children. And now there is the question of control over genetic resources, conceived of as a new set of property relations to be negotiated by legislation and court decisions. But there are clearly salutary consequences, as well, of the breakdown of the symbolic order, as it were, since kinship ties that bind persons to one another may well be no more or less than the intensification of community ties, may or may not be based on enduring or exclusive sexual relations, and may well consist of ex-lovers, non-lovers, friends, community members. In this sense, then, the relations of kinship arrive at boundaries that call into question the distinguishability of kinship from community, or that call for a different conception of friendship. These constitute a "breakdown" of traditional kinship that not only displaces the central place of biological and sexual relations from its definition, but gives sexuality a separate domain from that of kinship, allowing as well for the durable tie to be thought outside of the conjugal frame, and opening kinship to a set of community ties that are irreducible to family.

## Notes

16. See Lévi- Strauss's discussion of "ethnocentrism" in *Race et histoire* 1–26.
17. See Clastres, *Society Against the State* and *Archeology of Violence*. For a consideration of anthropological approaches to kinship after Lévi- Strauss, see Carsten and Hugh-Jones *About the House: Lévi- Strauss and Beyond*.

## Works Cited

Carsten, Janet, and Stephen Hugh-Jones, editors. *About the House: Lévi-Strauss and Beyond*. Cambridge UP, 1995.

Clastres, Pierre. *Society Against the State: Essays in Political Anthropology*. Translated by Robert Hurley, Zone, 1987.

Lévi-Strauss, Claude. *Race et histoire*. Denoël, 1987.

Schneider, David. *A Critique of the Study of Kinship*. U of Michigan P, 1984.

———. *American Kinship: A Cultural Account*. 2nd edition, U of Chicago P, 1980.

# From Stevens, Jacqueline. *Reproducing the State*. Princeton UP, 1999.

The reason that marriage still constitutes gender difference is that the political statuses "husband" and "wife" are not as identical as they appear. As long as kinship rules exist, this is inevitable. Marriage statutes, as interpreted by the courts, position women as part of nature and men as part of political society. Marriage constitutes men's control over women's labor when it gives "husbands" custody rights that biological fathers per se lack.[38] The state, then, awards men control over the labor of women's bodies (children) by virtue of the political conventions of marriage. When married to a woman, a man is always the legal father of children he conceives with her, and often the presumptive father of any child she bears. Her relation to the child is by birth (natural), while his is by marriage (political). 'Matrimony' is the naming of the mother. This form suggests that mothers are just there, by nature, and it is the legal convention of marriage that constitutes fathers. To paraphrase Sherry Ortner, mothers are to nature as fathers are to politics.[39]

The politics/nature distinction has sometimes been gendered in an apparently opposite fashion as well. Rousseau's work is an example of this, as was the temperance movement in the late-nineteenth and early-twentieth centuries in the United States. During that period women's and Christian organizations figured the state as an institution that would domesticate the savage sexuality of its male citizens. It was also a "maternalist" institution that would protect its weaker members.[40] Law as a feminine, maternal force underscores the compensatory character of the state's masculinity. This conjunction may suggest that when men appropriate birth, qua "father"-s, their control of birth remains an ultimately feminine, i.e., maternal, activity.[41] They cannot **be** the mother, but through matrimony, they can have her. The state itself, by controlling reproduction, appropriates the reproduction for which mothers are otherwise responsible. The state is at once fatherly (political) and maternal (in charge of birth).[42] In its insistence on controlling marriage, the state positions itself as constitutive of intergenerational forms of being. It is the prerogative of the state to distinguish, and hence to constitute, the difference between what is **profane** (sex as "fornication,"

DOI: 10.4324/9781003203827-19

children as "illegitimate") and what is **sacred** (sex within marriage, legitimate children).[43] Not just United States custody law, but all kinship systems depend on the negation of mothers. As Kingsley Davis noted, the primary function of kinship systems is to bring men into a relation with children. Political societies reach out to give men authority they would otherwise lack.

A possible revisionist criticism of this view might point to examples of matrilineal societies. That is, some scholars might infer from matrilineal practices that kinship rules do not necessarily subjugate women to men. These matrilineal societies actually might be instances in which a high regard for maternity resulted in a higher status for women than for men.[44] Still, as long as paternity is regulated, and even when **mothers** seem to be at the center of what is sacred, figured as such by matrilineal rules of descent, kinship forms still adversely affect women, because matrilineality has no necessary relation to matriarchy. The main arguments that women have power in these and other contexts are largely heuristic, asserting that we "could" interpret events differently.

****

Any kinship system exists in relation to an otherwise unregulated process of reproduction. That is, kinship suggests the possibility of species reproduction absent kinship. Marking the activity as subject to certain distinctions imposed by a political society bestows certain meanings on these practices. When a political society takes charge of maternity, it performs associations between the maternal and the natural, not because kinship systems are necessary, but rather because they serve certain purposes that seem necessary but on closer inspection are not. Kingsley Davis and others have insisted on the opposite, Davis maintaining that "reproduction can be carried out in a socially useful manner only if it is performed in conformity with institutional patterns."[49] Elsewhere Davis writes that "every family is actually a biological group," but after noting tremendous variation among kinship forms, he observes, "The structure of the human family is rooted not in biology, but in the folkways and mores."[50] One way to reconcile these claims is to note, as Davis does, that the human species is one that "interbreeds" and so, depending on the remoteness of ties one traces, it can be said that we are "all biologically related," which simply illustrates the uselessness of biological arguments about kinship. If biology means we are all interrelated, then it cannot be the basis of kinship forms that establish an "us" distinct from "them."

Why is reproduction regulated by political societies per se? One argument, put in practice in Rome and in modern Italy, Germany, and the nineteenth-century United States (among other places), is that augmenting the legal family unit will increase the population.[51] The so-called "bachelor taxes" under Augustine and current tax credits for children born to married couples associate marriage with species reproduction. Yet other writers construed marriage as an impediment to reproduction. Eighteenth-century French thinkers argued that one way to increase the population was to make divorce easier and marriage generally less restrictive.[52]

It is true that reproduction is necessary for the species to survive. It is not true that reproduction must be gendered. Many activities are necessary for humanity's sustenance. People need shelter, food, and water. The production and collection of all of these has been in certain places and times gendered. Why is it more difficult to imagine that yam collection need not be gendered than that child production need not be gendered? Just as yam collection may be but need not be associated with kinship roles, the same holds true for childbirth. Rules specifying roles in kinship systems themselves mark these practices as gendered. They do not follow from something like the-practice-in-itself. Kinship regulations are not in place because of "givens" such as human nature or biology.

We regulate kinship because of beliefs such as this:

> We have seen that throughout history civilizations that have allowed the traditional bonds of family to be weakened—those civilizations have not survived. America has, and always should be, a nation that prioritizes traditional family values and the tradition of a one man and one woman marriage.[53]

Yet of course weakened civilizations have died, but the human species survived well enough for Rep. Ron Packard to cast his vote. The marriage form exists to maintain ongoing political communities, not humanity itself.

* * * *

**Family Court**

It is through the operation of marriage law that particular political societies reproduce as such. In the United States the marital status of "husband father" trumps a biological father's claim to his children, and it also trumps a mother's "natural" status—as the laws on surrogacy, discussed below, make clear. A woman's right to make decisions about her children is substantially undermined if she is married to the father. Not biological paternity but marriage creates this form of dependence for her.

Insofar as the courts associate women with nature, the state's articulations of the maternal relationship appropriate and displace this feminine status. Luce Irigaray writes:

> Historically, the obligation for women, to give birth to children within their husbands' genealogy corresponds to the beginnings of *non-respect*

> *for nature*, to the establishment of a notion or concept of nature that is substituted for the fertility of the earth . . . Paradoxically, the cult of the mother often goes hand in hand, in our cultures, with scorn for or neglect of nature.[54]

Explicitly and in the more nuanced metonymic associations that follow from its interventions, the state's control of reproduction through marriage disempowers mothers by associating them with a view of nature that is itself constituted by the grammar of the dichotomy of political society/ nature imposed by the very form of political societies.

The court decisions most constitutive as well as illustrative of the politicization of fatherhood consider child, really infant, custody. In these cases, which include surrogacy cases, adoption cases, and cases of artificial insemination, the biological parents are not married.[55] According to most statutes and court decisions, when parents are unmarried, and when the father has demonstrated no interest in either the mother or the pregnancy, the mother has the prerogative to determine whether to allow the child to be adopted. The permission of the father is not required.

Apparent exceptions to this rule are emerging, although all are cases in which the father has shown an interest in the pregnancy and in the child. In these cases the courts have named an equivalence between the mother who bears a child and the father who, for instance, establishes a trust fund in the child's name. On this basis, biological fathers have custody rights similar to those of married fathers. In all of these cases the state holds the prerogative not simply to enforce "the law," nor to use the law to enforce contracts and status relations decided in civil society. Rather, the state assigns status. "Wife," "Husband," Father," and "Mother" are all state creations. As Judge Montgomery said: "We know what a child is. But what is a father, mother, or parent? It is time to redefine such once simple words from a perspective of the law. . . . [W]hat exactly *is* a daddy? Is it a noun or a verb?"[56]

In addressing similar questions the courts have established the following system of custody rights. Marriage statutes are largely the work of state legislatures, which means they vary, but every state has laws defining marriage.[57]

## Notes

38. By positioning children as the objects of women's labor, the state defines children as property. Though this contributes to an alienated concept of personality (as children "belong to" their parents, not themselves), that alienation is not the focus of this chapter.
39. Sherry Ortner, "Is Female to Male as Nature is to Culture?" in *Women. Culture, and Society*, ed. Michelle Rosaldo and Louise Lamphere (Stanford: Stanford University Press, 1974), pp. 67–88. As examples of the devaluation of females, Ortner writes: "female exclusion from a most sacred rite or the highest political council is sufficient evidence." The fact that the state constitutes the sacred

quality of marriage, one that excludes women from the sacred position of "husband," similarly situates women in the realm of nature and men in the realm of politics. Ortner writes: "[M]y thesis is that woman is being identified with—or, if you will, seems to be a symbol of—something that every culture defines as being of a lower order of existence than itself." This realm, according to Ortner, is nature, or the prof.me. But whereas Ortner develops an essentialist argument about women's "natural procreation functions" as the root of this identification, mine is a phenomenological argument about the juridical rendering of this dichotomy.

40. Theda Skocpol, *Protecting Soldiers and Mothers: The Political Origins of Social Policy in the United States* (Cambridge: Harvard University Press, 1992).
41. Norman O. Brown makes this point, in *Love's Body* (New York: Random House, 1966).
42. Another parallel worthy of note is the state's monopoly on the legitimate imposition of death. This appropriation of the power over life and death reflects that maternal relation to her newborn child, who depends on her for survival.
43. See also Fineman, *Neutered Mother*, pp. 146–47.
44. These women-as-agent accounts take two forms. One shows instances of matrilineal societies that are also matriarchal; the other re-reads the significance of the roles women play in societies that appear to be juridically dominated by men. For examples of the former, see Ladislav Holy, *Strategies and Norms in a Changing Matrilineal Society* (Cambridge and New York: Cambridge University Press, 1986); Michael Peletz, "The Exchange of Men in 19th-century Negeri Sembilan (Malaya)," *American Ethnologist* 14 (3) (August, 1987), 449–69; and Karla Poewe, *Matrilineal Ideology: Male-Female Dynamics in Luapula, Zambia* (London and New York: Academic Press, 1981). The latter, by far the more popular approach, includes Eleanor Burke Leacock, *Myths of Male Dominance: Collected Articles on Women Cross Culturally* (New York and London: Monthly Review Press, 1981); Sherry Ortner, "Gender Hegemonies," *Cultural Critique* 14 (Winter, 1989–90), pp. 35–80; Michelle Rosaldo, "The Use and Abuse of Anthropology: Reflections on Feminism and Cross-Cultural Understanding," *Signs* 5 (3) (1980), pp. 389–417; Karen Sacks, *Sisters and Wives: The Past and Future of Sexual Equality* (Westport, London: Greenwood Press, 1979).
49. Davis, "Illegitimacy and Social Structure," *American Journal of Sociology* 45 (1939), p. 259.
50. Davis, *Human Society* (New York: MacMillan, 1949), pp. 387, 399.
54. "The Necessity for Sexuate Rights," in *The Irigaray Reader*, ed. Margaret Whitford (Oxford and Cambridge: Blackwell, 1991), p. 200.
55. See *Child Custody and the Politics of Gender*, ed. Carol Smart and Selma Sevenhuijsen (London and New York: Routledge, 1989). Smart points out that the rhetoric on the child's need for the father aligns the father and child against the mother: "The more men's interests and children's interests are seen to coincide, the more mothers are disempowered" (p. 10); Nancy Erikson, "The Feminist Dilemma over Unwed Parents' Custody Rights," *Law and Inequality* 2 (1984), pp. 447–72; Kathryn Katz, "Ghost Mothers: Human Egg Donation and the Legacy of the Past," *Albany Law Review* 57 (1994), pp. 733–80. For a review of cases focused on problems of illegitimacy, see Martha Zingo and Kevin Early, *Nameless Persons: Legal Discrimination against Non-Marital Children in the United States* (Westport and London: Praeger, 1994).
56. "Child Abuse and Changing Definitions," address at the annual meeting of the Child Abuse and Neglect Committee, published in *Texas Bar Journal*, 57 (September, 1994), p. 886.

57. One difference is the person or organization designated to signify that a wedding has been performed. Most states require a religious official or state magistrate; hut some states exclude certain minister-by-mail "denominations." A few allow anyone to sign the form. Also, some of what follows is taken from state supreme court opinions, and these also reveal discrepancies. When it is relevant, I have provided information on the frequency of certain policies, such as surrogacy laws. These decisions are on cases the courts themselves deem "unique," "exceptional," or "unusual," and so one might wonder whether they help us understand the daily practices of most citizens. However, it is law that renders these situations marginal, not the parental disputes per se; without marriage law there is no "unique" marriage arrangement. In prompting a careful consideration of the "logic" of marriage rules, these cases provide insights that otherwise normalized understandings of marriage preclude.

# From Briggs, Laura. "The Intimate Politics of Race and Globalization." *Adoption Across Race and Nation*, edited by Silke Hackenesch, The Ohio State UP, 2023, pp. 15–37.

I argue that there are at least two traditions from which the border policy, and adoption and foster care more broadly, derives. One is a humanitarian history in which parents willingly relinquish their children to protect them from harm or to promote their well-being. The period of the rise of European fascism in the 1930s and '40s gives us these humanitarian roots, when children were sent away from Spain and Germany to protect them from Francoism and Nazism, particularly Basque and Jewish children, to be fostered during the war in places that were safer for them. The second tradition is older, with origins in slavery in the Americas and US Indian policy, of separating children from parents to break resistance and to build wealth, as when children were torn from their mothers on slavery's auction block in the New World. The separation of children from tribal nations in Canada, Australia, and the US and the legacies of slavery and child separation were contested and debated through the transnational abolitionist movements and Indian policy reform movements in the Americas from the nineteenth century through the twentieth.[5] In the US, the long arc of these political movements was crystalized as reform of child-taking in the Indian Child Welfare Act of 1978 and the National Association of Black Social Workers statement on where Black children belong of 1972. Both traditions are nodded to in the 1948 Convention on Genocide, which identifies one of the elements of the crime of genocide as "forcibly transferring children of the group to another group." This law was referencing a history that was well known in 1948—recalling the hiding (and baptizing) of Jewish children during the war, as well as the more than 11,000 Jewish children who were rounded up by the French police at the urging of the Gestapo and sent to the camp at Drancy, where only 300 survived.[6]

As the border separation of children from parents in 2018 and 2019 makes painfully evident, there is not always a bright line between the hostile, weaponized tactic of tearing children from parents and the humanitarian history. These currents have flowed apart and then together again, with the violence and cruelty of the former sometimes trying to disguise itself as the

DOI: 10.4324/9781003203827-20

latter. In Europe and the Americas, the political history of the nation has alternated between a racial nationalism, associated with fascism and other hard-right formations, and a civic nationalism, which while often racist nevertheless imagines the nation as composed of different racial groups.[7] The history of child separation follows these broad contours, where an overt racial definition of the state allows for the genocidal separation of children, and a civic nationalism often demands a fig leaf to cover its racism, and so requires that racialized child separation look humanitarian. In what follows, this chapter begins with the paradigmatic case of producing child separation that was essentially genocidal as humanitarianism: the US Indian policy designed to "kill the Indian to save the man"—ending the nineteenth-century wars against Native people west of the Mississippi by taking their children. It then turns not to slavery's auction block but to the mid-twentieth-century reckoning with it in the US civil rights movement, sometimes called the Second Reconstruction.[8] Finally, in a nod to contemporary struggles over transnational adoption policy and the Hague Convention, it turns briefly to US evangelical Christians and the fight over adoption from Uganda. Again and again, I argue, we see the lines between caring for children by separating them from their families and child separation as a tactic of terror blur.

****

Yet there was one official inquiry into boarding schools in the US. Throughout the 1920s Indian policy reform advocates ran ever more vociferous campaigns about the horrors of Indian policy, including ongoing land theft, detribalization, and the suppression of Native culture, language, and religious practices, and insisting that child separation and boarding school policies were a keystone of all these other processes. As a result of this public pressure, Hubert Work, the Secretary of the Interior, commissioned an independent report by the Institute for Government Research aiming to prove that the public campaign was rank exaggeration. The 1928 report, *The Problem of Indian Administration* (better known as the Meriam Report, for its author), suggested that things were, if anything, worse than the press accounts had had it, with special reference to boarding schools. It described children living in overcrowded dormitories, without even adequate toilet facilities at times, subsisting on a vastly inadequate diet, subject to terrible health conditions, ill-clad. Boarding schools "operated below any reasonable standard of health and decency," as Lewis Meriam wrote. Children suffered high rates of illness and death and were subject to a curriculum of little value; the report noted continued high rates of illiteracy. They had virtually no leisure time and were forced to do manual labor to support the school (in apparent violation of child labor laws, the report noted). It urgently recommended that children be returned to their parents and communities. "The continued policy of removing Indian children from the home and placing them for years in boarding schools largely disintegrates the family and interferes with developing normal family life."[28]

The report's effect was electric. President Herbert Hoover immediately and publicly increased the allocation to boarding schools for food and clothing for children. Within a few years, a leader of the reform campaign, John Collier, was heading up the Bureau of Indian Affairs and introduced significant changes designed to recognize tribal organization and Native religion and culture, halt the reduction of the land base of Indian country, and close boarding schools in favor of day schools.[29]

The effects of boarding schools on children and Native communities were devastating. Mortality rates among children were very high. Those children who did return had often forgotten their native language and sometimes had no language in common with their parents. As one agent with the Indian Service, Dane Coolidge, noted, "Back in the hogans of their people the returned school[children] are quite unfitted for their life. [. . .] They start in all over again to learn to spin and weave and handle their sheep and goats."[30] Many attribute high rates of violence, family dysfunction, alcoholism, and drug abuse among some Native communities to the legacies of the boarding school experience and to the fact that for years, many Indian children were raised away from their parents. One scholar wrote, "I have attended several Native wellness workshops in which participants are asked to draw a family tree that shows the generation in their family in which violence, substance abuse, and other related problems develop. Almost invariably, these problems began with the generation that first went to boarding school."[31] In the 1970s the American Psychiatric Association published an influential editorial that called boarding schools "a hazard to mental health."[32] In 1977 psychiatrist Joseph Westermeyer testified before Congress that Native families were in "crisis" as a result of the "ravages" of boarding schools and other familial separations, citing alcoholism and suicide attempts by parents who had lost their children.[33]

The legacy of boarding schools is not past; it lives in people who are currently alive and among us. Although day schools became more common in the 1930s, and boarding schools were largely phased out in the 1970s, the harm of being separated from parents at a young age continues into the present. In 1974 a survey by the Association of American Indian Affairs found one in three Native children separated from their parents, either in boarding school, foster care, or adoptions.[34] That number had risen by 1987, when another survey found even higher rates of children separated from their Native parents.[35] Scholars, mental health professionals, and activists may debate the proportions in which this is a legacy of policy—the habit of and deeply ingrained belief in separating Native children from parents—or of familial pain in the aftermath of the trauma of the boarding school experience. Regardless, it is amply clear that Indian families continue to suffer because of federal policy that separated children from parents, even many generations later.

When children who had been separated at early ages from their parents grew into adults, they often passed their trauma to their own children. In 2006 mental health professionals who surveyed nearly 500 Native American adults and youth found not only that the boarding school attendees in the group had much-elevated rates of suicide attempts, alcoholism, and drug abuse, but that children raised by boarding school attendees "are significantly more likely to have a general anxiety disorder, experience posttraumatic stress disorder symptoms, and have suicidal thoughts in their lifetime compared to others."[36]

****

## Native American and Black American Children: Communities in Rebellion

As with so much else in the US, racially minoritized populations within the country had a complex relationship to US foreign policy. On the one hand, as Kim Park Nelson among others has suggested, children brought to the US as refugees, or through private adoptions, have had to fit themselves into existing racial formations—including those from Asia, Latin America, and, in more recent times, Africa.[41] On the other hand, those groups who one way or another are or have become native to North America—Indigenous people on the one hand and the Black American descendants of slaves on the other—have troubled histories with adoption. In some ways, these were the communities most intimately connected to the shift from the widespread movement of children having something to do with refugees to the ways adoption began to traffic with something even darker—a response to political rebellion in a deeply paranoid, dualistic Cold War world of communists and anticommunists. Black and Native communities were among the first to raise the alarm that families and communities were losing their children to punish them for political activism at a time when political rebellion was quickly tied to communism.

We all know the number produced by the Association of American Indian Affairs in the 1970s to demand greater legal protections for Native communities and families: that, at that time, one in three Native American children were in out-of-home care. One thing that became clear from that group's investigations into children who were sometimes taken from reservations—without any color of law—is that involvement with Indigenous sovereignty movements, particularly the American Indian Movement, put people at risk for losing their children.[42] It was a conspicuous echo of the use of boarding schools a century and a half earlier to effect the final end to the nineteenth-century Indian Wars on the North American continent. Taking people's children and attempting to strip them of their languages and traditional ways of life is a remarkably effective way of stopping rebellions.

The other thing that put people at risk was when single mothers got welfare—the Aid to Families with Dependent Children program that was the largest government program providing support for children from the 1930s to the 1990s. When activists insisted that women in Native communities were entitled to access to these programs, state governments and social workers saw this as effectively ending claims to self-government and sovereignty for tribal nations with respect to children. And so with welfare came state governments' right to take children—which they did, in massive numbers, ignoring the orders of tribal courts about children's placement. In 1978 the Association of American Indian Affairs succeeded in passing the Indian Child Welfare Act, which was supposed to return control of child placement to tribal courts. But that measure has been under constant assault in one way or another ever since—whether from social workers who argue that alcoholism, meth, or crack cocaine are such public health crises in Native communities that kids must be placed off the reservation or, alternately, by the conservative Goldwater Institute trying to wrest control of lucrative Indian gaming from tribal nations through a sideways attack on Native sovereignty, by going after their control of their children.[43]

Black communities in the US in some ways fared even worse, and for some of the same causes—single mothers receiving welfare and political rebellion. In the 1950s and '60s, in the context of the civil rights movement, the racist right tried to turn the tables on the upstanding church folk who were the movement's public face by insisting on the sexual immorality of the majority of Black folks. Throughout this period, at a regional and local level, shaming unmarried mothers was a tactic of white segregationists. Children became a crucial issue in the movement, one of the front lines of civil rights. After 1954 and the *Brown v. Board of Education* decision and Emmett Till's murder in 1955, children were the public face of the desegregation of public spaces. In 1963 it was the Children's Crusade in Birmingham that cost high-profile white supremacist Bull Connor of Birmingham his job, as their courage in facing down his fire hoses and dogs was splashed across every newspaper in the country.[44]

White segregationists fought back by suggesting that their mothers were immoral, sexually loose women. From 1958 to 1964 in Mississippi, the legislature tried to pass mandatory sterilization laws for Black women who had "bastard" children. As lawyers and the incipient welfare rights movement pressed on the de facto exclusion of Black, Native, and Puerto Rican women from AFDC programs, welfare officials played cat and mouse with these new clients, trying to catch them with a man in the house by surprising them late at night and stationing someone at the back door or window, searching for men's underwear or shaving things, getting the scoop from gossipy neighbors. If they found evidence of heterosexual sex, they would argue that the children had a "substitute father" who should pay for their support and throw the woman and children off welfare. The more Black Americans in the South fought for civil rights, the more officials cut benefits to working-class women and children; between 1957 and 1967 the city of Birmingham decreased its total yearly expenditures on welfare from $31,000 to a mere $12,000.[45]

Throughout the 1940s and 1950s, progressives and conservatives clashed over whether giving cash benefits to impoverished people kept women and children alive or were a wasteful exercise in taxing and squandering money that simply contributed to immorality and wastefulness among those who received benefits. In the context of desegregation and rising Black unemployment (as defense jobs vanished with the end of the Second World War, and plants and other businesses were asked to lay people off to make way for returning soldiers—explicitly, women, but often Black American men were fired, too, for good measure), welfare was often weaponized as a tool to fight Black communities in rebellion. All over the South and the North, Black women lost benefits for failing to keep a "suitable home" or for having "illegitimate" children. In Louisiana in 1960, the legislature cut off thousands of children as part of a "segregation package" of legislation designed to punish the Black community for the radical act of sending four little girls to two white first grades in New Orleans. Governor Jimmie Davis called unmarried mothers "prostitutes"; hundreds were urged to "voluntarily" relinquish their children now that they had no way to feed them. The National Urban League responded with "Operation Feed the Babies," which became an international effort to raise money to help mothers pay for rent and clothing, while Black churches cooked meals and distributed thousands of pounds of food to help families keep body and soul together through the crisis.[46]

The culmination of these processes happened in 1961, when Congress authorized funding for the program known as ADC–Foster Care, which provided welfare funds for states to take the children of welfare mothers and put them in foster care. In the first year of the program alone, 150,000 southern children were placed in out-of-home care.[47] In subsequent years, ADC and foster care were transformed from a system that ignored Black children to one that acted vigorously to take them in the name of protecting them from the consequences of poverty. Although the Urban League fought vigorously for welfare payments that would keep children in their homes instead, the Eisenhower administration insisted that it was a "states rights" issue in which they could not intervene.[48]

It's worth noting, also, that the ADC–Foster Care program was what the much-maligned 1972 National Association of Black Social Workers statement was about: trying to find a tactic that protected Black unmarried mothers from losing their children. Black children were rarely being placed for adoption voluntarily; this was a fight about what became of children who were taken, sometimes maliciously, by welfare officials who found the state of Black communities' housing, poverty, and morals wanting. By claiming that Black children belonged in Black families, the NABSW was trying to shine a light on the positive resources of Black families: the ability to provide their children the wherewithal to survive and find psychic wholeness in a culture that often hated them. When white families adopted Black children, they took the cost of raising them off the hands of the state and vastly expanded the child welfare system's ability to take them in the first place. This was, and remains, the crucial issue in all fights about adoption policy, domestic and foreign: there is not and never has been a fixed number of children who are simply out there, "available" for adoption, and any time you make adoption easy, you also make it easy for birth families to lose their children.

## Notes

5. See Jacobs, *White Mother to a Dark Race*; Jacobs, *Generation Removed*; Briggs, *Somebody's Children*; Briggs, *Taking Children*.
6. Roiphe, "Holocaust's Children." One Nazi legal theorist, Heinrich Krieger, provided a memo detailing US federal Indian law and Jim Crow for a National Socialist meeting on the Nuremberg laws that set out the special limitations on Jews, including stripping them of citizenship. Krieger published extensively on US race law, mostly in Germany. In one article in English, he argued that the best way to understand reservation policy (including reservations founded as camps for prisoners of war), the denial of US citizenship to American Indians (until 1924), the denial of the right to vote in elections (still not won by the time Krieger wrote in the 1930s), and the whole contradictory character of Indian law was to see it as a species of race law: "The proper nature of the tribal Indians' status is that of a racial group placed under a special police power of the United States." Whether this was the only or best understanding of Indian law, it is clear that boarding schools *could* be understood as a special instance of race laws under federal military power. See Blackhawk, "Federal Indian Law as Paradigm"; Krieger, "Principles of the Indian Law."
7. Stern, *Proud Boys and the White Ethnostate*.
8. Woodward and McFeely, *Strange Career of Jim Crow*.

****

28. See, for example, Collier, "America's Treatment of Her Indians"; Collier, "American Congo"; Philp, *John Collier's Crusade for Indian Reform*; Institute for Government Research, *Problem of Indian Administration*, 348, 15.
29. Philp, *John Collier's Crusade for Indian Reform*.
30. Coolidge, "'Kid Catching' on the Navajo Reservation."
31. Smith, *Conquest*, 44.
32. Beiser, "Hazard to Mental Health."

33. US Congress, Senate, Select Committee on Indian Affairs.
34. Myers, *They Are Young Once*, 92–93.
35. Plantz, *Indian Child Welfare.*
36. Evans-Campbell et al., "Indian Boarding School Experience."

****

41. Park Nelson, *Invisible Asians.*
42. Unger, *Destruction of American Indian Families.*
43. Briggs, *Somebody's Children*; Jacobs, *Generation Removed*; Cohen, "Indian Affairs, Adoption, and Race."
44. De Schweinitz, *If We Could Change the World.*
45. Kelley, *Race Rebels*, 95; Solinger, *Beggars and Choosers.*
46. Lindhorst and Leighninger, "Ending Welfare as We Know It"; Bell, *Aid to Dependent Children.*
47. Altstein and McRoy, *Does Family Preservation Serve?*, 6–7; Schene, "Past, Present and Future Roles." This pattern was not limited to the South; in New York City, for example, the percentage of Black and Puerto Rican children (vs. white children) also soared after 1960. See Grant, *Politicization of Foster Care*, 31.
48. Lawrence-Webb, "African American Children"; Lindhorst and Leighninger, "Ending Welfare as We Know It"; Bell, *Aid to Dependent Children*; Brissett-Chapman and Isaacs-Shockley, *Children in Social Peril.*

## Works Cited

Altstein, Howard, and Ruth G. McRoy. *Does Family Preservation Serve a Child's Best Interest? Controversies in Public Policy.* Georgetown UP, 2000.

Beiser, Morton. "Editorial: A Hazard to Mental Health: Indian Boarding Schools." *American Journal of Psychiatry*, vol. 131, no. 3, 1974, pp. 305–306.

Bell, Winifred. *Aid to Dependent Children.* Columbia UP, 1965.

Blackhawk, Maggie. "Federal Indian Law as Paradigm Within Public Law." *Harvard Law Review*, vol. 132, no. 7, 2019, pp. 1787–1877.

Briggs, Laura. *Somebody's Children: The Politics of Transracial and Transnational Adoption.* Duke UP, 2012.

———. *Taking Children: A History of American Terror.* U of California P, 2021.

Brissett-Chapman, Sheryl, and Mareasa Isaacs-Shockley. *Children in Social Peril: A Community Vision for Preserving Family Care of African American Children and Youths.* CWLA, 1997.

Cohen, Andrew. "Indian Affairs, Adoption, and Race: The Baby Veronica Case Comes to Washington DC." *The Atlantic*, 12 Apr. 2013. www.theatlantic.com/national/archive/2013/04/indian-affairs-adoption-and-race-the-baby-veronica-case-comes-to-washington/274758/.

Collier, John. "America's Treatment of Her Indians." *Current History*, vol. 18, no. 5, 1923, pp. 771–781.

———. "The American Congo." *The Survey*, vol. 50, 1923.

Coolidge, Dane. "'Kid Catching' on the Navajo Reservation." *The Destruction of American Indian Families*, edited by Steven Unger, Assoc. on American Indian Affairs, 1977, pp. 18–21.

De Schweinitz, Rebecca. *If We Could Change the World: Young People and America's Struggle for Racial Equality.* U of North Carolina P, 2011.

Evans-Campbell, Teresa, et al. "Indian Boarding School Experience, Substance Use and Mental Health Among Urban Two-Spirit American Indian/Alaskan Natives." *American Journal of Drug and Alcohol Abuse*, vol. 38, no. 5, 2012, pp. 421–427.

Grant, Trevor L. *Politicization of Foster Care in New York City*. Yacos, 1996.

Jacobs, Margaret D. *A Generation Removed: The Fostering and Adoption of Indigenous Children in the Postwar World*. U of Nebraska P, 2014.

——. *White Mother to a Dark Race: Settler Colonialism, Maternalism, and the Removal of Indigenous Children in the American West and Australia*. U of Nebraska P, 2011.

Kelley, Robin D. G. *Race Rebels: Culture, Politics, and the Black Working Class*. Free, 1996.

Krieger, Heinrich. "Principles of the Indian Law and the Act of June 18, 1934." *The George Washington Law Review*, vol. 3, no. 3, 1935, pp. 279–308.

Lawrence-Webb, Claudia. "African American Children in the Modern Child Welfare System: A Legacy of the Flemming Rule." *Child Welfare*, vol. 76, no. 1, 1997, pp. 9–30.

Lindhorst, Taryn, and Leslie Leighninger. "'Ending Welfare as We Know It' in 1960: Louisiana's Suitable Home Law." *Social Service Review*, vol. 77, no. 4, 2003, pp. 564–584.

Meriam, Lewis. *Problem of Indian Administration: Report of a Survey Made at the Request of Honorable Hubert Work, Secretary of the Interior, and Submitted to Him, February 21, 1928*. Johns Hopkins UP, 1928.

Myers, Joseph A. *They Are Young Once But Indian Forever: A Summary and Analysis of Investigative Hearings on Indian Child Welfare, April 1980*. American Indian Lawyer Training, 1981.

Park Nelson, Kim. *Invisible Asians: Korean American Adoptees, Asian American Experiences, and Racial Exceptionalism*. Rutgers UP, 2016.

Philip, Kenneth R. *John Collier's Crusade for Indian Reform, 1920–1954*. U of Arizona P, 1977.

Plantz, Margaret C., et al. "Indian Child Welfare: A Status Report." *Children Today*, vol. 18, no. 1, 1989, pp. 24–29.

Roiphe, Anne. "Holocaust's Children, One by One by One." *The New York Times*, 7 Feb. 1997, p. C1.

Schene, Patricia A. "Past, Present and Future Roles of Child Protective Services." The Future of Children, *Protecting Children from Abuse and Neglect*, vol. 8, no. 1, 1998, pp. 23–38.

Smith, Andrea Lee. *Conquest: Sexual Violence and American Indian Genocide*. Duke UP, 2015.

Solinger, Rickie. *Beggars and Choosers: How the Politics of Choice Shapes Adoption, Abortion, and Welfare in the United States*. Hill and Wang, 2002.

Stern, Alexandra Minna. *Proud Boys and the White Ethnostate: How the Alt-Right is Warping the American Imagination*. Beacon, 2019.

Unger, Steven, editor. *The Destruction of American Indian Families*. Association of American Indian Affairs, 1977.

Woodward, Vann C., and William S. McFeely. *The Strange Career of Jim Crow: A Commemorative Edition with a New Afterward by William S. McFeely*. Oxford UP, 2001.

# From Novy, Marianne. *Reading Adoption: Family and Difference in Fiction and Drama*. U of Michigan P, 2007, pp. 56–86.

One moment in *The Winter's Tale* particularly exemplifies the ideology of resemblance as a sign of family relationship: the moment when Paulina enumerates all the details in the baby girl's face that are like Leontes' to prove Hermione's faithfulness. When Paulina refers to the baby as having "the trick of 's frown, his forehead, nay, the valley,/ The pretty dimples of his chin and cheek, his smiles,/ The very mold and frame of hand, nail, finger" (2.3.101–3), she is describing details that the audience must find impossible to see; indeed, most likely the baby would have been "played" by a doll, not a live baby at all. This passage briefly pictures Leontes as himself an infant (there is no other passage I know of in Shakespeare where the "pretty dimples" of an adult male are mentioned); more significantly here, it evokes the persistent tendency to *look for* details of resemblance between family members, and to imagine them into existence, especially in relation to babies. Clearly it is part of a still dominant ideology that babies are supposed to look like someone else in the family, and if that resemblance is not obvious, it will be imagined. In the theater, the question of what members of the audience believe about the baby's similarity to Leontes could be like the question of whether they believe the idealistic Gonzalo or the villainous Antonio about the island in *The Tempest*. Paulina may be credible in her description to the extent that she seems to be morally reliable in general; yet already in Jacobean times it must have been obvious that even if the baby was not as identical to Leontes as she claimed, it would not necessarily have meant that Leontes did not beget it. Some might well consider any exaggeration on Paulina's part justifiable as an attempt to save the baby and Hermione from Leontes' rage. This would then suggest how the desire to preserve a child—not just by confirming its paternity, as here, but also by flattering parents' frequent desire to see themselves re-created—may generate the ability to imagine resemblances between child and parents. Ultimately Leontes' recognition of Perdita as his daughter takes place offstage, and the play subordinates the question of whether Perdita looks like him; the emphasis on her resemblance to her mother, which has nothing to do

DOI: 10.4324/9781003203827-21

with fidelity in marriage, testifies to the fact that Leontes has regained his belief in Hermione.

The recognition scenes of these plays in general tend to develop the perspective of the genetic fathers much more than the perspective of any one else in the large family constellation. We see the anxieties of Pericles and Leontes, and we hear their joys in much more intense language than their children's. There is no attention to how Perdita, Guiderius, and Arviragus feel about discovering a different set of parents, or how they come to terms with those they earlier thought of as their only parents. (In his rewritten last act of *Cymbeline*, George Bernard Shaw imagines that Guiderius would say, "We three are fullgrown men and perfect strangers. / Can I change fathers as I'd change my shirt?" and then refuse to inherit the throne.)[27] Nor are they much concerned with the feelings of the foster parents, though the foster fathers receive somewhat more attention than the foster mothers. With the exception of the shepherd's wife and Euriphile (significantly both deceased), foster mothers are characterized in a way congruent with the general cultural prejudice against stepmothers.[28] And although birth mothers are recovered in two of these plays, the final reunion is clearly seen from their husbands' points of view, not theirs.

Many of Shakespeare's plays can be discussed with reference to an absent mother. Romance is the genre in which he gives mothers, comparatively, the most attention, and an idealized image of motherhood is evoked most vividly in the return of Hermione in *The Winter's Tale*.[29] Her silence to Leontes may be, as Gail Paster suggests, a sign of her diminishment by patriarchal discipline (she would be justified in reproaching him, as she does at the beginning of the play for lesser faults); yet in her words of affection and attention to Perdita, suggesting that it is through concern for her daughter alone she has preserved herself, she is the mother that any separated daughter would want.[30] The fact that Hermione speaks only to Perdita, and indeed says that it was because of hope to see her that she remained alive, appeals to the fantasy that any child might have, that it was she her mother loved best after all. When she asks, "Where hast thou been preserv'd? Where liv'd?" (5.3.124), she is, in a sense, the perfect mother, because she wants to know about the other family without criticizing them, giving her daughter room to assimilate the complexity of her experience.

The idealized birth mothers Hermione and Thaisa contrast sharply to the evil foster mothers, Dionyza and Cymbeline's nameless queen. While Stephen Collins relates the negative view of stepmothers in the Renaissance to a general misogyny, these plays show that misogyny could be part of a polarized view of women.[31] Hermione and Thaisa, in their return, are as idealized as a dead or absent mother is likely to be by a child who lives with an unsatisfactory substitute. And indeed they are accompanied in the romances by a third idealized birth mother, appearing only in a dream-vision, Posthumus's mother, who died at his birth.[32] Perhaps the point is to focus dramatic attention on the birth mother (recovered at the end of *Pericles* and *Winter's Tale*) by removing motherly competition from her. When women do foster maternally in Shakespeare—Lychorida, Paulina—they are no threat to the prerogatives of the birth mother. Indeed, they present her or her memory to her daughter.

The recognition scenes of all these plays emphasize bodily connections in the family. The characters' words are often, among other things, stage directions indicating that characters should embrace. Rediscovered relatives are introduced to each other as "Flesh of thy flesh" (Pericles says this of Marina to Thaisa [5.3.47]) or "The issue of your loins . . . and blood of your begetting" (Belarius thus returns Cymbeline's sons [5.332–33]). The plays are full of the imagery of birth, pregnancy, and conception—most often in literal references to characters' origins.[33] This imagery reinforces the plays' mythology of "blood" and their emphasis on biological relatedness. But it is often used metaphorically, and sometimes the point of the metaphor is to make the reunion of parents and children into a rebirth or a reconception. Pericles, seeing Marina, says, "I am great with woe, and shall deliver weeping" (5.1.109). Cymbeline, recognizing his sons upon Belarius's proof, says, "O, what, am I/A mother to the birth of three? Ne'er mother/Rejoiced deliverance more" (5.5.370–72). And Pericles welcomes Marina as "Thou that beget'st him that did thee beget," using of her generative power a word primarily used of male actions. These images stand out because of the intense moments in which they are uttered, but birth/pregnancy imagery is also used at other times—Camillo alludes to folklore about pregnancy when he describes his desire to see "Sicilia" (a name that refers to both his king, Leontes, and his country) as "a woman's longing" (4.4.671) and Imogen describes her desire to see Posthumus by saying, "Never long'd my mother so/To see me first, as I have now" (3.4.2–3). Though good mothers here are largely absent or dead, imagery of biological maternity is frequent in the words of both male and female characters.[34] Concern with the link between generations is so strong that images of pregnancy and childbirth appear frequently partly because they are the most vivid way to picture that link, and occasionally images of begetting also figure. But the plays also show, and use for images, child rearing as well as childbearing. A memorable line when the young Pericles declares his love of Thaisa puts "fostering" and "blood" together and suggests fostering may be seen as just as basic.

*Simonides:* What, are you both pleased?
*Thaisa:* Yes, if you love me, sir.
*Pericles:* Even as my life my blood that fosters it. (2.5.88–90)

In each of these plays, the characters raised in a second family are described by others as extraordinary. Marina and Perdita speak exceptionally well and outshine others in beauty and talents; Guiderius and Arviragus are brave, ambitious, yet gentle and civil. Marina transcends the brothel, and Perdita surpasses all expectations for shepherdesses. Belarius comments on the boys whom he has raised, "How hard it is to hide the sparks of nature," and many critics have analyzed these plays in terms of the supremacy of heredity. The tendency of the romance genre to idealize its central characters (found also in the portrayal of Imogen and Miranda, raised by the fathers who begot them) here uses the lost child theme among its strategies. But in spite of all the blood- and-birth imagery, much of these plays' presentation of heredity could be seen as a construction mediated by the good foster parent. Belarius knows the boys are princes; the old shepherd infers that Perdita, found with fancy clothes and gold, comes from a wealthy and perhaps aristocratic background; and Lychorida passes on to Marina the image of Pericles' bravery. Perhaps each of them makes a connection comparable to Paulina's emphasis on the similarity between Leontes and his infant. Is modern psychology necessary to imagine this? The only concept required is the self-fulfilling prophecy, a dynamic arguably exemplified in many of Shakespeare's plays. Nevertheless none of these plays makes this aspect of the foster parent's role explicit, and only the dead Lychorida receives tribute for the memories she has passed on.

The family separations and reunions in Shakespeare's plays have many possible relations to early modern family psychology. Adoption was not part of the legal code under that name in Renaissance England, but there were many different ways in which children were raised by people who did not give birth to them, and the word might even be used, as it is when the countess in *All's Well that Ends Well* says, "Adoption strives with nature, and choice breeds/A native slip to us from foreign seeds" (1.3.142–43).[35] The word was also familiar from various biblical passages, especially in the Epistles of Paul, where Christians are referred to as adopted children of God.[36] But the events in the plays also connect with everyday family experience in Shakespeare's time. Gail Paster writes, in *The Body Embarrassed*, that Perdita's experience is "a version, romantically heightened, of what happened soon after birth to countless babies in the wet-nursing culture . . . inexplicable extrusion from the birthing chamber, enforced alienation from the maternal breast, and a journey to the unknown rural environment of a foster family lower in station than its own. Even though the birth parents knew where they had placed their baby and occasionally visited it, the physical and social separation of the two environments was virtually as complete as it is here."[37] A similar analysis could be made, though with more qualifications, of Marina's, Guiderius's, and Arviragus's experiences. Perhaps these events glamorize also the many other family separations common in Shakespeare's culture; from about ten years of age on, upper-class children might be sent to other families to learn manners and to bond dynasties, middle-class children to learn trades and professions, and lower-class children to become servants.[38] Here these ordinary separations are transformed into the more dramatic separations of abandoning, kidnapping, and shipwrecking. Perhaps these romance plots also provided a fantasy transformation for the more permanent separations caused by frequent mortality, which was much higher than ours for both parents and children, and highest, it seems, in London, where the plays were performed. At the beginning of the seventeenth century, the life expectancy in London was only 22.3 years, and "by age twenty forty-seven percent of women born in London had suffered the death of their fathers."[39] Furthermore, infant and child death rates were, in general, high in early modern Europe. "An infant in the first four months of life had in general a 20 to 40 per cent chance of dying before his or her first birthday. . . . the chances of surviving to age twenty were in general no better chances fifty-fifty."[40] Shakespeare's own son Hamnet had died at the age of eleven.

Members of the original audiences in different family circumstances probably differed to some extent in their responses to these plays, just as do members of the audience in different circumstances today. Paster has argued, for example, that the emphasis on the difference in behavior between Perdita and her foster family and on characters' identification of her with nobility "offers a powerful counternarrative for the specific fears and repressed anxieties of the wet-nursed child."[41] We could imagine that the play could also soothe anxieties of parents of wet-nursed children. Similarly, the emphasis on resemblances between biological family members might have reinforced the sense of solidarity between those who had been wet-nursed or fostered out in childhood and their parents.

On the other hand, what of the many audience members whose parents had died early and who had been raised by stepparents? How important was it to them to emphasize their connections with their deceased parents? How much did their stepparents take on parental roles in their imagination? The orphaned Posthumus, who has been raised by Cymbeline, is left without a household again when he is banished for marrying Imogen; in absence from her, his suspicion of women alienates him from her as well as the memory of his parents ("That most venerable man which I/Did call my father was I know not where/When I was stamp'd" [2.5.3–5]).[42] How much does this dramatize anxieties of the time? For some members of the audience, who could never hope for a reunion in real life, Posthumus's dream-vision of his family could have served as a reassurance of their continued connection with their family, but Posthumus's marriage to Imogen reconnects him with his foster-father Cymbeline as well as with her. In *All's Well*, Helen's strong bond with the Countess of Rousillion, her foster mother as well as Bertram's mother, coexists with her frequent references to her dead father (even though at 1.1.84 she claims to have forgotten him to emphasize her obsession with Bertram).

## Notes

27. Shaw, "Cymbeline Refinished" (1937), quoted in Thompson, "Cymbeline's Other Endings," 213.
28. On that prejudice, see Stephen Collins, "'Reason, Nature, and Order': The Stepfamily in English Renaissance Thought," *Renaissance Studies* 13 (1999): 312–24; see Neely, Broken Nuptials, 174, on the desexualization and sanctification of mothers in the romances through real and mock deaths. The foster mother in Pandosto begins as a misogynist caricature who threatens to cudgel her husband "if he brought any bastard brat within her dores," though eventually she nourishes "it so clenly and carefully as it began to bee a jolly girle, in so much that they began both of them to be very fond of it" (Greene, Pandosto, in Bullough, *Narrative and Dramatic Sources*, 8:174, 175).
29. See Adelman, *Suffocating Mothers*, 9–10 and passim, for a detailed analysis of the varying roles of mothers and fantasies about mothers in Shakespeare's canon. Hermione and Thaisa are less idealized early in the play than after they reappear. Only two other plays, *Romeo and Juliet* and *Merry Wives of Windsor*, include mother-daughter relationships; in both, those relations are rather cool and distant, to tragic effect in *Romeo and Juliet.*
30. Paster, *Body Embarrassed*, 179.
31. Collins, "Reason, Nature, and Order," 320–21. On polarization in views of women, see for example, Mary Beth Rose, *The Expense of Spirit* (Ithaca, N.Y.: Cornell University Press, 1988), 4–5.
32. Compare the presence of the idealized mothers Ceres and Juno in the masque of *The Tempest.*
33. Doreen Delvecchio and Antony Hammond give a list of examples in *Pericles*: see their introduction to *Pericles, Prince of Tyre*, ed. Delvecchio and Hammond (Cambridge: Cambridge University Press, 1998), 47–49. See also Neely, *Broken Nuptials*, 191–92; and Marianne Novy, *Love's Argument: Gender Relations in Shakespeare* (Chapel Hill: University of North Carolina Press, 1984), 171–74.
34. For an interpretation of the cross-gendered imagery emphasizing male nurturance, see Novy, *Love's Argument*, 174; for the view that it involves male appropriation of female procreative power that excludes women, see Adelman, *Suffocating Mothers*, 197–98 (which also emphasizes the repression of sexuality); and Marilyn Williamson, *The Patriarchy of Shakespeare's Comedies* (Detroit: Wayne State University Press, 1986), 165.
35. Bevington glosses this passage as referring to grafting, a metaphor also used of adoption in some twentieth-century writing, such as *Perspectives on a Grafted Tree*, ed. Patricia Irwin Johnston (Indianapolis: Perspectives Press, 1983).
36. See Gal. 4:5–7 and Rom. 8:12–17. Gager has speculated that, in spite of clerical hostility to adoption discussed by Jack Goody, "the Christian theology of adoption through baptism' might very well have aided in sustaining adoption traditions for families interested in having a non-natal child to stand as their heir" (*Blood Ties*, 69; see also 44–46). Perhaps some ambitious historian will discover records notarizing adoption in England as Gager has done in France. But see Goody, *The Development of the Family and Marriage in Europe* (Cambridge: Cambridge University Press, 1983), 77–75, 99–402.
37. Paster, *Body Embarrassed*, 273.
38. Beatrice Gottlieb, *The Family in the Western World from the Black Death to the Industrial Age* (New York: Oxford University Press, 1993), 160; these customs are discussed with specific reference to the late sixteenth and early seventeenth century in Ivy Pinchbeck and Margaret Hewitt, *Children in English Society*,

vol. 1 (London: Routledge and Kegan Paul, 1969), 25–26. Gottlieb claims that apprenticeship often began around age seven, but Ilana Krausman Ben-Amos finds that ten, twelve or later were much more likely ages, though younger children could be boarded out for such reasons as schooling, outbreaks of plague, poverty, or parental death; see her *Adolescence and Youth in Early Modern England* (New Haven: Yale University Press, 1994), $4–64. Her view of the ages of apprentices is supported by Paul Griffith, *Youth and Authority: Formative Experiences in England, 1560–1640* (Oxford: Clarendon Press, 1996), 33. Lawrence Stone discusses what he calls a "mass exchange of adolescent children, which seems to have been peculiar to England," in *The Family, Sex, and Marriage in England, 1500–1800* (New York: Harper and Row, 1977), 107. Lori Humphrey Newcomb discusses *The Winter's Tale*'s source, Pandosto, in relation to the widespread institution of adolescent service, in "The Romance of Service: The Simple History of Pandosto's Servant Readers," in *Framing Elizabethan Fictions: Contemporary Approaches to Early Modern Narrative Prose*, ed. Constance Relihan (Kent, Ohio: Kent State University Press, 1996), 117–39. I am grateful for a prepublication copy of this essay, which now has been revised into a chapter in Lori Humphrey Newcomb, *Reading Popular Romance in Early Modern England* (New York: Columbia University Press, 2001).

39. Hather Dubrow, *Shakespeare and Domestic Loss: Forms of Deprivation, Mourning, and Recuperation* (Cambridge: Cambridge University Press, 1999), 162. She deals with the relation of the romances to the threat of parental death on pp. 166, 189–93. See also her comments on parental death, step-parenting, and theatricality on pp. 165 and 170. I am grateful for a prepublication copy of this chapter, which is expanded from "The Message from Marcade: Parental Death in Tudor and Stuart England," in *Attending to Women in Early Modern England*, ed. Betty S. Travitsky and Adele F. Seeff (Newark: University of Delaware Press, 1994).
40. Gottlieb, *Family in Western World*, 133. Frances E. Dolan, *Dangerous Familiars: Representations of Domestic Crime in England, 1550–1700* (Ithaca, N.Y.: Cornell University Press, 1994), 168, has argued that *Winter's Tale* in particular is a displaced, aestheticized resolution of anxiety about infanticide.
41. Paster, *Body Embarrassed*, 276.
42. See Adelman, *Suffocating Mothers*; and also Skura, "Interpreting Posthumus' Dream."

# From Dorow, Sara K. *Transnational Adoption: A Cultural Economy of Race, Gender, and Kinship*. NYUP, 2006.

The "matching" of children in the Chinese welfare system with prospective parents in the United States—and some twenty other countries—is largely a mundane, march-step affair done by workers in Beijing. Files of parents and files of children work their way through various departments in the offices of the China Center of Adoption Affairs (CCAA), meeting in what is called, predictably enough, the "matching department." The political economy of kinship desires, but also of particular networks between overseas agencies and Chinese orphanages and officials, has already determined how some of that matching will go. Meiming, a woman who works in the CCAA offices, tells me it is fairly bureaucratic and straightforward: parents and children are matched in bunches by order of entry into the system, depending on such factors as age and location. (Special-needs matching goes through a separate process and is by necessity less mechanical.) But then Meiming gets animated and wonders out loud, how are we supposed to know we are matching the right child with the right family? How do we know the family will like the child matched with them? Of course, she adds, all those American parents want young, beautiful, smart children—like any parent would want. I commiserate with her about the strange role of matching children and parents across oceans and bureaucracies, and she smiles and says that even so, parents will ask her and her colleagues, "How did you know she was just the right child for us?" Bureaucratic process can and perhaps must be constructed as a conduit for fate.

The centerpiece of the package sent from Beijing to waiting American parents, which includes limited health and background information on the child, is the photo. In the first decade of the program it was usually a passport-size shot of a child's head, poking out from layers of clothing. Photos have become an increasingly important piece of what Cartwright (2003) calls "adoption image culture"; they serve as advertisements, family artifacts, and medical diagnostic tools. But what is so crucial about the referral photo is that it performs these functions around the individual child that a family will adopt. Along with the sparse information accompanying it,

DOI: 10.4324/9781003203827-22

the photo is scrutinized and fetishized as a dense matrix of potentially fulfilled expectations. Is this the child we expected? Is she of the health status and age we hoped for? Can we imagine her as ours? Much of the work of fulfilling these expectations happens, as described in the previous chapter, through the trans-Pacific exchange of resources that produces particular kinds of children and parents for each other even before they are matched. But those general assurances of a kinship that will work for both parents and children are now translated into a child, into "the one." The referral photo equally, and paradoxically, grounds parents in the reality of their adoption and magnifies the fantasy of connected fate: the magical whisper of "yes" of which poet Mary Cummings writes. These are both at work in the stories parents tell of the phone call they first received from the agency about the child referral, of their mad rush to go pick up the photo, of the mixture of anxiety and anticipation that surrounded opening the package of materials about the child. Some women likened these mixed sensations to those of pregnancy, as did adoptive mother Eileen Kretz: I felt like all of a sudden I was pregnant. It was like, we get this picture, and it's like, "Aagh!" (laughs) I really did! I felt like—actually it felt that way the whole way through, except the procedure was so slow, and then all of a sudden you have this baby waiting for you. As with ultrasound images, the referral photo makes the child real. But a decision must also be made about whether to accept or deny a referral. This often means scrutinizing the photo and the scant medical information for signs of trouble. In fact, agencies encourage parents to have the information looked at by a physician, while making disclaimers about the possible inaccuracies of information sent by China—a real and notorious possibility, especially in the early years of the program. Josh and Gretta Peterman had expected a healthy toddler but were worried when the head circumference readings they received were quite small. After much agonizing consultation with their physician and some initial ire from Chinese officials, they turned down the referral and were assigned another toddler. Such scrutiny is also about other forms of belonging: the photo might be screened, however innocently, for ethnic desirability (Cartwright, 2003) and for a sensibility of "right fit."

****

Preadoption "contact," especially in the form of the referral photo, takes on a life of its own that continues even beyond the adoption. As the first and one of the few pieces of tangible evidence of a child's life before adoption, it becomes emblematic of that preadoption life. But perhaps most important, the referral photo becomes a memento that links and invites comparison of the child's past and future. It is a piece of identity narrative that kick-starts the compulsive search for coherence between there and here, then and now, and in particular ways (Wheeler, 1999; Hall, 1990); it produces history as a way of making sense of what has happened in both continuous and comparative terms. Many times when I visited adoptive families' homes in San Francisco or the Twin Cities, out would come life books and photo albums of their adoptive journey. And quite often, the referral photo was displayed early in the book as a solemn representation of the life that was. In some cases, it was folded into a fuller story of the history that connected the child to both China and the United States. In other cases, it served as a comparative "before" picture to the improved new life displayed in later pages of photos. Parents would then sometimes tell me, with a mixture of sadness and joy, "I can't believe she's the same child." Making such comparisons requires that she be, in some fundamental way, the same child. But with this mix of continuity and dislocation comes its own set of uncomfortable, ghostly presences of inequitable racial, familial, and national splitting—borders that are produced and made more visible with the migration of the child. The child is transformed, but never completely, and the next step in the process—the trip to China—helps reveal why: she is object and subject of multiple sets of social relations, making her many things at once.

## Works Cited

Cartwright, Lisa. "Photographs of 'Waiting Children': The Transnational Adoption Market." *Social Text*, vol. 21, no. 1, 2003, pp. 83–109.

Hall, Stuart. "Cultural Identity and Diaspora." *Identity, Community, Cultural Difference*, edited by Jonathan Rutherford, Lawrence & Wishart, 1990, pp. 222–237.

Wheeler, Wendy. *A New Modernity? Change in Science, Literature and Politics.* Lawrence & Wishart, 1999.

# From Franklin, Sarah. *Embodied Progress: A Cultural Account of Assisted Conception.* Routledge, 1997.

## Assisted Conception in the Enterprise Culture

These two features of the Thatcherite redefinition of British citizenship during the 1980s had important consequences for the population discussed in this study, who were consumers of private healthcare, aiming to produce a family, on whose behalf they could exercise the kinds of consumer choices valorised within the enterprise culture. For Thatcher, the right to exercise choice in general, and consumer choice in particular, was the carrot at the end of the antiwelfare state stick. Reproductive choice fits neatly into this equation. Consumers of private reproductive medicine in Britain during the 1980s were able both to take advantage of the many clinics eager to establish themselves in this rapidly expanding sector, and, indirectly of the tax incentives provided by the government to encourage such entrepreneurial activity. Although assisted conception was not 'big business' in Britain in the immediate wake of the birth of Louise Brown in 1978, by the mid-1980s it had gained momentum, and by the late 1980s it was expanding very rapidly.[4] In the city of Birmingham alone, the number of IVF clinics tripled from two to six between 1986 and 1989. The 'enterprising up' of conception thus exemplified the broader context of celebratory political initiatives aimed to enhance entrepreneurial activity, and consequently widen consumer choice.

Although some IVF clinics were established within large, urban NHS hospitals in cities such as London, Manchester and Birmingham, these were an exception to the rule of largely private services on offer.[5] At a time of cuts to the NHS, infertility services were not a priority, and without the efforts of individual consultants who prioritised this area, they were unlikely to be offered through NHS hospitals. In the private sector, on the other hand, IVF could be offered at especially low rates due to the possibility of having the necessary prescriptions for expensive hormone dosages met through a woman's own NHS GP. Since these expensive pharmaceutical products account for nearly half the overall cost of each IVF cycle, clients of private

DOI: 10.4324/9781003203827-23

reproductive healthcare in Britain essentially received a large government subsidy for treatment.[6] This made IVF more affordable in Britain than it is, for example, in the US. Still, the average cost of a cycle at several hundred pounds made it available to a limited population.

****

## Popular Representations of Assisted Conception

I have written elsewhere on the popular media representation of assisted conception in England in the late 1980s (Franklin 1990), and in particular of the idiom of 'desperateness' which so often was used to characterise the quest for conception of infertile women and couples (see also Pfeffer 1987). While I do not wish to rehearse that argument in detail here, a few points are worth repeating in the interests of contextualisation. It should be noted that beginning with the birth of Louise Brown, which received worldwide media attention in the summer of 1978, conception narratives derivative of the world of achieved conception have provided a steady supply of late twentieth century procreation stories (see also Franklin and McNeil 1993). A compilation of such accounts, modelled on Montagu's famous catalogue of Australian conception accounts (1937) could likewise be entitled *Coming Into Being Among the Euro-Americans.* In England, popular media accounts of assisted conception were distinctively formulaic in their narrative structure, combining established generic and sequential conventions to organise a telling tale of missed conceptions. These media accounts were accompanied by a flurry of popular handbooks and guidebooks to the world of achieved conception. Since these were among the most important means by which a wider public became acquainted with the new reproductive technologies, they offer an important perspective on the changing cultural meanings mobilised in and through conception stories. In the account below, I draw on only some of these accounts to explore certain key features of popular representations of infertility.

****

The representation of a powerful genetic drive to reproduce, coupled with the influence of social pressures, establishes the 'social and natural facts' of infertility, much as this dichotomy structured earlier accounts of kinship, family and procreation in anthropology. The view that the urge to found a family has evolutionary significance, and derives from a primordial human desire, also recalls the importance of such arguments to turn-of-the-century debates about the origins of sociality, the beginnings of the pair bond, and the regulation of sexuality and marriage. The model of society being, in this sense, 'after nature' is clearly evident in these accounts, as they are in the myriad others of which these are typical. This connection, however, takes an interesting turn in relation to the introduction of new technology.

If 'the desire to found a family' is a primordial drive that 'rises unbidden from our genetic souls', then 'life's progression' from marriage to childbirth is not merely a social convention, but part of the flow of life itself. It is, in this sense, a naturalised progression. However, this natural sequence of events has also to take a particular social form. It is implicit in the account of couples 'feeling excluded from a whole range of activities' and experiencing a loss of 'the kind of life they would have led' in order to 'fulfil their own or other peoples' expectations' that the desire is to conform to established social conventions. When Patrick Steptoe argues that it is a 'biological fact' that women possess a 'biological drive to reproduce', he is not concerned with lesbian or single women, whose exclusion from conventional social arrangements may lessen the likelihood of their having children. To the contrary, he firmly opposed such women having children at all, on the grounds that it is unnatural and morally wrong. In this sense, the social conventions are also naturalised, in the sense of being 'modelled on', or 'rooted in' or 'determined by' nature.

Reproduction is, of course, a highly naturalised activity in the Euro-American cultural tradition. Into this highly naturalised domain, then, enters medical science, on behalf of the 'desperate' infertile couples for whom 'life's progression' has been held hostage to the random injustice of nature's lottery in making them unable to conceive. This is the critical link in popular media representations, such as the one described earlier, through which the 'desperate' desire for a child provides the lead-in to the 'medical hope for a cure'.

* * * *

These personal details perform an important function in providing narrative closure. Their presence indicates the need for more than a medical 'solution' to the problem of infertility. Through details about their jobs, houses, holidays and happiness, these accounts not only provide a 'good story', but they do so through creating a traditional happy ending, which re-establishes the couple within the conventions of heterosexual romance, confirming the unity of the conjugal and the procreative function, buttressed by references to upward mobility, social approval and establishment through becoming a family. The themes of hope, fulfilment and 'dreams come true' are thus linked to the 'miracle of modern science', a 'test-tube baby'. Hence, as the 'desperate' infertile couple narrative begins by describing the emotional desires of the would-be parents, so it also closes by referring back to their emotions and fulfilment, thereby enclosing the interior narrative of scientific progress within a frame of reference to heterosexual reproductive desire and the maintenance of established social conventions.

In a sense, then, the 'desperate' infertile couple narratives 'embody' or enclose scientific process by re-embedding it within familiar, recognisable details of ordinary, everyday life. The point is that this containment of the potentially quite disruptive or troubling implications of a 'test-tube baby' is evident in the very structure of these narratives. This is very characteristic of *popular* narrative, which works by inviting identification and then rewarding, or 'satisfying' it. The narrative tension, provided by an 'obstacle' to fulfilment is overcome, followed by celebratory closure. It is significant that the 'happy couples' stories present both a continuity and a commensurability between biological science and the biological family. The achieved route of conception stands in for conjugality and family as *social* achievements, 'after nature', though in this context, 'after technology' as well. In sum, it is the substitutability of natural, social and technological 'facts' these narratives demonstrate which indexes particular features of the kinship universe within which they are operative, and of which they are also transformative.

Together, then, these elements of the achieved conception success story articulate core features of both the 'enterprise culture' context in which they are produced, and the wider set of cultural values attached to conjugality, procreativity and family in English society. As purchasers of private healthcare services, couples 'buy in' to the 'dream come true' of a family of their own. In turn, they sell their two-bedroomed semi to purchase a larger home. Through these means they become established, and are enabled to realise the way of life they had imagined for themselves, before 'life's progression' was brought unexpectedly to an impasse. As self-reliant individuals, seeking to extend conjugality into family and home-ownership, they express a desire for social achievement through biological reproduction. Assisted conception, in these representations, precisely reproduces the core analogies of English kinship, just as it also fulfils the promise of the enterprise culture in the form of widened consumer choice through market deregulation and expansion.

The language of hope, miracles and progress are also significant features of these accounts. 'Hope' is the important flip-side of the fact that assisted conception usually does not work. This has important implications for the next three chapters, where it is explored in greater depth. 'Progress' is like 'hope' in this respect, for it signals the continuing effort to overcome obstacles, to transcend limits and to explore new horizons. 'Progress' also importantly signifies the desire for improvement, which is what society also imposes on the 'nature' it is 'rooted in' or 'based upon'. Assisted conception is to reproduction what progress is to nature: it is a 'helping hand' assisting nature to progress as it was meant to do. Likewise, assisted conception is to reproduction what enterprise is to the national economy—a vital force for change, improvement and achievement.

At the same time, the neat symmetry of the 'dominant' cultural logic valorising assisted conception is somewhat contradicted by the language of 'miracles.' To begin with, the miracle is both 'of modern science' and of nature. The miracle baby both attests to the miraculous powers of science and to the miracle of new life, that is, of nature. In so far as the 'miracle' is of modern science, it is no longer 'after nature', but displacing it; technology also 'does service for' ideas of the natural. The 'helping hand' is more like a corporate takeover, through which the agency of technology becomes dominant, not merely 'assisting' conception but literally removing it from the body altogether. It is the disembodiment of conception that effects this shift, through which the 'facts of life' are not only relocated to the Petri dish, but subject to retemporalisation, through cryopreservation, and redirection through modification and alteration. This 'assistance' has various consequences of displacement which are discussed in more depth in the conclusion. Here, I wish to conclude this section through a brief consideration of the formula of natural science in the service of the natural family which so thoroughly characterises the representation of assisted conception as 'giving nature a helping hand'.

## Notes

4. Although assisted conception was expected to become highly profitable in England, as in other parts of the world, it has not, on the whole, proved so successful in business terms. It is instead the large pharmaceutical companies, such as Organon and Serono, who made the largest profits on IVF through their patent-protected monopolies on Clomid, Metrodin, Perganol and other drugs essential to the IVF technique. The far greater success of the pharmaceutical industry in making profits on IVF was epitomized by the purchase of Bourne Hall, Steptoe and Edwards' flagship enterprise near Cambridge, in the late 1980s by Serono, subsequent to the clinic's bankruptcy.
5. For an account of the development of infertility devices in Britain between the private and the public sectors, and for a critical account of their provision, see Pfeffer and Quick 1988.
6. Full details of the IVF procedure are provided in the following chapter. See also Fishel and Symonds 1986.

## Works Cited

Fishel, Simon, and Edwin Malcolm Symonds, editors. *In Vitro Fertilisation: Past, Present, Future.* IRL, 1986.

Franklin, Sarah. "Deconstructing 'Desperateness': The Social Construction of Infertility in Popular Representations of New Reproductive Technologies." *The New Reproductive Technologies*, edited by Maureen McNeil, et al., Macmillan, 1990, pp. 200–229.

———. "Redefining Reproductive Choice: The Changing Landscape of Reproductive Politics in the Context of the New Reproductive Technologies." Conference presentation, London School of Economics, 1990.

Franklin, Sarah, and Maureen McNeil. “Reproductive Futures: Recent Feminist Debate of New Reproductive Technologies.” *Feminist Studies*, vol. 14, no. 3, pp. 545–574.

Pfeffer, Naomi. “Artificial Insemination, *In Vitro* Fertilisation and the Stigma of Infertility.” *Reproductive Technologies: Gender, Motherhood and Medicine*, edited by M. Stanworth, Polity, 1987.

Pfeffer, Naomi, and Allison Quick. *Infertility Services: A Desperate Case*. Greater London Association of Community Health Care, 1988.

Steptoe, Patrick C., and R. G. Edwards. “Birth After the Reimplantation of a Human Embryo.” *Lancet*, vol. 12, no. 2, 1978, p. 366.

# From Fedosik, Marina. "The Power to 'Make Live': Biopolitics and Reproduction in *Blade Runner 2049*." *Adoption & Culture*, vol. 7, no. 2, 2019, pp. 169–175.

The problematics of reproductive difference raised by *Blade Runner 2049* may appear idiosyncratic to the sci-fi imagination concerned with reproductive options that are not available to us, but we can see threads of similar thinking about kinship and personhood when adoption is culturally understood through ideas grounded in heterocoital human reproduction as a basic fact *of* life. A significant body of scholarship on this issue exists in CAS, which Sally Sales, in her Foucauldian analysis of open and closed adoptions, sums up. Sales shows that, in agreement with the structures of western kinship, in both closed and open adoption "the blood tie occupies a foundational place" even though adoption seems to decouple kinship from heterocoital reproduction (7). Culturally, the blood tie is central to individuality and personhood. Uncertainty around this tie may bear on a person's individuation and socialization. Sales explains that this is why in both open and closed adoption, the adopted family is expected to "provide the child with a new foundation, but simultaneously sustain the old foundation of the [biological] family origin" (8). This duality serves simultaneously to ensure the adoptive family's unity and to legitimize the adoptee's personhood in a culture that relies on the knowledge of biological origin as the basis of identity and belonging. Sales recognizes that "[w]hether by adoption or by technological innovation, these artificially achieved families certainly rewrite the originary place of the blood tie for those growing up outside of their biological blood line" (8). And yet, her evidence shows that "the rooting of identity in an originary biological heritage appears to be an abiding practice at the heart of western kinship" (8). Even though (or maybe because) adoption, as a family-making technology, denaturalizes kinship, it is haunted by heterocoital reproduction and the knowledge of biological origin. The heterocoital biological origin thus remains a necessary condition for individuation, and this frame of reference is considered by most western cultures necessary for cultural (self)recognition of the person who deserves inclusion into the system of human relatedness as a legible and legitimate human subject.

DOI: 10.4324/9781003203827-24

The emergence of new reproductive technologies does not seem to revise radically this cultural orthodoxy. Strathern observes that in "twentieth-century culture, nature has increasingly come to mean biology . . . [and] the idea of natural kinship ha[s] been biologized" (19). This return to essentialism, according to Mark Jerng, has "recentered biology and genetics as primary ways of thinking about who we are," but Jerng speculates that "this development" could be more than "just pendulum shift back to nature in the old nature-nurture binaries, although that is how it is often framed" (209). If anything, assisted reproductive technologies are geared towards imitating natural biological reproduction and downplaying their artificial qualities. The growing cultural understanding of "nature" not as given and immutable but as open to human manipulation seems to create cultural anxieties that are met by attempts to tether technologically managed life processes to familiar ideas about kinship based in blood ties. While biogenetically based reproduction may no longer be strictly heterocoital, the normalizing cultural script with which we describe these procedures still calls for imagining kinship and personhood through a conventional metaphor. Alternative methods of reproduction and kinship-making inevitably give rise to complications if we insist on thinking of technologically mediated kinship[8] through heterocoital metaphors. In CAS we see such complications, for example, in the struggles around articulations of identities produced in adoption. Changing the ideas we think ourselves into being with is not easy, especially if we tap into such a fundamental one as reproduction. By thinking of nature as malleable and biology as a "knowledge-producing practice" (Haraway 323) we open to revision not only a personal understanding of selfhood and relatedness to others, but, as Strathem puts it, "the relationship of human society to the natural world" as well as the "ideas about passage of time, relations between generations, and, above all, the future" (5). This may be the reason why the narratives of the future that trouble familiar reproductive scenarios bend towards the apocalyptic or at least imagine nonheterocoital forms of reproduction as a threat to the future of humanity. We can clearly see this threat in the two *Blade Runners.*

## Note

8. Adoption is understood here as a technology of kinship.

## Works Cited

*Bladerunner 2049.* Directed by Denis Villeneuve, Warner Brothers Pictures, 2017.

Haraway, Donna. "Universal Donors in a Vampire Culture: It's all in the Family: Biological Kinship Categories in the Twentieth-Century United States." *Uncommon Ground: Rethinking the Human Place in Nature*, edited by William Cronon, Norton, 1996, pp. 321–366.

Jerng, Mark. *Claiming Others: Transracial Adoption and National Belonging*. U of Minnesota P, 2010.

Sales, Sally. *Adoption, Family, and the Paradox of Origins: A Foucauldian History*. Palgrave McMillan, 2012.

Strathern, Marilyn. *Reproducing the Future: Essays on Anthropology, Kinship, and the New Reproductive Technologies*. Manchester UP, 1992.

# From Eng, David L. *The Feeling of Kinship: Queer Liberalism and the Racialization of Intimacy*. Duke UP, 2010.

**Psychic Diasporas**

For the transnational adoptee, where does history begin?

In the opening minutes of *First Person Plural*, we are given several conflicting answers to this question. The filmmaker presents a complex montage sequence that combines family photographs, her adoptive father's home movies, which include scenes of Borshay Liem's arrival at the San Francisco airport on March 3, 1966, and her own footage, shot thirty years later, of her American parents and siblings watching these home movies and recalling their feelings about her arrival. The sequence begins with Denise, Borshay Liem's sister, explaining the excitement of getting a sister, "someone to play with," as she puts it. "I remember getting my hair done to go pick you up at the airport, and I was really jazzed about that," she tells us, an image of her younger self in front of the bathroom mirror flashing up before us. But despite her excitement about picking up Cha Jung Hee, her new little sister from Korea, Denise's investment in feminine self-display reflects a narcissistic logic that underlies the Borshay family's initial encounter with their eight-year-old adoptee. Unlike Binh and Lattimore's asymmetrical reflection in the mirror stage of Stein's salon, this mirror stage of the Borshay family is capable of reflecting only upon itself, capable of entertaining only its own wishes and desires. With a chortle, Denise readily admits: "I think mother went up to the wrong person. Yeah, I think we didn't know until we checked your name tag or something who told us who you were. It didn't matter. I mean one of them was ours."

Here, the language of ownership and possession, along with the assumed exchangeability of the variously tagged adoptees disembarking from the plane, constitutes a clear violation of the exclusive bond thought to exist between mother and child, a bond thought to exist outside the logic of the market.[35] This violation opens immediately upon the terrain of an unacknowledged commodification. Significantly, . . . [images from *First Person Plural* removed] Deann's "acquisition" by the Borshay family is

DOI: 10.4324/9781003203827-25

accompanied by the simultaneous erasure of Cha Jung Hee's Korean identity and past through the dismissal of her prior family and history. "You know, to us an orphanage meant that you had no family," the adoptive white mother Alveen Borshay later explains. "This way you were going to have a family." Suggesting that Borshay Liem's history only begins with her entry into their particular family unit, Denise concludes: "From the moment you came here, you were my sister and we were your family and that was it. And even though we look different—different nationality or whatever—we were your family."

Echoing Alveen's and Denise's sentiments, Donald Borshay's account of that fateful day is remarkably similar. Although the father recalls a momentary emotional wrinkle after Borshay Liem's initial arrival, this problem is quickly smoothed out through its concerted repression and willing away: "I remember very clearly your first meal," Donald recalls. "Mother prepared something that was very nice. And we were sitting at the table and you just kind of dropped your head and the tears started to come down. No words were spoken. Mother could see what was happening, and she simply took you away from the table and you were excused and from then on it was perfect."

"*From then on it was perfect.*" I have spent some time detailing the various recollections of the "from then on" moment of Borshay Liem's arrival in the United States. I do so because these comments collectively illustrate the ways in which Borshay Liem is commodified as an object to be enjoyed while, in the same breath, her Korean past is effaced and denied, a forgotten history repressed and passed over. In Denise's, Alveen's, and Donald's recollections, history proper begins only at the moment of Borshay Liem's arrival "over here," the privatized language of family and kinship working to overwrite histories of militarization and suffering as well as the particularities of Cha Jung Hee's past in Korea.

Alveen admits quite forthrightly that her initial desire to adopt Deann stemmed from watching Gary Moore commercials on NBC television. These advertisements, depicting the plight of Korean War orphans, outlined the "Foster Parents Plan," to which Alveen cathects as a substitute for the church from which the family has become estranged. "Daddy had gone into real estate and was doing really well," Alveen recounts, "and I said we should do something for somebody because life has been really good for us, and I watched the TV and Gary Moore came on." One cannot describe Alveen's attachment to Cha Jung Hee, the foster child Donald and she initially sponsor from afar, as anything but sincere and enthusiastic (albeit unreflective) American liberalism. Still, this narrative of liberal benevolence cannot be easily reconciled with Borshay Liem's painful past. Public histories of colonialism, civil war, social conflict, and abject poverty in Korea cannot be easily connected to the domestic sphere of the prosperous American home.

Moreover, while there is no such thing as a motherless child, the opening sequence of *First Person Plural* highlights the management of Borshay Liem's past history through the vicissitudes of nomination, through the problem of her proper name. Sent to the United States at eight years old, Borshay Liem has a series of proper names and identities that are erased through her multiple exchanges. "My Name is Kang Ok Jin," Borshay Liem begins in the opening lines of *First Person Plural.* As her face flashes onto the screen and fades into an eerie solarized silhouette, she continues: "I was born on 14 June, 1957. I feel like I've been several different people in one life. My name is Cha Jung Hee. I was born on 5 November 1956. I've had three names, three different sets of histories. My name is Deann Borshay. I was born 3 March 1966, the moment I stepped off the airplane in San Francisco. I've spoken different languages, and I've had different families." First "Kang Ok Jin" and then deliberately substituted for another child, "Cha Jung Hee," by the Korean adoption agency, "Deann Borshay" is finally born on 3 March 1966, not by her Korean birth mother, but by her arrival on the San Francisco Jetway. Ultimately, through the animating desires and projections of her American family, she enters what they consider to be her history proper. Indeed, to the extent that adoptees are born *legally* at the moment of the transfer of parental rights from the (absent) birth mother to adoptive parents—with the rewriting of the adoptee's birth certificate to reflect this exchange and new family genealogy—there is no maternal origin to which they can return. As far as the law is concerned, the birth mother and "back there" no longer exist.

It is important to note that the repression of Borshay Liem's past is carried out not only as a collective family project but also, and more importantly, through the *strict management of the adoptee's affect.* That is, the contraction of Korean history into the privatized boundaries of the white American family is finessed through the management and control of Borshay Liem's emotional life. The silent tears that mark her traumatic arrival and the negation of her past is a language of affect—a feeling of kinship—that cannot have symbolic life or recognition. These . . . [images from *First Person Plural* removed] tears must necessarily be refused, as Donald Borshay does indeed first deny and then excuse them, such that Borshay Liem has little psychic recourse to work through her considerable losses.[36]

How might we begin to analyze Borshay Liem's affective losses? A number of years ago, in response to a series of Asian American student suicides at the university where I was teaching at the time, I co-wrote with Shinhee Han an essay entitled "A Dialogue on Racial Melancholia."[37] In this article, we analyze Freud's theories of mourning and melancholia as presenting a compelling framework to conceptualize registers of loss and depression attendant to the conflicts and struggles associated with immigration, assimilation, and racialization for Asian Americans. As described by Freud, melancholia—in contrast to his concept of normal mourning, where libido is eventually withdrawn from a lost object to be invested elsewhere—is a pathological mourning without end. As Freud's privileged theory of unresolved grief, melancholia delineates a psychic condition whereby certain losses cannot be avowed and, hence, cannot be properly mourned. In our argument, racial melancholia describes both social and psychic structures of loss emerging from Asian immigrant experiences that can be worked through only with considerable pain and difficulty.

Here it is important to emphasize that the immigration process is based on a structure of loss. In "Mourning and Melancholia," Freud describes the lost object as embodying a person, place, or ideal. When one leaves a country of origin, voluntarily or involuntarily (as in the case of transnational adoptees), a host of losses both concrete and abstract must be mourned. To the extent that lost ideals of Asianness—including homeland, family, language, property, identity, custom, status—are irrecoverable, immigration, assimilation, and racialization are placed within a melancholic framework, a psychic state of suspension between "over there" and "over here." In Freud's theory of mourning, one works through and finds closure to these losses by investing in new objects and ideals—in the American dream, for example.

However, to the extent that Asian Americans are perpetually consigned to foreigner status and continue to be considered eccentric to the U.S. nation-state, and to the extent that ideals and standards of whiteness remain unattainable for them, it might be said that Asian Americans are denied the capacity to invest in new people, places, and ideals. This inability to invest in new objects is a crucial part of Freud's definition of melancholia. Racial melancholia thus describes a psychic condition by which vexed identification and affiliations with lost objects, places, and ideals of Asianness, as well as whiteness, remain estranged and unresolved.

In *First Person Plural*, we witness the numerous ways in which Borshay Liem's past is repressed, the continuous ways in which her racial difference and past history are managed, denied, and forgotten, so that she cannot mourn what she has lost in Korea. Furthermore, the documentary portrays Borshay Liem's frustrating and impossible identifications with ideals of whiteness that remain perpetually elusive. Speaking about her vain attempts to mimic the "American ways" of her siblings, Denise and Duncan, Borshay Liem presents us with a series of home movies documenting her tortured development into adolescence: Deann sitting amidst her white dolls; Deann dressed up like a Korean doll; Deann the prom queen; Deann with her towering white high school boyfriend; Deann as a perky college cheerleader.

In an especially harrowing episode recounted by her mother, a young Borshay Liem is shown in a home movie combing the very blond hair of a doll. In a disturbing voice-over commentary that could easily be described as an Asian version of Toni Morrison's *The Bluest Eye*, Alveen tells Borshay

Liem, "You said, 'Mother, my ears always stick out. I hate that.' I said, 'Honey, that can be fixed if you want,' and you wanted." At this point, Donald Borshay chimes in, "So we went to the plastic surgeon in San Jose . . . and when they went to take the bandages off, then you began to cry." Again, the family is faced with an overflow of tears—an overflow of affect—that is met with bafflement and thus remains outside the parameters of symbolic inscription. Throughout the documentary, we witness in everyday acts, gestures, and offhand comments by her entire family, the active production of Borshay Liem's Korean otherness, accompanied by its simultaneous reinscription and containment, a whitewashing and effacing of this difference through what I have been calling the racialization of intimacy. In the opening minutes of Borshay Liem's documentary, her brother Duncan, in what can be described only as a simultaneous tone of self-congratulation and discomfort, tells her: "You didn't come from my mommy's womb. You don't have the family eyes, but you've got the family smile. Color and look doesn't make any difference. It's who you are. You're my sister." And in response to Deann's admission to Denise that "I always thought you had the perfect eyes. It was always frustrating because I couldn't get my eyelashes to look like yours," the latter immediately retorts: "People would see us or whatever and they'd say 'Is that your sister? You guys look just alike.' "

Duncan's and Denise's statements collectively underwrite the tenets of an emergent multiculturalism under neoliberalism—the acknowledgment and dismissal of difference—that provides a contemporary twist to what Homi Bhabha earlier described as the irreducible failure of mimicry: "*Almost the same, but not quite . . . Almost the same but not white.*"[38] This imperative to conform—what Deann describes as the impulse to "create a collage of things and [make] myself over to fit all the little things I had seen"—implicates Deann's desire to blend in as well as her siblings' simultaneous acknowledgement and refusal of such efforts. This dynamic underscores a new form of passing in our putatively color-blind age, which is less about the concealment of difference than about our collective refusal to acknowledge it, as I noted above. From a slightly different perspective, we might describe this new logic of passing as marking the coming together of a prior history of the Asian model minority stereotype, as "whiter than white," with a neoliberal multiculturalism under which race only ever appears as disappearing, a racial politics that acknowledges difference only to dismiss its importance. In short, this coming together installs the law of colorblindness under the sign of an anti-racism, whose stuttering logic goes something like this: *we are all different, but we are all the same, too . . . but it doesn't really matter.*

Freud maintains in "Mourning and Melancholia" that melancholia emerges from a pathological disposition and can be distinguished from regular mourning by its inability to end.[39] In "A Dialogue on Racial Melancholia," . . . [images from *First Person Plural* removed] Han and I contest

Freud's distinction between mourning and melancholia. If experiences of immigration, assimilation, and racialization in the United States are fundamentally determined both through the forced relinquishing of lost but unspeakable Asian ideals and through foreclosed investments in an idealized whiteness, then we might justifiably describe racial melancholia as a normal everyday group experience for Asian Americans. This insight places Asian American subjectivity and racial melancholia on the terrain of conflict rather than damage. In this respect, racial melancholia might be better described as a depathologized structure of feeling, pointing to those unidentified affects marking emergent group formations and identities.[40] Operating less as an individual than a group dynamic, racial melancholia for Asian Americans and transnational adoptees involves not just mourning or melancholia, but a continual negotiation between mourning *and* melancholia

Significantly, this negotiation is often and even exclusively configured within Asian American cultural politics as an *intergenerational* and *intersubjective* negotiation. That is, problems and contradictions arising from Asian American immigration are often interpreted in terms of master narratives of intergenerational cultural conflict between parents and children, between older and younger generations. The tendency to reduce all social issues, including those resulting from institutional racism and economic exploitation, to first-generation versus second-generation cultural struggles, threatens to displace them from the public domain and into the privatized space of the family.[41] In the process, it effaces what are necessarily public histories and conflicts, absolving the state and mainstream community from responsibility, from proper political address or redress.

While pointing out this palpable danger, I would like to emphasize in the present analysis of transnational adoption the elimination or attenuation of this intergenerational and intersubjective process, the loss of the communal nature of racial melancholia. As a collective social unit, the family cannot recognize Borshay Liem's racial melancholia: Borshay Liem's losses remain unaffirmed and unacknowledged by those closest to her, by her own family, by those most affectively immediate to her. This is the striking difference concerning the ways in which racial melancholia is often negotiated collectively within Asian American immigrant families, in contrast with the ways in which it is often negotiated in isolation by the Asian transnational adoptee. Earlier, I asked whether the transnational adoptee, as well as her adoptive family, was Asian American. To the extent that Borshay Liem's adoptive family recognizes her as a racialized subject—while not recognizing themselves as such—we witness an emotional cleaving of great consequence in the intimate space of the family. This failure of recognition serves to redouble the effects of racial melancholia, severing Borshay Liem from her family unit, affectively segregating her, and ultimately forcing her to negotiate her losses in silence and isolation. In short, what should necessarily be an *intergenerational* and *intersubjective* negotiation of loss is transformed into an *intrasubjective* negotiation of loss in its inexorable singularity. This is the feeling of kinship—the psychic life of race and the racialization of intimacy—that haunts Borshay Liem in this documentary of affect.

"There was an unspoken contract between us, which we had all agreed upon, that I was an orphan with no family ties to Korea," Borshay Liem later explains, referring to the public language of contracts and exchange to pierce the bubble of the private nuclear family. In an emotional voice-over, one hand covering over her mouth as she speaks, Borshay Liem offers this painful insight: "I belonged only to my American parents. It meant I didn't have a Korean history or Korean identity . . . I think being adopted into my family in some ways brought a lot of happiness for both me and for my parents, my American family. But there was also something that was—there was also a lot of sadness that we couldn't deal with as a family. And a lot of that sadness had to do with loss." She adds, "I was never able to mourn what I had lost [in Korea] with my American parents," attempting to explain the years of clinical depression from which she suffered after leaving her family and Fremont to attend college at Berkeley.

What is especially disturbing here is not just the fact that the family cannot recognize Borshay Liem's racial melancholia, that they cannot easily conceive of her adoption as involving loss, or that they cannot easily imagine her arrival in the United States as anything but an unequivocal gain. Equally distressing is the fact that Borshay Liem's clinical depression marks a sphere of intense sadness, an excess of and excessive affect that is (mis)read by those involved in her psychic plight as ingratitude. Such interpretations only serve to exacerbate her enduring feelings of disloyalty and shame. What, after all, could be less grateful on the part of an adoptee than depression?

Hence, what is justifiably felt to be a happy event from the point of view of the Borshay parents and siblings comes to overdetermine the adoptee's affect and feelings of kinship. Deann's melancholia is countered by an overpowering joy on the part of the other family members, such that their collective emotional will comes to overwrite her affective states and experiences. In the end, Borshay Liem tells us, "I forgot everything. I forgot how to speak Korean. I forgot any memory of ever having had a family, and I even forgot my real name . . . the only memories I have of my childhood are the images my father filmed while growing up. I relegated my real memories into the category of dreams."[42]

For Borshay Liem, racial melancholia involves the overwriting of all her childhood memories of and affective ties to Korea. In this regard, the psychic predicament of the transnational adoptee might be described as the containment of her emotional agency. Indeed, though I earlier described the practice of transnational adoption as one of the most privileged forms of diaspora and immigration, Borshay Liem's experiences also underscore it as a process largely devoid of affective self-determination. In her attempts to mourn the unspeakable losses initiated by her (involuntary) exchange, the transnational adoptee might also be said to function under an affective embargo, making it particularly difficult to negotiate her melancholia and transform it ever gradually into mourning. Here, I am delineating a profound form of racial melancholia, which, in Borshay Liem's words, reduces memories to dreams and agency to fantasy.

Ultimately, it is only the mother who notices this affective discrepancy. Reviewing some thirty years later the family movie of her arrival on the San Francisco Jetway, Alveen discovers Borshay Liem's stricken facial expression. In a voice-over accompanying this visual segment, she admits to her daughter, "When you arrived—little stoic-face and bundled up in all those clothes—we couldn't talk to you. You couldn't talk to us. I realize now that you were terrified. Because we were so happy, we just didn't think about that." Alveen's delayed recognition and acknowledgement of Borshay Liem's terror some thirty years after the fact creates what I would like to describe, borrowing a term from Walter Benjamin, a "dialectical image."[43] This dialectical image joins together two disparate times and spaces, shocking us out of an account of history as the way-it-really-was and creating an alternative story and historical narrative. In *First Person Plural*, the emotional clash between the Borshay family's affective joy and the young adoptee's obvious terror is transformed into a repetition compulsion, becoming a return-of-the- repressed, psychically negotiated between daughter and mother. . . . [image from *First Person Plural* removed]

Here, let us remember that adoption, especially in our contemporary moment, is not only bound up in the outsourcing of reproductive labor to the global South, but also with questions of faltering maternity, failed reproduction, and proper mothering. To the extent that adoption, rather than having no children, is often viewed as the last alternative to biological reproduction, the bond between adoptive mother and child is continually overdetermined. In the case of transnational adoption, these issues become especially problematic because of the child's tenuous place within the biologized ideal of the nuclear family and blood-line kinship. Because the racialized difference between the white mother and Asian daughter can elicit comment, because it can become something demanding explanation, the maternal bond often appears as something unnatural and in need of support.[44] "Some people would ask and others would kind of look," Alveen tells Borshay Liem, "and you knew they were wondering, but we didn't care." Given the challenge to negotiate racism and alterity within the intimate public sphere of the white family, Alveen's reaction follows a logic of colorblindness that wills away difference even as it installs the traumatic effects of its denial in Borshay Liem's psyche. The mother is not just responsible for removing Borshay Liem from the dinner table; she is literally burdened with handling her daughter's disjunctive affect. Ultimately, she is blamed for the daughter's psychic predicament: "Emotionally," Borshay Liem concludes, "there wasn't room in my mind for two mothers."

## Notes

35. Upon learning that she was switched for another child, Alveen tells Borshay Liem, "Well, I didn't care that they had switched a child on us. You couldn't be loved more. And just because suddenly you weren't Cha Jung Hee, you were Ok Jin Kang—Kang or whatever—didn't matter to me. You were Deann and you were mine."
36. Attitudes toward adoption (in general) and transnational adoption (in particular) have shifted considerably from forty years ago. However, given the ways in which racial difference is often appropriated and reinscribed by a politics of neoliberal multiculturalism, the current acknowledgement of the adoptee's racial, ethnic, or cultural difference may not have shifted the need for this management of affect in any significant manner.
37. See David L. Eng and Shinhee Han, "A Dialogue on Racial Melancholia."
38. Homi Bhabha, "Of Mimicry and Man: The Ambivalence of Colonial Discourse," 126; 130.
39. See Sigmund Freud, "Mourning and Melancholia." Later, in "The Ego and the Id," Freud comes to revise this distinction between mourning and melancholia, noting that the ego is, in fact, comprised of its abandoned and lost objects. See Sigmund Freud, "The Ego and the Id," 28–29.
40. See Williams, Marxism and Literature, 128–35.
41. See Lowe, Immigrant Acts, 63.
42. In another part of *First Person Plural*, Borshay Liem adds, "When I had learned enough English to talk to my parents, I decided that I should tell them who I really was. I remember going up to my mother and telling her 'I'm not who you think I am, I'm not Cha Jung Hee. And I think I have a mother and brother and sisters in Korea still.' And she turned to me and said, 'Oh honey you've just been dreaming. You don't have a mother. And you never had brothers and sisters. Look at these adoption documents. It says that you're Cha Jung Hee and your mother died giving birth to you.' And she said. 'You know what, this is just a natural part of you getting used to living in a new country. Don't worry about it. They're just bad dreams. They're going to go away soon.' "
43. Walter Benjamin, *The Arcades Project*, 456–75.
44. Here, I draw on this argument from Anagnost, "Scenes of Misrecognition," 395.

## Works Cited

Anagnost, Ann. "Scenes of Misrecognition: Maternal Citizenship in the Age of Transnational Adoption." *Positions: East Asia Cultures Critique*, vol. 8, no. 2, 2000, pp. 389–421.

Benjamin, Walter. *The Arcades Project*. Translated by Howard Eilan and Kevin McLaughlin, Harvard UP, 1999.

Bhabha, Homi. "Of Mimicry and Man: The Ambivalence of Colonial Discourse." *October*, vol. 28, Spring 1984, pp. 125–33.

Borshay Liem, Deann, writer and director. *First Person Plural.* National Asian American Telecommunications Association, 2000.

Eng, David L. and Shinhee Han. "A Dialogue on Racial Melancholia." *Psychoanalytic Dialogues: A Journal of Relational Perspectives*, vol. 10, no. 4, 2000, pp. 667–700.

Freud, Sigmund. "Femininity." 1933. *The Standard Edition of the Complete Psychological Works of Sigmund Freud*, Volume XXII (1932–1936), translated and edited by James Strachey et al., Hogarth, 1960, pp. 112–135.

———. "Mourning and Melancholia." 1917. *The Standard Edition of the Complete Psychological Works of Sigmund Freud*, Volume XIV (1914–1916), translated and edited by James Strachey et al., Hogarth, 1957, pp. 243–258.

———. "The Ego and the Id." 1923. *The Standard Edition of the Complete Psychological Works of Sigmund Freud*, Volume XIX (1923–1925), translated and edited by James Strachey et al., Hogarth, 1961, pp. 12–66.

Lowe, Lisa. *Immigrant Acts: On Asian American Cultural Politics.* Duke UP, 1996.

Silverman, Kaja. "Girl Love." *James Coleman* by Kaja Silverman, Lenbachhaus München, 2002, pp. 150–171.

Williams, Raymond. *Marxism and Literature.* Oxford UP, 1977.

# Part 3

# Adoption Narratives

## Introduction: Telling Stories

In this section, readers encounter work that addresses adoption narratives and narrative structures that scholars in CAS engage, largely to critique. In particular, these works look for, and at, the effects of fiction on the stories we tell ourselves about adoption and adoption identities; the way in which we define what constitutes a "true" adoption narrative and how these narratives might narrow what adoption experiences actually are; how narratives in and of adoption interact with narratives of nation, race, gender, or sexuality, supporting them or undermining common understanding of these and other categories of knowledge; and how genealogy and origins-work is narrativized and for what purpose, among many other questions we ask about the role of story in creating, supporting, critiquing, or confirming adoption difference. One of the more disputed narratives in adoption is confronted by Barbara Melosh: "Adopted persons themselves contested the narrative of 'best solution.'" That is, the story often told of adoption is that it is "in the best interests" of the child/adoptee, is the "best solution" to any crisis. Children need families, we tell ourselves, but adopted people started asking whether any family or any family formation would do, and "women who had relinquished children for adoption soon followed" in asking the same questions. Melosh is observing here both the story's inherent weaknesses and the historical progression of its critique from adoptees to their natal mothers. Her larger point is to notice how and through what mechanisms ideas about adoption changed, pointing in particular to the power of first-person stories of adoption to steer the discourse. "Adoption stories," she writes,

> offer evidence of dramatically changing views of the institution while suggesting the ways that autobiographical narrative operates to shape, circulate, and reframe ideas about adoption. Most adoptive parents' accounts validate the postwar consensus in stories that celebrate alternative family formation. By contrast, many memoirs of adopted persons and birth

DOI: 10.4324/9781003203827-26

> mothers challenge tenets of the postwar consensus by reclaiming blood ties supposedly erased by adoption. All signify the difference of adoption.

Margaret Homans calls our attention to such stories *as stories* rather than data, particularly the stories that elevate blood ties and origins as their ends. She employs what CAS scholars and many adopted people consider an Ur–adoption narrative, *Oedipus Rex*, as well as narrative theory framed by J. Hillis Miller, to suggest adoption stories' complex relationship to time: that the ends of the adoption narrative may not really be satisfying or truthful ends at all.

> For Miller, the play [*Oedipus Rex*] dramatizes the failure of ends to proceed logically or deterministically from origins. . . . Oedipus goes backwards in time, trying out various theories about his birth and then stringing together an unlikely series of events to make up the origins narrative on which he settles, the narrative that has come to stand, improbably, for the truth itself.

Homans's point is that all narrative is constructed and in a sense, perhaps in that precise sense, arbitrary, especially as to where it comes from and where it ends. In believing in these stories as truth, we miss their essentially fictive nature. The fictiveness of narrativized adoption stories, especially "finding origins," should free adopted people into self-creation and agency. However, Homans finds,

> the adopted, including Oedipus, are haunted by the conviction that there is an origin. They do not necessarily find the 'absence at the origin' [which is Miller's observation] intellectually or personally liberatory. Instead, adoption narratives are generally about the work of making an origin, which is often the work of refusing to accept such a view as Miller's.

"Origins," she continues, "are felt to be 'obscured' rather than absent."

The importance of, and changes in, stories about transnationally and transracially adopted people concern Catherine Ceniza Choy, who notes that

> the significance of these stories [of transnational adoption] is not simply their portrayal of rough spots in global family making; when read together they present a more nuanced and honest portrayal of the emotional work undertaken by American families who adopted Asian children.

Some scholars look to such stories for the way in which they represent the political and historical conditions that frame them: global resource inequities, war, power politics, and other institutional and systemic factors that end up endangering children by destroying the capacity of their natal families to care for them—or perhaps simply creating the opportunity for narratives that designate some families as destroyed and some children in need of rescue, regardless of whether that story is fabricated, too simple, or simply convenient. Choy regards first-person narratives of transnational transracial adoption as a kind of corrective:

> the adoptee's painful perception of the experience is strikingly different from most accounts at the time [in the mid- to late twentieth century], which represented the adopted child as a blank slate or as an American-already-in-progress after his or her first day in the United States.

In looking at the difference between the adoptee experience and that experience reported more generally, Choy wants us to see not just that adoptee stories have weight but that stories of easy and quick assimilation falsify and obscure the emotional labor of adoption and the complexity of human experience, especially of family-making. The mismatch between these stories is the source of some of the harm of adoption for everyone involved. An early adoptive parent and adoption facilitator, Pearl S. Buck, is the subject of Kori A. Graves's observation about the way in which adoption narratives were instrumentalized in order to promote adoption as a solution to many global problems. "Buck crafted an adoption narrative for the media that highlighted the successes she observed," Graves writes; "in order to appeal to a larger audience, Buck's narrative also recast mixed-race children of Asian descent as the embodiment of the best characteristics of every part of their heritage." In essence, the narratives selectively presented both adoption and potential adopted children in a light that made both seem better than they may have been—better in the sense of more beneficial, less problematic, more in line with the values and preferences of the adoptive parents, less emotionally complicated and fraught. In a sense, however, this practice was itself corrective of ideas about the potential for inherited (and unknown) evils in the unkinned, origin-less potential adoptee. That is, Buck's narratives reformed the idea of sin-through-blood to present blood qualities favorably or as lacking the kind of significance that meant children were judged and denied families because of their race: "Buck challenged the lingering influences of eugenics and the one drop rule of racial identity, which became the foundation for her sustained critique of what she considered to be racist adoption policies."

Buck's work was supported by a larger movement, especially associated with Korean transnational adoption. Arissa Oh points out that

> Christian and Christian Americanists who launched Korean adoption as a systemic practice sparked a revolution on a number of fronts: they opened the floodgates of intercountry adoption, triggered important

> changes to US immigration laws, changed Americans' ideas about what families looked like and how they should be made, and overturned social work doctrine about race and adoptability.

This change came largely from the way in which adoption narratives circulated among potential adopters. Oh looks at media coverage of Korea and the Korean War, Korean children, and adoption from Korea, noting how that coverage shifted the way people understood the conflict: "The American media," Oh writes, "was particularly adept at showing that it was Korea's children who were the true victims of communist aggression, the 'real' reason their nation was involved in the war on that little-known, faraway peninsula." Here, fiction—simplification and narrow focus—abets shifts in the conception of adoption from Korea: every war is, of course, about some kind of rescue of someone, but in this case, the shift to the rescue of Korean children fitted neatly with narratives about how to win the ideological war against communism: "Stories showed how orphans teetering on a razor's edge between life and death made it clear that America could win the ideological battle with North Korea and its allies by helping these orphans." In framing adoption to submerge racial difference between adoptees and their adoptive families, stories of salvation, identification (especially around the mixed-race children of GIs whose treatment as pariah triggered American fantasies of America as a haven for the persecuted), and competition for the ideological high ground undermined narratives of the "as-if" matched family that had predominated. As Mark Jerng describes it, "The child becomes subject to competing projections and desires, highlighting the processes of racial identification—in both the sense of identifying someone *as* X and identifying *with* someone—as an effect of anxieties over transmission," particularly of race or racial characteristics. Matching had created race-unified families who reproduced the (illusion of the) race of the family, but Jerng notes that matching "encapsulates this production of race as a negotiation of [those competing] projections," with race "not [articulated] as a social category and static, given that it's imposed on individuals, but rather produced through the interplay of projections among social workers" who are composing what constitutes matching through race. It is not, after all, "a purely empirical practice," Jerng notes, "but rather one that often calls upon narrative to fill the gaps." In Sandra Patton's research, we encounter some of these competing projections around race in the later quarter of the twentieth century, which can be seen narrativized, Patton asserts, in films such as *Losing Isaiah*. In such narratives

> of transracial adoption and welfare reform, Black women are represented as drug addicted and poor, and thus "fit" as breeders but "unfit"

> as mothers. Black children are shown as fragile, frail, drug addicted, unwanted and indeed disposable. In stories like *Losing Isaiah*, Black children are uncared-for and unwanted by their Black families, and thus must be saved by those fit to save, and redeem those lost children—White women.

This narrative racializes children in competing narratives of worth: too bad to be wanted by their families, good enough to be saved, if only they can be freed from the families that don't want them. But the children are also part of a larger narrative about the role of the family in making and sustaining civil society: as Patton notes, "Public discourse has been saturated with rhetoric about 'family breakdown' as the cause for contemporary social ills. . . . [T]his supposed 'breakdown of the family' fails American society through a failure of *socialization*." That is, beside a narrative of inherited negative characteristics through race sits a narrative that insists on the potential of nurture against race.

One of the ends of an origins search, as we encountered earlier, is the narrative of belonging to a group of people recognized generally, to groups of other people, as providing identification. The origins story is perhaps the one that adoption writers engage most fully—how and why do origins stories matter, what do they mean, what constitutes them, and who do they serve? For Gabrielle Glaser, looking at early Adoptee Rights activist Florence Fisher's work, the then-absolute-secrecy even about the adoption itself that was one of the public narratives about adoption in the mid- to late-twentieth-century iteration of the practice meant withholding critical information about identity. Glaser notes that Fisher

> began a twenty-year search to find her true identity, just as the postwar adoptions were in full swing. Public opinion about adoption, and the rights of adopted people to know their origins, had hewed toward complete secrecy. But [in order to know herself, Fisher] longed to know—*had* to know—more about her origins.

But Sally Haslanger's work decouples origins knowledge from the creation or understanding of who one is and certainly from the idea that without origins knowledge, an adopted person is without a self and thus without access to a good life. She asserts that "neither knowledge of others who are by virtue of biological relatedness, nor biological narratives that draw specifically on such knowledge, are necessary for developing full selfhood." Though "adoption is a significant factor in identity development, . . . whether an adoptee struggles with identity is to a significant extent a matter of context, where context includes both immediate family and society." Haslanger's claim is that the "struggle" is inherent not in the missing knowledge but in the expectation of having knowledge in the context of normative expectations of that knowledge. In other words, if most people know their biological parents and a few people don't, that can create difference that manifests as struggle and a sense of partialness and lack in the few who don't. "In our current cultural context," Haslanger writes, "the natural nuclear family schema plays an important role in forming identities—including healthy identities." The stigma of not knowing is created by the feeling of not fitting that schema, which, "in . . . early 21st century American culture is bio-normative." Haslanger locates the problem—that is, the struggle and the difficulty with selfhood for the adoptee—in "the reification of the [natural nuclear family] schema as universal, necessary, and good," rather than allowing for "the families that fail to match it."

It is with motherhood as an identity that both Heather Jacobson and Frances J. Latchford contend in their work here, Jacobson with narratives of maternal attachment, Latchford with the narrowness of the available stories for women who decide to relinquish their children. Jacobson notes that

> Surrogacy challenges basic cultural ideologies of motherhood—those deeply held, socially constructed cultural beliefs that women are the mothers of the children they gestate, that women bond deeply with their gestating babies and newborns, and that women who birth children want to mother them.

Those beliefs "cast surrogates negatively as workers: either they are capitalizing on their fertility to swindle . . . or they are forced by the larger structural forces of poverty and gender inequity to capitalize on their reproductive abilities." Women are trapped in narratives about fertility (and infertility), labor, pregnancy, attachment—what's natural and normal or framed that way in these stories—and surrogacy confronts people with the falseness of naturalizing such stories. Instead, surrogates themselves often embrace other narratives of their motivations, feelings, and work, ones that are also gendered and perhaps too narrow but at least provide options for difference among them. These, Jacobson notes, are stories that "frame their work as sacrifice, neatly positioning surrogacy alongside other forms of female-dominated labor." For Latchford, it's "the discourse of naturalized motherhood that surrounds birthmothers [that] enables us to look at how women's agency is effaced by bio-essentialist views of motherhood within and without adoption, search, and reunion discourse." In these narratives of what's "natural" about birthmotherhood, we can see more clearly how women's individual choices—even the concept of choice—disappear. When motherhood can be only one thing, when there's only one story of birthmotherhood, we lose the sense of the women (the individual, individually motivated, feeling, human people) birthmothers are. "In the simplest terms," Latchford continues, women are cast as "innately driven toward motherhood and bio-narcissistic nurturing," but birthmothers, in resisting nurturing, upset the apple cart and thus must be pathologized. "The pathology of these women stems," so the story goes,

> from the trauma that surrounds their inability, or perceived failure, as women and *ipso facto* as mothers to nurture the children they bear. . . . [B]irthmothers are pathologized as incapable of either inner peace and/or a normal sense of self because they are denied a social role and recognition as mothers.

But birthmothers "*are* agents. . . . [I]nsofar as the stories of autonomous birthmothers are erased, so too is the political import of their decisions and experiences as sites of resistance against imperatives of naturalized motherhood." In thinking about how stories work—to express the differences of adoption, to repress those differences, to understand their relationship to data or to fiction, to watch as stories manipulate readers into actions that have consequences hardly yet to be understood—this is how CAS scholars confront and engage the stories by which we live.

# From Melosh, Barbara. "Adoption Stories: Autobiographical Narrative and the Politics of Identity." *Adoption in America: Historical Perspectives*, edited by E. Wayne Carp, U of Michigan P, 2004, pp. 218–246.

Adoption is Other in a culture and kinship system organized by biological reproduction. This essay examines autobiographical narratives of adopted persons, birth mothers, and adoptive parents as uneasy negotiations of identity.[1] Memoirs of adoption by adoptive parents first appeared in the 1930s, but adoption autobiography was not established as a recognizable subgenre until the 1970s, when first adopted persons and then women who had relinquished children for adoption published their stories as testimony of their critique of adoption practices. Some of these accounts have been written by the founders of and activists in the adoption rights movement; virtually all acknowledge its influence. At the same time, the increasing number of such accounts and their broader audience suggest their wider cultural resonance. Even as the number of adoptions has fallen sharply since 1970,[2] adoption stories have claimed a heightened public visibility.

Autobiographical construction of self is social and historical. These narratives illuminate the experience and cultural meaning of adoption, even as their explorations of anomalous families illuminate, by contrast, contemporary discourses of motherhood, family, and cultural identity more generally. I read these narratives as memoirs that write the self in negotiation with wider cultural positions or discourses on adoption. After World War II, adoption became more common and more widely accepted than it had been before. For the first time, a broad white middle-class consensus proclaimed adoption the "best solution" to the "problem" of pregnancy out of wedlock. Regina Kunzel has traced the shift of white middle-class response from the evangelical reform of the early twentieth century, which saw the pregnant woman as a sinner in need of moral redemption, to the expert professional consensus of the 1930s and 1940s, which viewed out-of-wedlock pregnancy as the "symptom" of neurosis: their clients were not fallen women but problem girls. After World War II, rising rates of pre-marital pregnancy among white teenagers further tempered white middle-class zeal for condemning the sinner. At the same time, the pronatalism of the 1940s

DOI: 10.4324/9781003203827-27

and 1950s generated new public discussion and sympathy for the plight of infertile couples. In this context, adoption became widely accepted as an alternative route to family formation. The boundaries of adoptive families widened, too, as some agencies began to place African-American and American Indian children with white adopters.[3]

"Expert" narratives of adoption both reflected and codified these conditions. Professional literature—primarily that of social work but also that of psychology and psychiatry—advocated adoption as the "best solution" to the "problem" of out-of-wedlock pregnancy, at least for white women. In this narrative, adoption served all three parties in the relationship. The unwed mother might recover from the stigma of pregnancy out of wedlock, gaining a second chance for marriage and respectable motherhood. The child surrendered for adoption would benefit from the improved life chances afforded by growing up in a two-parent family. And the adoptive parents could recoup the losses of infertility by forming families through adoption (though not all adoptive parents were infertile or childless, most "stranger adoption" was motivated by infertility, and the discussion tends to focus on this kind of adoption, which constitutes on average about half of all adoptions).

During the period 1945–1965, adoption practice became more uniform than it had been before or would be after. Though adoption was and remains controlled at the state level and therefore operates under varying legal codes, most adoptions were mediated by public or private agencies under the control of social workers. Courts widely accepted social workers' legitimacy as experts qualified to counsel relinquishing parents, to assess adoptive homes, and to defend the best interests of the children.[4] Confidential adoption became standard practice—that is, birth and adoptive parents generally did not meet, birth parents had no contact with their children after they were relinquished, and most states used sealed records that concealed the identity of birth parents and substituted the names of adoptive parents on the birth certificate of adopted persons.[5] This practice powerfully symbolizes the cultural status of adoption as substitute family: the amended birth certificate rewrites the actual circumstances of the adoptive family in a document that makes their relationship indistinguishable from blood kinship, at least in the public record. Concern for matching—placing children with adoptive parents who were similar in appearance, temperament, and intelligence—also attests to the interest in effacing the difference of adoption, of making the adoptive family indistinguishable from the biological family. As anthropologist Judith Modell has observed, this embrace of adoption embodied a telling contradiction.[6] On one hand, in the United States adoption is the full legal equivalent of biological kinship: adoptive children are represented "as if begotten," an equivalence expressed through physical similarities in matching families. On the other hand, the biological family remains the standard of kinship: the mark of the acceptance of adoption is the cultural denial of its difference from biological relatedness.

Still, the social kinship of adoption enjoyed remarkably widespread support in the two decades following World War II. Experts and the lay public participated in a broad proadoption consensus whose tenets might be summarized as follows: as the full equivalent of biological family, adoptive families were permanent. What law had ordained was not subject to disruption or renegotiation, except under the same extraordinary circumstances that might call for the disruption of families joined by blood. Adoptive families were singular and exclusive: adoption permanently severed the bonds of blood kinship, replacing them with the legal ties of adoption. Favorable views of adoption rested on assumptions that nurture figured more prominently than nature in shaping human development. Expert and popular opinion alike approved relinquishment, portraying it as a difficult but loving and responsible response to pregnancy out of wedlock. Both experts and lay persons affirmed the power of love to heal the wounds of adoption—the disappointments of infertility, the pain of relinquishment for mother and child, even the damage of deprivation or abuse.

By 1970, that broad consensus began to crumble. Further liberalization of sexual attitudes, improved birth-control technology, and legal abortion made the "best solution" seem anachronistic. Women could terminate unwelcome pregnancies or raise children born out of wedlock without automatically forfeiting middle-class prospects of respectability. The political ferment of the 1960s challenged the consensus around adoption in other ways. At home and abroad, nationalist movements produced sharp critiques of interracial and transnational adoptions. In 1972, the National Association of Black Social Workers declared its opposition to white adoption of black children, a position that reversed a growing trend toward such adoptive families in the 1950s and 1960s.[7] Activists defending tribal autonomy forced the termination of the American Indian Project, a national effort, jointly sponsored by the Child Welfare League and the Bureau of Indian Affairs, that sought to place Native American children with white adopters between 1958 and 1967.[8] As American leftists responded to nationalist movements in the Third World, some castigated international adoption as a form of imperialism. Around the world, in places that had become well-known sources of adoptive children, governments reassessed their participation in the international movement of children, and many moved to restrict out-of-country adoption. In scientific and popular discourses, environmentalism gradually yielded to a pervasive biological determinism that renewed old fears of the risks of adoption.

Adopted persons themselves contested the narrative of the "best solution," and women who had relinquished children for adoption soon followed. The sunny optimism of the "best solution," they argued, denied the trauma of adoption's rupture of biological kinship. Adopted persons protested the idea that legal identity could erase blood kinship. In a growing search movement, they fought cultural and legal prohibitions to establish ties with biological kin. Women who had relinquished children for adoption began to speak out. Rejecting the shield of silence provided by confidential adoption, they challenged the postwar consensus. In an autobiographical act of renaming and self-construction, they claimed the new identity of "birthmother," a neologism that repudiated the fundamental doctrine of adoption, that blood ties could be permanently severed by law. By the early 1970s, this growing critique of adoption had begun to take on the organization and self-consciousness of a social movement, later named the adoption rights movement.[9]

Adoption stories offer evidence of dramatically changing views of the institution while suggesting the ways that autobiographical narrative operates to shape, circulate, and reframe ideas about adoption. Most adoptive parents' accounts validate the postwar consensus in stories that celebrate alternative family formation. By contrast, many memoirs of adopted persons and birth mothers challenge the tenets of the postwar consensus by reclaiming the blood ties supposedly erased by adoption. All signify the difference of adoption in one way or another: these stories are notable because they explore kinship that violates the cultural expectations attached to biological family. And, in one way or another, all register the stigma attached to that difference: they are negotiations of what sociologist Erving Goffman called "spoiled identity."[10] These accounts illustrate fractures in the cultural ideology that proclaims adoption the equivalent of biological kin by exploring the ways in which adoption figures as difference, absence, and stigma, Other and inferior to blood kinship. Accounts by adoptive parents (usually mothers) struggle with the losses of infertility, the formation of a substitute identity of parenting not based in biology, and, often, the search for a child. Autobiographies by adopted persons deal with the absence and loss of the birth mother and the gaps and silences of adoption secrecy: most of these are narratives of a psychic and actual search for the birth mother. Birth mothers' memoirs offer poignant testaments to the experience of spoiled identity. Their stories are efforts to overcome the stigma of the "bad mother" and to find and reclaim children they relinquished for adoption. Adoption life writing is a genre heavily dominated by women. Most of these accounts are written by women—adoptive mothers, adopted persons, and birth mothers. Motherhood still figures more prominently in women's social and cultural identities than fatherhood does in men's, perhaps explaining the over-representation of female authors in adopters' accounts. Strikingly, adoptees' searches are dominated by the search for the birth mother, with birth fathers assuming greatly attenuated roles. Most accounts of adopted persons in search are written by women, reflecting women's predominance among searchers.[11] So far, birth fathers have remained silent in this literature, which includes no full-length account of a man's experience of relinquishment. Most likely, birth mothers rather than birth fathers are telling stories of relinquishment and regret because the unwed mother's "moral career" is more dramatically disrupted by out-of-wedlock pregnancy. Her transgression is more visible to others and to herself through the embodied experiences of pregnancy and childbirth. And motherhood still carries more cultural weight than does fatherhood: *mother love*, signifying an enduring and unconditional nurture, is a phrase without a male-gendered equivalent.

Stories of adoptive parents are negotiations of identity that proclaim the equivalence of biological and adoptive kinship. They are also quest narratives, tales of obstacles overcome on unconventional roads to parenthood. Accounts written since 1975 detail long searches for children, serving as advice manuals to other potential adoptive parents and as critiques of the restrictions of contemporary adoption practice. In the stock plot of these narratives, a heterosexual couple decides to have a child, encounters unexpected obstacles, pursues medical treatment for infertility, and then turns to adoption. Then, the couple encounters more obstacles—the scrutiny of social workers, the scarcity of children available for adoption, the maze of adoption law. The tale ends with joyful scenes of parenthood claimed through adoption and with affirmations of the bonds and satisfactions of adoptive kinship. That point of closure implicitly endorses the logic of the "as if begotten" family: once the family is formed, the difference of adoptive kinship disappears.

## Notes

1. There is no comprehensive bibliographic aid to accounts on adoption, though Library of Congress subject headings now identify some of these. I think I have read most of the full-length accounts written by birth mothers, about three-quarters of those written by adopted persons, and perhaps a quarter of the accounts written by adoptive parents (by far the most prolific of the triad). I know of no full-length memoir by a birth father. For a collection of accounts from birth fathers, see Mary Martin Mason, *Out of the Shadows: Birthfather's Stories* (Edina, Minn.: O. J. Howard, 1995), which uses birthfathers broadly to include various experiences that separate men from children: several (but not all) of the essays are about fathers of children relinquished for adoption.

   The best bibliography for these purposes is Susan G. Miles, *Adoption Literature for Children and Young Adults* (New York: Greenwood Press, 1986), which, despite its title, includes autobiographies and other material directed to adult audiences. I have found Miles quite comprehensive for the period before 1986—indeed, her bibliography includes books by small presses and vanity presses that are not even in the extensive collections of the Library of Congress. For more recent accounts, I rely on book reviews and the online catalog of the Library of Congress. Birth mother is now a Library of Congress subject heading. Miles lists fifty-one accounts by adoptive parents, eight by birth mothers, and twenty-three by adopted persons.

I have limited this discussion to full-length memoirs or autobiographies. Several published volumes include compilations of firsthand accounts. I do not consider those in detail here because of the additional interpretive issues introduced by procedures of editorial selection, interviewing and transcription, and selective compilation.

2. Although births out of wedlock increased after 1970, the number of "stranger" (nonstepparent) adoptions dropped steadily. In 1970 there were 89,000 adoptions; by 1975, there were 48,000. The federal government has not collected national statistics on adoption since 1975, but subsequent estimates suggest that this number has remained relatively constant. See Christine A. Bachrach, "Adoption Plans, Adopted Children, and Adoptive Mothers," *Journal of Marriage and the Family* 48 (May 1986): 243–53, esp. 245; and C. A. Bachrach, K. London, and P. Maza, "On the Path to Adoption: Adoption Seeking in the U.S.," *Journal of Marriage and the Family* 53 (Aug. 1991): 705–18.
3. For example, see Leontine R. Young, *Out of Wedlock: A Study of the Problems of the Unmarried Mother and Her Child* (New York: McGraw-Hill, 1954), 160–61. For discussion and critique of the treatment of pregnancy out of wedlock during this period, particularly of the racial politics that prescribed adoption for white women while largely ignoring black women altogether, see Rickie Solinger, *Wake up Little Susie: Single Pregnancy and Race before* Roe v. Wade (New York: Routledge, 1992). In *Fallen Women, Problem Girls: Unmarried Mothers and the Professionalization of Social Work, 1890–1945* (New Haven: Yale University Press, 1993), Regina Kunzel examines the emergence of expert views of pregnant women as neurotic. For a summary of the development of adoption as a formal institution with widespread popular support, see E. Wayne Carp, *Family Matters: Secrecy and Disclosure in the History of Adoption* (Cambridge: Harvard University Press, 1998), 1–35.
4. See Viviana A. Zelizer, *Pricing the Priceless Child: The Changing Social Value of Children* (New York: Basic Books, 1985), 263 n.119. In 1941, she notes, only about a quarter of nonrelative adoptions were done by agencies. In 1971, nearly 80 percent took place under agency supervision. For a fascinating account of the history of secrecy and disclosure in adoption and the emergence of confidential adoption, see Carp, *Family Matters,* 102–37.
5. For a fascinating account of secrecy and disclosure in adoption and the emergence of confidential adoption, see Carp, *Family Matters,* 102–37.
6. Judith Modell, *Kinship with Strangers: Adoption and Interpretations of Kinship in American Culture* (Berkeley: University of California Press, 1994), 225–27.
7. For a discussion of the National Association of Black Social Workers' statement, see Mary Kathleen Benet, *The Politics of Adoption* (New York: Free Press, 1976), 140.
8. For a history and assessment of this project, see David Fanshel, *Far from the Reservation: The Transracial Adoption of American Indian Children* (Metuchen, N.J.: Scarecrow, 1972).
9. On the origins and development of the adoption rights movement, see Carp, *Family Matters,* 138–66.
10. Erving Goffman, Stigma: *Notes on the Management of Spoiled Identity* (Englewood Cliffs, N.J.: Prentice-Hall, 1963).
11. Judith S. Gediman and Linda P. Brown, *Birth Bond: Reunions between Birthparents and Adoptees—What Happens After* (Far Hills, N.J.: New Horizon Press, 1989), xxxi, 55. In her study of Canadian adopted persons in search,

Karen March found that women outnumbered men by three to one, a distribution that she notes replicates that found by others studying search and reunion. March notes further that gender was the only distinguishing characteristic that separated searchers from nonsearchers (see *The Stranger Who Bore Me: Adoptee–Birth Mother Relationships* [Toronto: University of Toronto Press, 1995]). Katarina Wegar notes that most adoptees in search are white women in young adulthood (*Adoption, Identity, and Kinship: The Debate over Sealed Records* [New Haven: Yale University Press, 1997], 63–64).

# From Homans, Margaret. "Adoption Narratives, Trauma, and Origins." *Narrative*, vol. 14, no. 1, 2006, pp. 4–26.

To say that adoption is a fiction-generating machine is not to contrast it categorically with non-adoptive family formation, but rather to claim that it presents in a particularly acute form the problem of the unknowability of origins and the common tendency to address that problem with fiction making.[4] This essay uses narrative theory and a debate in trauma theory to read some nonfictional and fictional narratives involving the retrospective construction of adoptive origins; it also suggests how increased attentiveness to the subject of adoption might complicate narrative theory. I discuss some narrative consequences that flow from adoption's orientation towards a knowledge about the past that is intensely but apprehensively sought and that is not finally available. I argue that adoptive origins and origin stories are not discovered in the past so much as they are created in the present and for the present.

## Adoption through the Lens of Narrative Theory and Trauma Theory

Narrative theory, at least since Roland Barthes, has identified the story of Oedipus—his search for the truth about his parentage, his trust in language to tell that truth—as the paradigm of storytelling itself (see e.g. Miller 3–45, Rivkin 122–124). That this key western narrative is a story about adoption is a secret hidden in plain view. As Marianne Novy points out, adoption memoirs often reference Oedipus the adoptee, but literary theorists, starting as they do with Freud's view of the story as everyman's fantasy, have for the most part overlooked the adoption theme. For most readers, Oedipus's abandonment and "sealed records" adoption merely comprise the mechanism by which he is induced to commit his celebrated crimes. But the uncovering of adoption at and as the fountainhead of narrative theory should be suggestive for scholars both of narrative and of adoption. Without taking any special notice of the adoption theme, but in an approach compatible with the focus on adoption for which I am arguing, J. Hillis

DOI: 10.4324/9781003203827-28

Miller influentially reads *Oedipus Rex* against the grain as a demonstration of the unattainability of truth and origins.[5] Building on the classical scholarship of Sandor Goodheart, who showed that *Oedipus Rex* does not prove Oedipus's guilt, Miller emphasizes the irrationality, the implausible coincidences on which the denouement—the recognition of the alleged truth—of *Oedipus Rex* depends. For Miller, the play dramatizes the failure of ends to proceed logically or deterministically from origins. Like the adoption narratives I will discuss, Oedipus goes backwards in time, trying out various theories about his birth and then stringing together an unlikely series of events to make up the origins narrative on which he settles, the narrative that has come to stand, improbably, for truth itself. If Miller's reading holds sway today, it is worth pointing out that Oedipus's adoption, his departure from the Oedipal family and its causal logic, is not incidental but central to the capacity of his story to stand for the undoing of that logic. Perhaps the scandal of his story is not incest and parricide but adoption, which requires him to spin such racy yarns about his origins and their presumed but not proven consequences, and which can stand as a paradigm for all such retrospective and doubtful figurings of origins. But Oedipus's adoption story, taken up as it has been by the adopted to stand for loss and yearning, also quarrels with such deconstructive appropriations.

Building on his reading of Oedipus, Miller generalizes about the elusiveness and constitutive fictionality of origins. With reference to writers as diverse as Trollope, Valery, Hegel, Derrida and Said, Miller writes:

> The paradox of beginning is that one must have something solidly present and preexistant, some generative source or authority, on which the development of a new story may be based. That antecedent foundation needs in its turn some prior foundation, in an infinite regress. Any beginning in narrative cunningly covers a gap, an absence at the origin.
> (57–58)

Miller uses deconstructive reading here to show the impossibility of origins. Although he is also interested in the stories that rest on such thinly if "cunning[ly]" covered gaps, his language about origins is categorical: the "regress" is "infinite," there is "an absence at the origin."[6] To read his argument, presented as it is in so calm and genial a tone, is to be swayed by the pleasure of feeling scales drop from one's eyes and intellectual skies open up. But the adopted, including Oedipus, are haunted by the conviction that there is an origin. They do not necessarily find the "absence at the origin" intellectually or personally liberatory. Instead, adoption narratives are generally about the work of making an origin, which is often the work of refusing to accept a view such as Miller's. While Miller's magisterial view offers an astringent corrective to what are often false and sentimental (if arduously sought) truth claims about origins in adoption, it also does not sufficiently account for the imaginative work and emotional labor such claims can perform. Two recent narratological studies of stories thematically related to adoption suggest how Miller's observation about origins might apply, but with an adjustment of emphasis and tone, to the case of adoptive origins.

Catherine Romagnolo, reading Amy Tan's *The Joy Luck Club*, a novel of severe personal and cultural dislocations, reveals how ideologically freighted as well as elusive various kinds of narrative beginnings, especially "causal beginnings," can be ("Narrative Beginnings" 3). Drawing on the skepticism of postcolonial and feminist theorists such as Homi Bhabha and Trinh Minh-Ha, who debunk the possibility as well as the political desirability of cultural authenticity because of the invidious hierarchies it can foster, Romagnolo argues that contemporary novels may, through the ideological mobilization of formal devices, likewise expose as a dangerous fantasy the dream of recovering authentic origins. Tan, she argues, countering "a fixation" among advocates of Asian American culture "upon reclaiming authentic origins [that] can occlude the experiences of marginalized members of a community," destabilizes narrative beginnings by structuring her novel around multiple plots and points of view, in order to "critique . . . the very concept of origins [and] illuminate the discursive constructedness of authenticity, origins, and identity" (Romagnolo, "Narrative Beginnings" 2). According to Romagnolo, origins in Tan's novel are multiple and undecidable, but they nonetheless matter to the characters. Several older women search for something from the past (much as the adopted do), and although Romagnolo shows how the novel destabilizes or even "repudiates the existence of [each quest's] goal," she also stresses "the importance of the histories of these characters to their ongoing sense of agency" (6). Origins may be "irretrievable" (9), and for politically salutary reasons, but that makes the action of their incomplete reconstruction all the more vital.

Taking a related approach to the "discursive constructedness of . . . origins," Mark E. Workman moves narrative theory even closer to some specific characteristics of adoption narratives. Workman observes that certain personal narratives with "obscured beginnings" are " 'flawed' because of the narrator's awareness of and preoccupation with an originary event that the narrator strives to envelop within her story but that lies beyond her narratival grasp" (249). Workman's exemplary "flawed" narratives (recorded anecdotes rather than literary texts) are those of sexual jealousy, which compels imaginative reconstruction of an unexperienced event, and trauma, which compels imaginative reconstruction of an unremembered or uncomprehended event. The sequence of birth and abandonment prior to adoption has been linked to both of Workman's paradigmatic narratives, and so when it comes to adapting Miller's categorical remarks about "absence at the origin" to the specific case of adoption, Workman's thesis offers a particularly apt guide. Even more than in Romagnolo's reading of Tan, the emphasis in Workman's texts and in adoption narratives falls less on "absence at the origin" and more on creative, if compulsive, acts of reconstructing origins; origins are felt to be "obscured," not absent. Adoptive parents often describe their feelings about meeting their children as falling in love; like Workman's jealous lovers, such parents may feel compelled to imagine primal scenes they missed.[7] The linkage of adoption to trauma is more complex, since infant relinquishment is not only like trauma (an unremembered yet life-altering event): it has itself been called a form of trauma by such popular theorists of adoption as Nancy Newton Verrier and Betty Jean Lifton. While Romagnolo explains why stable, knowable origins are unlikely (if sometimes desperately sought) in narratives involving personal or cultural dislocations, Workman's specific concern with the reconstruction of traumatic origins can highlight the generative aspects of adoption narratives. Like (or as) trauma narratives, adoption narratives are often obsessively oriented towards an irretrievable past, and like (or as) trauma, adoption compels the creation of plausible if not verifiable narratives. Narratives of trauma and adoption (therapeutic and otherwise) are best understood not as about the unearthing of the veridical past, nor yet again about revealing the past to be what Miller calls the "absence at the origin," but about the creation of something new. I turn now to trauma theory to suggest how its handling of origins might contribute to our understanding of adoption narratives.

Adoption writers such as Verrier and Lifton subscribe to a theory of adoption as trauma that roughly corresponds to the theory of trauma as "unclaimed experience" articulated by Cathy Caruth, Shoshana Felman, Dori Laub, Bessel Van der Kolk and others in the early 1990s. (This is the definition of trauma on which Workman relies.) For Lifton, the adopted are "wounded psychically" (165). In Verrier's view, any separation from the biological mother from the moment of birth onwards, whether for relinquishment or merely for medical treatment, produces a "primal wound" that manifests itself in numbed affect, anxiety, depression, lifelong difficulty in trusting others, and in the same "intrusions" and "constrictions" suffered by survivors of wars, the Holocaust, or childhood sexual abuse. As sufferers of post-traumatic stress disorder (PTSD), in Verrier's view, the adopted act out rather than consciously recall their abandonment. Not only do the adopted experience "possession by the past," to borrow Caruth's formulation, its "insistent reenactments . . . bear witness to a past that was never fully experienced as it occurred [and] that is not yet fully owned" (151). Verrier tells an anecdote, for example, of an adoptee who helplessly mimed her own abandonment by her birth mother (Verrier 151). Lifton describes adoption as a disease not unlike the condition of survivors of Hiroshima: "We walk around seemingly normal like everyone else, but we've got taboos, guilts, and repressions lodging like radiation inside us" (156).[8] For Caruth and her fellow authors and the primary research on which they draw, such as that of analyst Pierre Janet, trauma has physical effects, as it does for Verrier and Lifton's adoptees, and it creates a "traumatic memory" system filled with literal but unrepresentable memories separate from the "narrative memory" that is available to conscious recall (van der Kolk and van der Hart 160). The task of the survivor and the therapist or witness is to move the traumatic event from the former to the latter, where it can be integrated into the sufferer's overall life narrative. Similarly, Verrier claims that the adoptee, even a days-old infant, remembers her abandonment, with memories that are deeply buried, even "cellular;" and she believes in the capacity of hypnosis to retrieve the events thus retained. The task for therapy, in Verrier as in Caruth, is to articulate and narrate what at first seems non-narratable.

Used as a model for narrative, Verrier's account of trauma would imply that the story of the past should and can be accurately told. Just as Caruth finds that "the images of traumatic reenactment remain absolutely accurate and precise," Verrier emphasizes the literality of the trauma and its residues. Unlike Caruth, however, with her deconstructive skepticism about the difficulties involved in narrating and integrating traumatic memories (those images are also "largely inaccessible to conscious recall" [151]), Verrier has little doubt that therapy can retrieve the past. But in Verrier's writing, this therapeutic work involves a surprisingly high degree of fiction making. When an infant arrives in its adoptive home, for example, Verrier encourages the parents to interpret any "unexplained sadness or crying" as "expressions of the child's loss of the biological mother. . . . It would be important to empathize with the loss and to talk about it—put it into words for him" (119). Perhaps so, but the parents could also be making this all up, imposing a fiction on the child and obliging her to mourn a loss she does not feel.

Moreover, Verrier's strategies for mourning also entail some unacknowledged temporal dislocations. Verrier urges the adopted to search for their birthmothers, and she calls this "[s]earching for that biological past" (153–4), as though a living and inevitably much changed human being could somehow make present or embody the past. This temporal confusion is common to many search narratives. As Barbara Yngvesson writes: "The search for roots assumes a past is there, if we can just find the right file, the right papers, or the right person" (13). But as Betty Jean Lifton says of her own search, "[t]he past was not there waiting to receive me" (118). Verrier elides such questions as why searching for the biological past would be a good idea or what it should accomplish. She emphasizes instead that if everyone speaks honestly about "what they are truly feeling" in the present, all will go well. "These feelings do not have to be denied or apologized for. But if they are not owned, they will be projected upon another member of the triad" (166). In other words, for the "unclaimed experience" of the past of Caruth, Felman, and Laub's model, Verrier substitutes feelings in the present that must and can far more easily be "owned." "How is it possible . . . to gain access to a traumatic history?" asks Caruth (151); Verrier's inadvertent answer is that there is no history; there is only the present. Her literalism about the past (her insistence that it can be retrieved) has the paradoxical effect (because it cannot be) of making history disappear.

## Notes

4. That orphanhood (and by implication adoption) is a rich resource for narrative has long been recognized. For example, orphanhood is among the most common ways of producing an interesting hero and plot in the classic English novel from Fielding to the Brontës, Dickens, Eliot, and Hardy.
5. Alternatively, but with aims analogous to Miller's, feminist scholars have been showing that the Oedipal plot, with its emphasis on constitutively male filial discoveries that model linear thinking and action, is not the only possible plot (see for example Friedman, Winnett). Julie Rivkin shows how the dismantling of Oedipal family structure can also undo the cause and effect sequences of Oedipal narrative, and Judith Butler proposes Antigone as the founding figure of a new psychoanalytic theory, one that would defy the heteronormativity founded on Oedipus's narrative. These critical gestures seek alternatives to the lockstep linearity of Oedipus. Novy likewise, exploring alternatives to Oedipus not as narrative model but as model for thinking about adoption, proposes Euripides's pro-adoption *Ion*.
6. I am staying here as much as possible within the realm of narrative theory, but the groundlessness and impossibility of origins, and of meaningful distinctions between originals and copies, is found in other theoretical discourses as well, notably in the work of Donna Haraway (whose admirable cyborg refuses to sustain a connection to organic origins) and Judith Butler.
7. A recent example is Kathleen Tolan's play *Memory House*, produced at the Playwrights' Horizons theatre in New York (May 2005), in which the character playing the adoptive mother, narrating the adoption story, says, "then I fell in love" (to which the cynical teenager replies, "too bad it didn't last"). Predictably, the daughter picks a fight about the mother's supposed disregard for the birth family and place of origin, which the mother counters—confirming Workman's thesis—by insisting that she thought constantly about the birth mother.
8. Lifton also sees the adopted and their birth parents as just as much in need of reunion as families separated by the Holocaust (220–221, 227).

## Works Cited


Butler, Judith. *Antigone's Claim: Kinship between Life and Death*. Columbia UP, 2000.

Caruth, Cathy. "Recapturing the Past: Introduction." *Trauma: Explorations in Memory*, edited by Cathy Caruth, The Johns Hopkins UP, 1995, pp. 151–157.

———. *Unclaimed Experience: Trauma, Narrative, and History*. The Johns Hopkins UP, 1996.

Friedman, Susan Stanford. "Lyric Subversion of Narrative in Women's Writing: Virginia Woolf and the Tyranny of Plot." *Reading Narrative: Form, Ethics, Ideology*, edited by James Phelan, Ohio State UP, 1989, pp. 162–185.

Lifton, Betty Jean. *Twice Born: Memoirs of an Adopted Daughter*. McGraw Hill, 1975.

Miller, J. Hillis. *Reading Narrative*. U of Oklahoma P, 1998.

Novy, Marianne. *Reading Adoption: Family and Difference in Fiction and Drama*. U of Michigan P, 2005.

Rivkin, Julie. *False Positions: The Representational Logics of Henry James's Fiction*. Stanford UP, 1996.

Romagnolo, Catherine. "Back to the Beginning[s]: A Feminist Reconsideration." Conference paper, Narrative: An International Conference, April 2005.

———. "Narrative Beginnings in Amy Tan's *The Joy Luck Club*: A Feminist Study." *Studies in the Novel*, vol. 35, 2003, pp. 89–108.

Van der Kolk, Bessel A., and Onno van der Hart. "The Intrusive Past: The Flexibility of Memory and the Engraving of Trauma." *Trauma: Explorations in Memory*, edited by Cathy Caruth, The Johns Hopkins UP, 1995, pp. 158–182.

Verrier, Nancy Newton. *The Primal Wound: Understanding the Adopted Child*. Gateway, 1993.

Winnett, Susan. "Coming Unstrung: Women, Men, Narrative, and Principles of Pleasure." *PMLA*, vol. 105, 1990, pp. 505–518.

Workman, Mark. "Obscured Beginnings in Personal Narratives of Sexual Jealousy and Trauma." *Narrative*, vol. 12, 2004, pp. 249–262.

Yngvesson, Barbara, and Maureen A. Mahoney. " 'As One Should, Ought and Wants to Be': Belonging and Authenticity in Identity Narratives." *Theory, Culture and Society*, vol. 17, no. 6, 2000, pp. 77–110.

# From Choy, Catherine Ceniza. *Global Families: A History of Asian International Adoption.* NYUP, 2013.

This chapter critiques the notion that the adopted child experienced a smooth and joyful transition upon arrival in the United States by featuring less well-known stories. These stories are archived by the ISS-USA, but most of them were not distributed to the general public. They reveal breakdowns in adoptive family placements and the need for family replacements; the stress created by the financial costs of international adoption; and one family's story about the mundane, but also highly emotional, challenges of adopting a Chinese child in the early 1960s. The outcomes of these adoptions are unknown, but the available archival records suggest that they would become successful placements. The significance of these stories is not simply their portrayal of rough spots in global family making; when read together, they present a more nuanced and honest portrayal of the emotional work undertaken by American families who adopted Asian children.

****

## Conclusion: Before *Ball Four*, "Kyong Jo—for Boutons"

If mainstream journalism perpetuated stereotypes of international adoption as totally joyful, it also had the power to debunk them. Unfortunately, the latter has been rare. The sportswriter Leonard Shecter's 1968–1969 feature article about the New York Yankees pitcher Jim Bouton's adoption of a Korean boy is one of these rarities.[43]

As a major league ballplayer and a well-known author, Jim Bouton is no ordinary American. But at the time of Shecter's interview for the article, Bouton's baseball career was almost finished. In 1963, he had won twenty-one games for the New York Yankees and made the all-star team. He won eighteen more games the following year and beat the Cardinals twice in the 1964 World Series. An arm injury in 1965 marked the beginning of the decline in his Major League career. As Sheeter writes, "His skills deserted him. Arm trouble, difficulty with Manager Ralph Houk, a slide down to the

DOI: 10.4324/9781003203827-29

minor leagues . . . all the indignities heaped on the professional athlete on his way down descended upon Bouton."[44]

Furthermore, Bouton's now-famous writing career was only in its infancy in 1968. Sheeter, who had befriended Bouton at the time Bouton had played for the Yankees, encouraged him to write a season-long diary for publication. The result, completed a little more than a year later, was *Ball Four: My Life and Hard Times Throwing the Knuckleball in the Big Leagues.* First published in 1970, Bouton's controversial, no-holds-barred account of his decline as a Major League pitcher, the antics of professional baseball players, and his rocky relations with management was a massive success. In 1995, the New York Public Library selected it as one of the "Books of the Century." And, in 1996, Bouton was featured in *The Sports 100: The 100 Most Important People in American Sports History*, published by Macmillan.[45]

During the low point of his baseball career, Bouton and his wife, Bobbie, adopted a three-year-old boy from Korea. Following the pattern of news articles about international adoption in the United States, Shecter's article began with the initial encounter between Kyong Jo and the Boutons at the airport:

> He was not yet four years old and he was a forlorn figure as he scuffed off the immense jet airplane at the Seattle airport. He wore a red shirt and baggy red trousers, a tiny blue hat on his head and broken-backed loafers on his feet. In one hand he clutched a sweater, in the other a passport. A handprinted tag pinned on his chest read, "Kyong Jo—for Boutons." That was all of it, all he had in the world. There was not even a paper sack to hold his sweater.[46]

The pathetic portrayal of the Asian child prior to and upon arrival was familiar. What was distinct about Shecter's writing about the airport encounter, however, was his depiction of Kyong Jo's fear about this new stage of his life alongside his American family's joy:

> His eyes, big and round and black, were tearless, but brimming with terror. When the lady from Travelers Aid tried to pick him up, he wrestled free and squatted on the ground, his elbows between his knees and his hands shielding his head. He was a despairing figure, a wounded animal, cringing, unmoving, apparently unhearing. Finally Jim Bouton, a large, pleasant-looking man of 29 with blond hair, deeply set blue eyes and a cheerful, gravelly voice, crouched down beside him and started speaking in heavily accented Korean. "Kyong Jo," he said, "do not be afraid. We will not hurt you. We will take good care of you."[47]

Jim and Bobbie Bouton had prepared themselves and their children, five-year-old Michael and three-year-old Laurie, for Kyong Jo's arrival. They had studied the Korean language. They planned to eat Asian food so that Kyong Jo would feel more at home. This well-intentioned preparation could not overcome the traumatic realities of the child's origins, however. In a stunning departure from the news stories about the smooth assimilation of the adopted child into the American family, Shecter contrasted the "heart-warming adventure" that the Boutons had hoped for with the "heartbreak" of Kyong Jo's personal history. The Boutons' welcoming gestures of language study and consumption of Asian food "meant nothing to a child given up by his mother and wrenched across the Pacific to a place where all the faces were pale and all the words were incomprehensible. Kyong just cried."[48]

The inclusion of the adoptee's painful perception of the experience is strikingly different from most accounts of the time, which represented the adopted child as a blank slate or as an American-already-in-progress after his or her first day in the United States. After several days passed and the Boutons were still unable to console Kyong Jo, they invited the Korean woman who had given them language lessons for a visit. She translated her forty-five-minute conversation with Kyong Jo to the Boutons. Shecter characterized Kyong Jo's story as a "long tale of woe." The sadness derived not solely from his plight in Korea but also from the confusion and anger experienced by a perceptive but very young adopted child separated from his mother and transplanted to the United States:

> Speaking rapidly and with a vocabulary and sentence structure that the teacher said were years beyond his chronological age, Kyong Jo said that he was very unhappy. He said he was angry at his mother for sending him away and that while he knew the Boutons were nice people who were trying to be good to him, they were simply not very bright. Every time he said anything to them, their only answer was that they didn't understand. Besides, they spoke funny and too rapidly and he wished they wouldn't talk so much, always gabble, gabble, gabble. Also, he couldn't understand why he was not living in America. Everybody told him that in America there were thousands of toys for everyone and each child had his own television set. The Boutons had only one. They had visited America briefly the other day, he admitted, where there were many toys and enough television sets for everyone (it was a department store), and perhaps he would be taken there for another visit soon. But by and large, he did not like living here and if he couldn't go back to Korea, he would at least like somebody to sleep with him as his mother did. No, not Bobbie. He preferred Jim.[49]

Another stunning element of Shecter's article is the discussion of Kyong Jo's Korean birth mother. Shecter explained that the mother who was "deserted by her American soldier, could barely afford to feed herself and her child. So she put him up for adoption, hoping that someone, somewhere, would do for him what she could not."[50] Kyong Jo, like an untold number of children in Asian orphanages, was not a true orphan. Not only did he have living birth parents, but he had lived a hybrid existence in Korea, split between institutional and parental care. Sheeter wrote that, "in a way, this made it especially difficult for Kyong Jo, for while he spent his days in an orphanage, his evenings were still spent with his mother. Leaving her was a great wrench."[51] Although Sheeter did not go into any more detail about the boy's past, he highlighted the existence of this relationship, while many other news stories of the time excluded mention of the birth mother and other relatives altogether. The erasure of the child's origins would become part of an increasing legal trend in international adoption in the second half of the twentieth century: emphasis on the adoptive families' and receiving nations' exclusive entitlement to the children.[52] Sheeter may not have anticipated the increasing interest in the adoptive child's birth family and especially the birth mother in the late twentieth century, but his writing revealed an understanding of the emotional significance of her presence in Kyong Jo's life.[53]

As Jim had to return to the ballpark, Bobbie had to handle the brunt of Kyong Jo's emotional distress. Their first evening together was especially difficult. Bobbie sadly reminisced:

> *Oma* is the Korean word for mommy. . . . That's all he would say. "*Oma, oma, oma*," over and over. I tried to get him to take a bath with the children. He wouldn't. I tried to get him into pajamas. He wouldn't let me. I laid him down in bed and told him everything I could say in Korean, that he was a good boy and we loved and would take good care of him. And he settled down for a while. Then I heard him get up and I came out and he was on the davenport, crying.[54]

According to Jim, "It tore you up to hear it. When I came home, I tried to comfort him and every once in a while he'd drop off to sleep. But then he'd wake up and sort of look around. As soon as he decided he hadn't been dreaming, he started crying again."[55] Kyong Jo's physical pain contributed to his incessant crying. His vitamin-poor diet had rotted his teeth so that most of them were black, with many rotted down to the gum line. The attempt to feed Kyong Jo Asian food—really, an Americanized version of Asian food—was a "disaster." He did not eat more than a spoonful of the rice with bean sprouts and vegetables for lunch or the chow mein for dinner. A change in his appetite came after a few days when the Boutons brought him to a hamburger place. Jim recalled, "He must've thought he was in heaven. He didn't stop eating until we dragged him away."[56]

Had the Boutons' story followed the pattern of most narratives, this promising turn would have marked the start of the swift and happy

Americanization of Kyong Jo, with the rejection of Asian food and the ravenous consumption of the all-American hamburger serving as the undeniable metaphor for Kyong Jo's assimilation. But in this narrative, [image and caption removed] the eating gave him energy for even more crying. In his interview with Sheeter about this time period, Jim revealed his serious self-doubt and lack of confidence:

> I began to think that I had wrecked the family. . . . For the first time in my life, I had trouble sleeping. I thought that I'd made a move which was a foolish one and that we'd done something we shouldn't have. There was so much tension, and we couldn't devote any attention to the other kids. Just that crying and sobbing. You couldn't get away from it. And while I agonized with him, I was afraid I had done a terrible thing.[57]

Jim Bouton's highly critical and desperate self-reflection is a dramatic departure from his and his wife's very thoughtful and well-planned decision to adopt an Asian child. Shecter's in-depth writing about their decision, which was steeped in the Boutons' personal as well as political views about their immediate family, population growth, and American racial politics, is the third major contribution of the article. On a personal level, the Boutons wanted a child who was healthy enough to endure their intense travel schedule and who was in between the ages of their other two children, Laurie and Michael, so that the younger Laurie would continue to be the baby of the family.

Their decision to adopt was also rooted in their political and ethical beliefs in zero population growth and Americans' moral responsibility to children fathered by Americans abroad. As Bobbie explained, "We wanted to give a home to someone who couldn't have it any other way. We'd sort of satisfied our desire for creating our own children. One of each. What more can you have?"[58] Jim continued, "We figured there are so many kids in the world who have no place to live and no family, that it's silly to just go on and have hordes of kids. Once your wife has had the pleasure of having her own child and you've satisfied your own ego, there are enough kids that don't have homes."[59] As a result of his deep concern about the overpopulation crisis, Jim openly advocated for men to have vasectomies and proposed a tax structure that would reward men who did so with a tax deduction. His proposal would also give tax deductions to families who adopted children, with larger deductions for families who adopted nonwhite and handicapped children. His proposal provided no tax deduction for "natural children," although he criticized the use of this term: "We had two of our children naturally (though what's unnatural about adoption?)"[60] Jim himself underwent a vasectomy in 1969 and wrote about this decision for a book titled *The Vasectomy Information Manual.*

Furthermore, by the late 1960s, the issues of race and racism continued to play central roles in shaping the practice of international adoption in the United States. Reflecting on his decision-making process, Bouton discussed these issues with a candor and complexity that is difficult to find in mainstream narratives about international adoption in the 1950s and early 1960s. His openness was, on one level, a reflection of his political engagement with the social protest movements of the times. Jim was a vocal opponent of apartheid in South Africa, and he had traveled to the 1968 Summer Olympics in Mexico City with a contingent of antiapartheid activists from Jackie Robinson's American Committee on Africa to protest the participation of South Africa's white-only teams.[61] On another level, the significance of racial issues in his decision to adopt an Asian child reflected increasingly controversial attitudes in the United States about transracial adoption, specifically the adoption of African American and Native American children by white American families.

## Notes

43. Leonard Shecter, "My Friend the Brother," publication name and date are not available on the photocopy in the archival records, pp. 38–43, ISS-USA papers, Box 12, File 7, SWHA. In an email message from Jim Bouton, dated May 11, 2011, he recollected that the article was published in *Signature* magazine in late 1968 or 1969. He also mentions that the article about Kyong Jo's adoption appeared briefly in *Ball Four*. See Jim Bouton, *Ball Four*, twentieth anniversary edition, edited by Leonard Shecter (New York: Wiley, 1990), 119. Even with advances in information technology and with the astute assistance of university librarians, I have been unable to locate the original magazine issue, which contains Shecter's article.
44. Shecter, "My Friend the Brother," 40.
45. "Jim Bouton Biography" in *NOW* with David Brancaccio, Politics and Economy, November 28, 2003, available at www.pbs.org/now/politics/bouton.html (accessed June 7, 2011). A fascinating transcript of Bill Moyers's interview with Jim Bouton about his crusade to save a historic baseball park in Massachusetts follows the biography, illustrating that Bouton's political activism and social commentary continued into the twenty-first century.
46. Shecter, "My Friend the Brother," 38.
47. Ibid.
48. Ibid., 40.
49. Ibid., 43.
50. Ibid., 42.
51. Ibid.
52. See Barbara Yngvesson, *Belonging in an Adopted World: Race, Identity, and Transnational Adoption* (Chicago: University of Chicago Press, 2010), 18–26.
53. Ibid., 1–2.
54. Shecter, "My Friend the Brother," 40.
55. Ibid.
56. Ibid.
57. Ibid.

58. Ibid., 42.
59. Ibid.
60. Jim Bouton, "One Man's Family Planning;" in Paul Gillette, *The Vasectomy Informational Manual* (New York: Outerbridge & Lazard, 1972), and reprinted in *New York Magazine*, April 10, 1972.
61. Douglas Hartmann, *Race, Culture, and the Revolt of the Black Athlete: The 1968 Olympic Protests and Their Aftermath* (Chicago: University of Chicago Press, 2003), 296.

# From Graves, Kori A. *A War-Born Family: African American Adoption in the Wake of the Korean War.* NYUP, 2020.

### Buck and the Narrative of Hybrid Superiority

When Welcome House expanded from a permanent foster home to a full-fledged adoption agency, Buck crafted an adoption narrative for the media that highlighted the successes she observed in the residential home. Whether speaking to small crowds, writing to women's organizations or for women's magazines, or soliciting money to support the Welcome House, Buck's goal was to change the opinions of people in areas where families were likely to adopt a Welcome House child. She always described the children as beautiful and intelligent, and this tendency rubbed off on some of the families who adopted from the agency. Alice Hammerstein Mathias was the daughter of Oscar Hammerstein, and one of the first to adopt a child from Welcome House with her husband Philip. She referred to the intellectual prowess of her half-white, half-Japanese American children in an interview she had with one Buck biographer. Mathias proudly proclaimed, "both of them are very bright;' and she called them "cute as a button."[36] Eve Eshleman, one of Buck's associates, remembered that Buck always described the Welcome House children as smart. Buck frequently mentioned the superiority of the Welcome House children to demonstrate that, unencumbered by the burdens of de jure and de facto segregation, the children's finest qualities would flourish.[37]

Buck's narrative of hybrid superiority contained elements of the model minority stereotype that emerged in the 1960s, in part, because of Chinese and Japanese activists' decades-long efforts to counter negative characterizations of their communities. These activists' goal was to improve Asians social and political standing in the United States. As historian Ellen D. Wu describes the process, Chinese and Japanese Americans utilized cultural, social, and political institutions to facilitate their transformation from "assimilating Other" to "model minority." Buck's narrative and institutional strategies to increase adoptions for mixed-race Asian children challenged negative stereotypes about the children by making them both the "assimilating Other"

DOI: 10.4324/9781003203827-30

and the model adoptee. However, scholars in Asian Studies, Asian American History, and Critical Adoption Studies have shown why the model minority idea that Buck promoted was and is troubling. Although Wu identifies the ways that Japanese and Chinese activists mobilized the idea to resist oppression, many scholars argue that the myth of the model minority actually obscures differences among and between Asians and Asian Americans, and it reproduces oppression and exclusion. Indeed, the idea of the model minority that gained traction in white popular culture and among white politicians in the 1960s allowed these communities to celebrate Asians' assimilation and achievements and condemn African Americans for failing to do the same. In this way, the myth became a tool that allowed white communities to deny institutional racism.[38]

Further, adoption scholars have described the ways the media, adoptive families, and child welfare officials had a hand in constructing the Korean adoptee as an ideal immigrant because of her or his youth and assimilability.[39] The idea undergirding these efforts was that the children's *Asianness* was inconsequential, even erasable. Buck's narrative also emphasized the assimilability of her mixed-race subjects, but she endeavored to reverse unfavorable assessments of the children's Asian identities. She suggested that circumstances—and in her construction the love of good families—would shape how the children's "superior" qualities developed. This strategy led some white adoptive parents, who had historically avoided transracial placements, to believe that adoptions of nonwhite children benefited them as well as the children. It also reduced the children to a set of stereotypes that Buck originally framed as positive attributes.

The language Buck used to rehabilitate the image of mixed-race adoptive children was always positive but varied based on the audience she needed to persuade. For example, she often changed the story of the first Welcome House child, Robbie, to make the circumstances of his birth more romantic. The basic story begins with the letter Buck received telling her about a child born to a white, American mother and an "East Indian" father. The only details this version includes are that Robbie's parents were unable to keep him even though the boy "was of high intelligence."[40] In another version, Buck described the relationship between the Indian father and white American mother as defined by love. Having moved to India with her missionary parents, this young woman believed the "gospel of love—the brotherhood of man" that her parents preached. But when she became pregnant, her missionary parents sent her back to the States "alone to bear her baby."[41] No matter which details were embellished or omitted, the significant message of the story was that mixed-race children were victims of racial intolerance who needed "superior families who have no fears."[42] With the help of such families, Buck believed that mixed-race children would be assets to their families and the nation.

In order to appeal to a larger audience, Buck's narrative also recast mixed-race children of Asian descent as the embodiment of the best characteristics of every part of their heritage. This shift was central to the development of her version of the model adoptee. Buck's emphasis on the beauty and intelligence of the Welcome House children resembled theories promoted by sociologists in the early twentieth century who challenged negative ideas about mixed-race Chinese children—based on the theory of hybrid degeneracy—by theorizing that mixed-race children possessed superior qualities from both sides of their ancestry. According to scholar Emma Jinhau Teng, sociologists developed the notion of hybrid vigor that characterized Asian hybrids as "intelligent, strong, fit, and beautiful."[43] Similarly, Buck's reconfiguration incorporated culturally salient signifiers to reverse the negative consequences associated with interracial intimacy. When she described the children as "superior in intelligence and certainly superior in beauty,"[44] Buck identified two major concerns that limited the adoption of mixed-race children. Opponents of interracial intimacy repeatedly charged that mixed-race children were a threat to the health and progress of the nation. These ideas flourished during the nineteenth century to ensure the legal and social inferiority of nonwhite peoples. But they took on new significance in the early twentieth century as fears of immigration and race mixing increased. Beginning with statutes prohibiting whites from marrying African Americans or Native Americans, states passed a host of laws to prohibit whites from marrying people identified by a range of racial, national, and religious labels including Chinese, Japanese, Korean, Malay, or Hindu. The proliferation of these anti-miscegenation laws allowed states to punish people who attempted to legitimate either their interracial intimacies or their interracial children.[45]

Although Pennsylvania did away with its anti-miscegenation laws in the late eighteenth century and outlawed school segregation in the late nineteenth century, resistance to racial equality persisted throughout the state. Events like the 1954 *Brown v. Board of Education* Supreme Court decision outlawing school segregation revived concerns throughout the nation that integration would lead to increased interracial intimacy. Even in communities like Doylestown that lacked any significant racial diversity, the prospect of interracial dating and marriage could create problems. Some residents of Doylestown based their disapproval of the Welcome House children on their fears of future interracial marriages. Buck claimed that one older man in her community railed, "If any of those damned half-breed children marries one of my grandchildren, I will see you goddamned to hell."[46] The first Welcome House mother, Viola Yoder, also remembered that some of her neighbors asked questions about whom the children would date when they got older.[47]

Buck did not shy away from the controversial issue of interracial dating. In 1955, she confronted the question of whom the Welcome House children would date by insisting that they were ideal dating prospects for any of the Doylestown youth. Citing the positive qualities they possessed that trumped any concerns about racial difference, Buck noted that the oldest of the Welcome House children "had more girls interested in him than the average boy has." Referring to the oldest Welcome House daughter, Buck assured that she was also a sought-after dating prospect. In both cases, she based her assessment of the young peoples' prospects on their physical appearances, winsome personalities, and gender appropriate behaviors. According to Buck, the young man was "a handsome fellow and a good athlete," and "a volunteer in the armed services:' She also bragged that the young woman was "pretty and sweet."[48] Here we see how Buck's efforts to make the Welcome House children's activities and attributes fit with postwar definitions of gender effectively essentialized both the gender and racial characteristics of the children.

When Buck's neighbors voiced concerns over the dating choices of Welcome House's mixed-race children, they were articulating long established fears of miscegenation as race suicide.[49] Buck observed these fears in one Junior League volunteer who panicked when her friends asked how she would feel if one of her children dated or married one of the Welcome House children. According to Buck, the woman told her she answered by explaining, "because I give money to help and because the children come and play with mine doesn't mean they have to marry them."[50] But she later discontinued her support of Welcome House. The prospect that a Welcome House child might date or marry with one of Doylestown's white children posed a threat to enduring beliefs that interracial intimacy led to genetically inferior offspring. Buck responded to these fears by proclaiming that "there are many Americans who would yield democracy itself rather than accept the scientifically proved fact that color does not decide the place of a human being in life."[51] Buck was referring to genetic research that, as early as the 1920s, had invalidated the scientific basis for these beliefs. But, as her neighbors' comments demonstrated, ideas about race as a marker and determining factor of a person's inferiority or superiority still held significant cultural influence throughout the twentieth century.[52]

The American eugenics movement of the early twentieth century encouraged the belief that genetically inferior people threatened society. Eugenicists believed that saving the nation from the so-called unfit required aggressive reproductive control. American eugenicists assumed that the unfit passed on their undesirable traits to their children. Thus, they promoted reproduction among white, middle-class couples positive eugenics—and discouraged reproduction in numerous communities defined as unfit—negative eugenics. Eugenicists counted immigrants, the impoverished, the mentally and physically disabled, and people of color among the unfit. Early twentieth-century eugenicists targeted several communities for negative eugenic interventions like sterilization without a specific focus on race, but they were still concerned that race mixing led to race suicide. Many policymakers who believed in eugenics were eager to save America from the degradation of race mixing, which was at odds with Buck's belief that race mixing was an undeniable characteristic of the nation.[53] Buck wrote, "the people of the United States . . . are certainly a mixed people, which may account for their energy and achievements."[54] Buck designed these statements to reverse ideas developed during the heyday of the American eugenics movement of the early twentieth century. Following World War II, eugenicists, efforts to *save* the white race through negative eugenics lost cultural and scientific support but not social currency.

Eugenics played a significant role in the legal and social policies that stigmatized mixed-race children and informed the adoption policies Buck found objectionable. Beginning in the 1920s, child welfare professionals had worked with doctors and psychologists to develop evaluative measures that would reduce certain risks in adoption. Many of these professionals believed that a child's nature and abilities were biologically determined. As mentioned in chapter 2, child welfare professionals also thought that by increasing standards and using tools to ascertain a child's mental and developmental status, including IQ tests, they could appropriately match children with families of similar status and aptitude. Child welfare professionals also judged the fitness of prospective parents based on interviews and home studies.[55] Although these measures often said more about prospective parents' social class and access to education than their intellectual abilities, social workers and adoption agencies used these practices, believing they were beneficial for both adoptive parents and children. These practices would become less influential in the 1950s and 1960s as popular and professional ideas about "children's hereditary taint [had] faded" for white children in the child welfare system.[56] But this transition was not as quick to take hold in the cases of nonwhite or mixed-race children in need of adoption.

Thus, Buck used a narrative reconfiguration of the Welcome House children's inherited characteristics to counter charges that they were inferior. Specifically, Buck relied on the language of hybrid superiority that originated in botanical science to reverse negative assessments of mixed-race children's attributes. When she compared mixed-race children to hybrid strains of corn and roses that possessed "rare qualities, so rare that the waste [of these children] was intolerable;' she echoed the ideas of geneticist George Snell.[57] Snell's survey of decades of research led him to conclude that hybridity was a vital element in the formation of civilized societies. He believed this pattern occurred because "race crossing . . . produces individuals of exceptional vitality and vigor:'[58] Buck was familiar with Snell's work and in one instance she paraphrased him, saying, "a hybrid people has always a higher intelligence and a beauty greater than is possessed by the so-called 'pure' races:'[59] Proponents of hybridity saw potential in selective race mixing that could lead to stronger traits among the hybrid generations. Though these scientists conducted most studies of hybridity on plants, some were willing to extrapolate their findings onto humans. Luther Burbank was one of the earliest horticulturalists to suggest that race mixing was positive for the US population. He aptly named his treatise on this subject *The Training of the Human Plant*. Anthropologist Ashley Montagu's writings on hybridity also influenced Buck's thinking. Peter Conn notes that Buck referenced Montagu's book, *Man's Most Dangerous Myth: The Fallacy of Race*, to support her claims that hybrids were superior.[60] The research and theories that challenged scientific racism became the basis of Buck's effort to undermine the suggestion that race mixing diluted positive characteristics from either side of a child's ancestry.

In addition to disputing adoption standards informed by eugenics, Buck publicized her objections to the ways adoption agencies adhered to a form of the one-drop rule that fixed mixed-race children's membership in communities of color. Based on the principle of race matching, agencies considered same-race adoptions healthiest for children, but mixed-race children confounded the logic behind this idea. As discussed in chapter 3, since these children did not fit one racial category, social workers attempted to match children with any known or visible nonwhite ancestry with families that represented that racial or ethnic identity. Buck challenged this practice of hypodescent by suggesting that love and not race should influence placement decisions. She rejected the justification for race matching by asking, "did it matter whether there was such matching? Who really matches his parents? The genes that carry the master plan of any human being may be given him by distant, even unknown, ancestors and not by his parents."[61] Buck insisted that love and compatibility mattered most in families. Describing Welcome House's successes with transracial placements she explained, "time and again we have proved that race and religion do not matter. All that matters is the ability to love."[62]

Buck challenged the lingering influences of eugenics and the one drop rule of racial identity, which became the foundation for her sustained critique of what she considered to be racist adoption policies. She hoped that more social workers would be willing to experiment with transracial placements. To foster this idea, she recommended that agencies abandon matching and rely on "criteria . . . from the human sources of experience and common sense to which textbook knowledge is helpful but secondary."[63] In many ways, Buck was reinforcing critiques that African American child welfare professionals with the NUL were making as they developed their Foster Care and Adoption Project discussed in chapter 2. However, instead of working through existing agencies to promote reform, which was the NUL model, Buck made the Welcome House the centerpiece of her reform plan. Buck imagined that Welcome House could provide leadership in this area. Buck's approach to these early transracial adoptions represented a significant departure from the matching standard that she had supported until the late 1940s, when she first began to identify matching as an impediment that kept eligible mixed-race children trapped in institutional settings.[64]

## Notes

36. Alice Hammerstein Mathias, Interview by Nora Stirling.
37. Eva Eshleman, Interview by Nora Stirling, August 27, 1976, Box 10, Folder "Eva S. Eshleman, PSB's French teacher, beginning in 1963; resident of Kutztown, PA," NS Collection.
38. For more on the model minority stereotype, see Hsu, *The Good Immigrants*; J. Kim, *Ends of Empire*; Lee and Zhou, *The Asian American Achievement Paradox*; Park Nelson, *Invisible Asians*; and Takaki, *Strangers from a Different Shore*.
39. Choy, *Global Families*; Pate, *From Orphan to Adoptee*; Oh, *To Save the Children of Korea*; Winslow, *The Best Possible Immigrants*; and Woo, "A New American Comes 'Home'."
40. Buck, "Notes on Welcome House," 34.
41. Pearl S. Buck, "Welcome House," *Reader's Digest*, July 1958, 46.
42. Rochelle Girson, "Welcome House," *Saturday Review*, July 26, 1952, 21.
43. Tent, *Eurasian*, 131.
44. Girson, "Welcome House," 21.
45. Pascoe, *What Comes Naturally*, 2–14; and Black, *War against the Weak*, 163–165. For more on miscegenation fears, see Kennedy, *Interracial Intimacies*, 18–19; and Spickard, *Mixed Blood*, 254.
46. Buck, "Notes on Welcome House," 37.
47. Viola Yoder, interview by Nora Stirling.
48. Buck, "Notes on Welcome House," 38.
49. Kennedy, *Interracial Intimacies*, 220; Pascoe, *What Comes Naturally*, 2–14; Romano, *Race Mixing*, 6–7; and Spickard, *Mixed Blood*, 254.
50. Buck, "Notes on Welcome House," 37.
51. Buck and Robeson, *American Argument*, 192.
52. For more eugenics, see Barkan, *Retreat of Scientific Racism*; and Alexandra Minna Stern, *Eugenic Nation*.
53. Kline, *Building a Better Race*, 2; 8–10, 20; Stern, *Eugenic Nation*, 4, 16–17, 18, 154; and Black, *War against the Weak*, 5, 23, 31, 378–391.
54. Buck, "Notes on Welcome House," 33.
55. Herman, *Kinship by Design*, 156–172; and Melosh, *Strangers and Kin*, 42–49.
56. Herman, *Kinship by Design*, 144.
57. Buck, "Notes on Welcome House," 35.
58. George D. Snell, "Hybrids and History: The Role of Race and Ethnic Crossing in Individual and National Achievement," *Quarterly Review of Biology* 26, no. 4 (December 1951): 331.
59. Buck, "Notes on Welcome House," 33.
60. Conn, *Pearl S. Buck*, 353. Sociologists also termed this type of selective race mixing constructive "miscegenation," and Teng explains that some theorists believed that only proximate racial groups produced superior offspring. Teng, *Eurasian*, 117–120.
61. Buck, *Children for Adoption*, 85.
62. Ibid., 90.

63. Buck, "Notes on Welcome House," 39.
64. For more on the activities of agencies experimenting with adoptions that placed children of color with white families, see Briggs, *Somebody's Children*, 35–37; and Herman, *Kinship by Design*, 204–215.

## Works Cited


Barkan, Elazar. *Retreat of Scientific Racism: Changing Concepts of Race in Britain and the United States Between the World Wars.* U of Cambridge P, 1992.

Black, Edwin. *War against the Weak: Eugenics and American's Campaign to Create a Master Race.* Four Walls Eight Windows, 2003.

Briggs, Laura. *Somebody's Children: The Politics of Transnational and Transracial Adoption.* Duke UP, 2012.

Buck, Pearl S. *Children for Adoption.* Random House, 1964.

———. "Welcome House." *Reader's Digest*, July 1958, p. 46.

Buck, Pearl S., and Eslanda Goode Robeson. *American Argument.* John Day, 1949.

Choy, Catherine Ceniza. *Global Families: A History of Asian International Adoption in America.* NYUP, 2013.

Conn, Peter. *Pearl S. Buck: A Cultural Biography.* Cambridge UP, 1996.

Eshleman, Eva. Interview by Nora Stirling, August 27, 1976, Box 10, Folder: "Eva S. Eshleman, PSB's French teacher, beginning in 1963; resident of Kutztown, PA," NS collection.

Girson, Rochelle. "Welcome House." *Saturday Review*, 26 July 1952, p. 21.

Herman, Ellen. *Kinship by Design: A History of Adoption in the Modern United States.* U of Chicago P, 2008.

Hsu, Madeline Y. *The Good Immigrants: How the Yellow Peril Became the Model Minority.* Haworth, 2007.

Kennedy, Randall. *Interracial Intimacies: Sex, Marriage, Identity, and Adoption.* Pantheon, 2003.

Kim, Jodi. *Ends of Empire: Asian American Critique and the Cold War.* U of Minnesota P, 2010.

Kline, Wendy. *Building a Better Race: Gender, Sexuality, and Eugenics from the Turn of the Century to the Baby Boom.* U of California P, 2001.

Lee, Jennifer, and Min Zhou. *The Asian American Achievement Paradox.* Russell Sage, 2015.

Mathias, Alice Hammerstein. Interview by Nora Stirling.

Melosh, Barbara. *Strangers and Kin: The American Way of Adoption.* Harvard UP 2002.

Oh, Arissa. *To Save the Children of Korea: The Cold War Origins of International Adoption.* Stanford UP, 2015.

Park Nelson, Kim. *Invisible Asians: Korean American Adoptees, Asian American Experiences, and Racial Exceptionalism.* Rutgers UP, 2016.

Pascoe, Peggy. *What Comes Naturally: Miscegenation Law and the Making of Race in America.* Oxford UP, 2009.

Pate, Soojin. *From Orphan to Adoptee: U. S. Empire and Genealogies of Korean Adoption.* U of Minnesota P, 2014.

Romano, Renee C. *Race Mixing: Black-White Marriage in Postwar America.* Harvard UP, 2003.

Snell, George D. "Hybrids and History: The Role of Race and Ethnic Crossing in Individual and National Achievement." *Quarterly Review of Biology*, vol. 26, no. 4, 1951, pp. 331–347.

Spickard, Paul R. *Mixed Blood: Intermarriage and Ethnic Identity in Twentieth-Century America*. U of Wisconsin P, 1989.

Stern, Alexandra Minna. *Eugenic Nation: Faults and Frontiers of Better Breeding in Modern America*. U of California P, 2002.

Takaki, Ronald. *Strangers from a Different Shore: A History of Asian Americans*. Little, Brown, 1989.

Teng, Emma Jinhaua. *Eurasian: Mixed Identities in the United States, China, and Hong Kong, 1842–1943*. U of California P, 2013.

Winslow, Rachel Rains. *The Best Possible Immigrants: International Adoption and the American Family*. U of Pennsylvania P, 2017.

Woo, Susie. "A New American Comes 'Home'": Race, Nation, and the Immigration of Korean War Adoptees, 'GI Babies,' and Brides." PhD diss., Yale U, 2010.

Yoder, Viola. Interview by Nora Stirling.

# From Oh, Arissa. *To Save the Children of Korea: The Cold War Origins of International Adoption.* Stanford UP, 2015.

A broad array of Americans embraced the adoption of Korean GI babies as a new kind of missionary work. Generally speaking, adoptive families adopted for religious or humanitarian reasons. They were a subset of a second, much larger group: Christian Americanists, as represented by the American mass media and Congress. This second group infused the religiously motivated adoptions with nationalist meaning and celebrated them as an affirmation not only of the adoptive parents' Christian goodness but also of their Americanness. In addition, Christian Americanists used the apparent colorblindness of the Christian adoptive families to support American Cold War claims of racial democracy. Through this interplay of religious and nationalistic concerns, what began as a mainly religious adoption movement became the shared crusade of devout Christians and Christian Americanists alike.

Harry Holt was the figurehead of this Christian Americanist project. In 1955, he brought twelve Korean GI babies to the United States: he and his wife, Bertha, had adopted eight, and the other four went to three other families. The publicity around this undertaking was so great that the Holts were inundated almost immediately with inquiries from Americans who wanted to adopt.[4] Seeing the need of the orphans in Korea and the demand for them in the United States, Harry Holt began shuttling between the two countries, bringing Korean GI babies to parents in the United States while simultaneously leading the fight for adoption-friendly immigration laws. In 1956, the Holts placed 211 orphans and established the Holt Adoption Program (HAP). (That agency, now called Holt International Children's Services, operates in more than a dozen countries and continues to be a leader in intercountry adoptions.) It is important to note that Harry Holt himself was not a Christian Americanist. He saw his work as serving God, and he never articulated a connection between his Christian faith and nationalistic beliefs. Nonetheless, he became emblematic of the Christian Americanist adoption movement through media portrayals that celebrated his good works as a Christian as an affirmation of his Americanness.

DOI: 10.4324/9781003203827-31

Korean adoption arose from a convergence between the Korean government's desire to remove mixed-race children and the American public's demand for these children, but that convergence would not have amounted to anything more without the catalyst of Harry Holt, who provided the channel through which Korean children could emigrate to the United States in great numbers. Holt restructured the rudimentary adoption mechanisms already in place and introduced two crucial innovations that made Korean adoption possible on a large scale: proxy adoption and charter flights. His Christian Americanist allies recast Korean adoption on an imaginative level, as a new kind of missionary work for a new kind of world, and helped expand the notion of the American family to include interracial and international adoption.

The Christian Americanism that powered the early Korean adoption movement was short lived, fading away in the early 1960s. In 1961, largely as a result of Christian Americanist lobbying, Congress made provisions for international adoption a permanent part of US immigration law. With Korean adoption becoming more mainstream, its advocates were no longer outsiders in need of a movement and a language for the movement. At the same time, the racial composition of the children being adopted shifted from mainly mixed race to mainly full Korean, reducing the potency of arguments that Americans were responsible for children fathered by American GIs. . . . Nevertheless, the Christians and Christian Americanists who launched Korean adoption as a systematic practice sparked a revolution on a number of fronts: they opened the floodgates of intercountry adoption, triggered important changes in US immigration laws, changed Americans' ideas about what families looked like and how they should be made, and overturned social work doctrine about race and adoptability.

****

In Christian Americanism, this religiosity intersected with American exceptionalism in two specific areas: in its sense of responsibility and its belief in the importance of families. With regard to the Korean situation, Americans believed they had a three-pronged responsibility: to the world, to Korea, and to the GI babies of Korea. The United States had a general charge to fulfill its new roles as world power, protector of democracy, defender of freedom, and bulwark against communism. These were some of the duties that the powerful publisher Henry Luce had famously outlined almost a decade before the Korean War began in his proclamation of "The American Century."[19] To support their country in these roles, it was important that patriotic American citizens take seriously their moral and civic obligations as leaders of the free world. If they failed to shoulder "the responsibilities of freedom" they would be victims and slaves.[20] As President

Eisenhower asserted, religious faith was essential to American success in this task: "religion nurtures men of faith, men of hope, men of love; such men are needed in the building of a new world reflecting the glory of God."[21] The United States, as the most powerful country on earth and the nation most loved by God, had a special responsibility to build a new, Christian, American world order.

Americans' second responsibility was to South Korea, where war had wreaked such havoc and produced such extraordinary numbers of refugees, orphans, and civilian dead. In the absence of a clear-cut victory against communist North Korea, the United States could salvage an ideological win by caring for Korea's people and helping with reconstruction.[22] The American media was particularly adept at showing that it was Korea's children who were the true victims of communist aggression, the "real" reason their nation was involved in the war on that little-known, faraway peninsula.[23] Their grimy little faces were oddly photogenic, filling article upon article about the Korean War. Such images were often accompanied by detailed descriptions of how orphans lived—where they slept, how they found food to eat and clothes to keep warm. A description of nine-year-old Tae in *Collier's* was typical of the stories that showed how orphans teetered on a razor's edge between life and death:

> During [the nearly three years that he'd been orphaned], the only food Tae had eaten was what he could steal or beg or buy with the few pennies he earned. His only home was the closest shelter he could find—a dry corner in some bombed-out building, a pile of boards in an alley. . . . But then Tae got sick. One of the worst things that can happen to a war orphan is to get sick. When you're sick, you can't work to get food and there's nobody to look after you. You may die for lack of treatment or you may starve to death because you can't help yourself.[24]

Stories in this vein made it clear that Americans could win the ideological battle with North Korea and its allies by helping these orphans. Even before the war had ended, popular magazines like *Life* and *Collier's* carried articles and photographs showcasing how GIs cared for Korean waifs: cuddling them, sewing handkerchiefs and overcoats and dolls for them from rags, feeding them, and distributing Christmas gifts. American military units built or supported orphanages and hospitals and gathered contributions of food, clothing, and money from friends and family back home. The story about the sick orphan Tae was representative not only because it described a Korean orphan's miserable life, but also because it included the stock character of a good Samaritan American GI: Tae met an American sergeant, who took him to a hospital for treatment. As in many other similar stories, it was the American who brought a ray of happiness and hope to a wretched orphan's life.

The third form of American responsibility—responsibility for children fathered by US troops—was the most specific and the most potent. Extensive media coverage alerted Americans to the ostracism and persecution that GI babies suffered, and although condemnation of the men who fathered the children was limited in the mainstream press, Americans betrayed a sterner attitude in their private correspondence. Pressing for the legislation that would allow them to adopt, prospective parents expressed a profound sense of national and personal responsibility towards the GI babies. "There is not only the moral obligation we Americans feel toward all uncared for children, but the more definite obligation, knowing our Armed Forces were responsible for these little Korean outcasts," wrote one couple. Another couple expressed a more prescriptive, though equally widespread, sentiment: "We feel it to be the duty of the United States Government to take over the care of these unfortunate children, for the United States Government sent the fathers of these children into the foreign countries and is therefore responsible for their conduct." A letter sent to Oregon Senator Wayne Morse and signed by more than thirty people stated: "We feel that since so many American boys have proved themselves delinquent fathers, that other American families who feel so inclined should be given the opportunity of taking these children who so badly need a home." These writers believed that private American citizens like them could act as proxies for their government and demonstrate their patriotism by "taking over the care" of these orphans themselves.[25]

The imperatives of anticommunism demanded that the country address the problem of the mixed-race children that American GIs had left behind all throughout Asia, for it would hardly do for the leader of the free world "to have half-American children running about as beggars and potential criminals in the streets of Asian cities." In announcing her own intention to adopt a Japanese-black GI baby in 1958, the novelist Pearl S. Buck reminded readers, "It is important from a political as well as a humanitarian view, to concern ourselves with the futures of those who will remain in Asia." Given the difficulty they would face in obtaining education and jobs, she warned, these children would be "the natural dissidents in coming years and prey to the worst Communist propaganda."[26]

## Notes

4. Bertha Holt, *Bring My Sons from Afar* (Eugene, OR: Holt International Children's Services, 1986), 9, 11.
19. Henry R. Luce, "The American Century," *Life*, 17 Feb. 1941, 61–65.
20. Harold Fey, "Will Korea Perish?" *Christian Century*, 16 Jan. 1952, 66; Klein, "Family Ties and Political Obligation," 40.
21. "Testimony of a Devout President," 13.
22. Rusk, "Voice from Korea," 187.

23. In case readers missed this message, editors were conscientious about spelling it out in photo captions that dubbed them "innocent victims of war." William J. Lederer and Nelle Keys Perry, "Operation Kid-Lift," *Ladies' Home Journal*, 12 Dec. 1952, 49.
24. Marvin Koner, "Korea's Children: The Old in Heart," *Collier's*, 25 July 1953, 24–25.
25. "Increase in Number of Visas to Be Issued to Orphans Under the Refugee Relief Act of 1953," *CR*, 84th Cong., 2nd sess., vol. 102 (26 July 1956): 14741–14743; [no first name noted] Adair to Arthur Watkins, 19 Sept. 1953, Box 58, Folder "I&N Act–Adopted Children," RG 46, National Archives, Washington, DC (hereafter "Archives I").
26. "Increase in Number of Visas to Be Issued to Orphans," 14742; Pearl S. Buck, *Children for Adoption* (New York: Random House, 1964), 167; "Author Pearl Buck to Adopt Part-Negro Orphan," *Chicago Defender*, 5 Apr. 1958.

# From Jerng, Mark. *Claiming Others: Transracial Adoption and National Belonging.* U of Minnesota P, 2010.

As adoption becomes a public, state-regulated institution explicitly aimed at family-making in the 1910s and 1920s, it more self-consciously produces the norms by which individual lives are cultivated, shaped, and made into proper persons. The shift toward state and federal involvement in the construction of adoption was in part a reaction to the often unregulated practices by evangelical reformers and religious institutions mentioned earlier. The modern twentieth-century institution of adoption was constructed in the context of Progressive reform, changing conceptions of motherhood and children, and the developing social science with regard to families and children.[18] Social work agencies armed themselves with the expertise of social science on issues of heredity, the impact of the environment, and child care in order to justify their work in deciding which babies fit with which families and in ensuring that the parents were fit and proper.

This social science of constructing "fit and proper" families relied on a tremendous production of knowledge about the mental, emotional, and physical fitness of both prospective adoptive parents and potential adopted children. As Barbara Melosh notes, " 'Fit' was professional shorthand for the goal of matching—through the skilled application of expert knowledge, social workers would design an adoptive family whose members would flourish together."[19] Adoption becomes the site of what Foucault has called "bio-power": "the right to intervene to make live . . . a power that has taken control of . . . life in general," or as Ann Stoler translates, "the right to intervene . . . in the manner of living, in 'how' to live."[20] Social workers self-consciously exercised a tremendous amount of power and knowledge over the manner of living and the raising of children—how to live the proper, normal life. One caseworker calls it "playing God."[21] Sophie van Senden Theis's placement guide, which became a standard for the field after its publication in 1921, calls for a "keen, close, and unprejudiced observation" of an applicant, arguing that it is "more important to know of a woman that she is easy going and indecisive than that she is a careless housekeeper. A child may grow up to be a satisfactory citizen in an untidy household . . . but

DOI: 10.4324/9781003203827-32

he has a poor chance of it if his foster mother changes her mind about what he must or must not do every day or so."[22] The exacting standards held by adoption professionals reaches into the motives and interior selves of both prospective adopters and potential adoptees. A sense of this regulatory power is captured in Irene Josselyn's assessment of what a child-conscious adoptive process should look at as opposed to earlier adoption practices:

> From the standpoint of the child, his needs were considered met, according to the policy of certain adoptive agencies, if the adoptive parents were of the proper religious faith and attended church. The meaning of their religion *in their actual living* was not explored. . . . Children require real parents, not stylized ones. To provide real parents, the adults seeking a child to adopt must be first appraised as real people with a recognition of the probability of their having the psychological needs, potentialities and limitations inherent in human beings. The *total personality* of the adults should be explored, and *only then* the evaluation made as to how that total personality will function in the role of a parent in relationship to a child
>
> (emphasis added).[23]

Not only should the parents' religion be known, but how that religion translates to their conditions of living should be investigated. This process seeks to capture nothing less than a holistic understanding of the adult and their modes and manners of living.

This process of shaping the integrity of children's and parents' relations is never free from anxieties about racial difference, framed as fears of unknown heredity—the baby's unknown "stock" or "background." Workers gathered "every scrap of significant information about his family" in the quest for a complete background of the child.[24] A questionable heredity or strange behavior could render a child "unadoptable."[25] Racism here emerges as a matter of degeneracy derived from discourses of social Darwinism.[26] In "The Illinois Adoption Law and Its Administration" (1928), Elinor Nims bemoans the lack of proper prohibition against transracial adoptions. She writes: "It is rather startling to discover that one judge considered the matter of race as of no account and would not make it a question of investigation."[27] She points to a case in 1924—very similar to that depicted in Chesnutt's novel—in which the adoptive mother, Mrs. Dunn, "returned the child to the hospital saying that her friends thought the baby was of negro blood. The management then got in touch with the mother, who admitted that the father was a colored man. The baby was then placed with Mr. and Mrs. Morton, a colored family."[28] Nims remarks that this case "is a striking illustration of the necessity for a careful inquiry . . . into the social and medical history of the child."[29] Likewise, Melosh notes a 1938 case record in which the "prospective adopters repeatedly raised concerns about 'colored blood.' They told their social worker that they knew of a white adoptive mother whose baby had turned out to have 'definite Negroid characteristics.' "[30] But these examples do not simply exhibit a fear of racial mixing or the need to uphold racial separation. Rather, they express a more generalized anxiety of what is "inside" the child—some latent, prior "trait" that will come out only later. The child becomes subject to competing projections and desires, highlighting processes of racial identification—in both the sense of identifying someone *as* "x" and identifying *with* someone—as an effect of anxieties over transmission.

Adoption practices thus produce the norms for who can relate to whom and for the conditions of individuation by regulating the identifications between parent and child. The policy of matching encapsulates this production of race as a negotiation of projections. It developed as a practice of placing children with parents based on similarities in race, religion, intelligence, personality, temperament, and a host of other factors. The idea behind matching is to construct the adoptive family "as if" it were biological, using likeness to sustain identification and deny difference within the family. As Ellen Herman puts it, "[modern] adoption has relied on the paradoxical theory that differences are managed best by denying their existence."[31] A closer look at practices of matching helps us see how race is articulated not as a social category and static given that is imposed on individuals, but rather produced through the interplay of projections among social workers. Far from denying the existence of racial difference, "matching" reproduced it as a condition of the child's potential individuation.

For example, a glance at a list of traits used as the bases for matching—everything from the supposedly empirical traits such as racial and religious background to less definable traits such as temperament, intelligence, and personality[32]—reveals the immaterial, projective quality of the traits in question. The listing of traits seems to suggest an ideal whereby these empirical and specific traits are supposed to add up to some kind of identification between parent and child. There is an odd tension in this list between the single trait and the long list of traits, begging the question: How many traits are needed to make a match? This process seems to suggest both that the whole (person) is simply the sum of these parts *and* that persons are synecdoches for a single trait. And yet the sheer proliferation of factors only highlights the impossibility that these traits could add up to any one thing. Matching is not a purely empirical process, but rather one that often calls upon narrative imagination in order to fill in the gaps. One social worker, for example, highlights her own narrative expectations in stating that she "believed that . . . applicants were not 'unreasonable or neurotic in requesting a child whose intelligence is in the superior group and whose background does not read like a story of William Faulkner's."[33] The fact that race and religion are singled out as more important than other traits suggests how crucial they have become for linking specific conditions of individuation with norms of familial and individual integrity.

It was often the case that orphaned children's parentages were unknown. Placing such children involved social workers, parents, and children themselves in a drama of locating race through how one relates to another. One case detailed by Barbara Melosh exemplifies how race and religion are not so much perceived as they are projected into a narrative that produces the conditions for proper individuation through a regulation of the parent–child relationship. In deciding on the proper placement for a particular child, a social worker and nurse alternate between speculations about the mother and then about the child:

> Anyone familiar with the Moors might recognize her [the mother] as Moorish . . . but otherwise I suspect that she would pass readily as Caucasian. . . . Both nurse and I feel we would think he [the child] was completely Caucasian if we did not know his mother is a Moor. Knowing this, however, there may be something just a little "different" about his nose and he has an abundance of thick straight black hair which stands out in all directions.[34]

What is most striking about these statements is the continual oscillation between the visible and invisible, the known and the unknown. What is perceived becomes the basis for seeing the child as "Moorish" ("Knowing this, however, there may be something just a little different . . .") at the same time that some "certain" knowledge is the basis for producing more perceptions: "Anyone familiar with the Moors might recognize her as Moorish." In other words, Moorishness is produced as both cause and effect. It functions as the unified background accounting for any and all perceptions with which it can be connected—even one as random as an "abundance of thick straight black hair which stands out in all directions." In the quest to fully know the child's background, whole ancestries and histories are constructed based on an upturned lip or a darker shade, and a fragment of biography or gossip make a feature visible. Racism has become a mode of thought that embodies, as Étienne Balibar puts it, "a very insistent *desire for knowledge*" that is "a way of asking questions about *who* you are in a certain social world."[35]

I have considered how the anxieties of adoption as a form of bio-power and regulation are projected onto the child, thus reproducing racial and religious identification as conditions of individuation. But what are the implications of this process for the object of anxiety—the adoptee's own subjectivity? How do children understand themselves in relation to this projective anxiety and insistent "desire for knowledge"? The anxiety of what is "inside" is shared by both adopter and adopted alike. This aspect of projection as part of the *relationship* between two subjects is illustrated by the example of a child who acts within the other's projection. Berebitsky recounts a 1901 case in which an adopted twelve-year-old child, Allen Rogers, shocks his adoptive parents by immediately telling them that "his mother was dead . . . that he had a colored brother[;] that his mother had this boy by a black man [and] he didn't seem to think there was anything wrong about it."[36] Supposing "everything was spoiled," the adoptive mother, Mrs. Widman, nevertheless "calmed her husband by telling him that 'no doubt Allen has misrepresented his mother I supposed she had a little colored fellow around the house and he thought it was a brother' "; she "admonished her children"—"if we ever heard another word we would punish them severely."[37] Though the boy's statements do not mean that he is black, Mrs. Widman takes this anecdote as if it spoils who he is in relation to her. She reacts to an anxiety about transmission and the fact that there is something prior that might impinge on her capacity to sustain an identification with her adopted child that hinges on race. The repression of any other "word" of the boy's history is the attempt to preserve the mother's identification of the child as something unspoiled, an identification that the child's own projection threatens by reopening the anxiety regarding the ever-present question: "How can we know?"

## Notes

18. Melosh argues for a sharper break between these two practices than I do, stating that "the developing profession of social work helped to displace the moralism of nineteenth-century evangelical reformers." *Strangers and Kin*, 19. As I demonstrate, the problem of individuation in relation to racial and religious markers demonstrates the uneasy coexistence of these two sensibilities.
19. Melosh, *Strangers and Kin*, 51.
20. Michel Foucault, *Society Must Be Defended*, trans. David Macey (New York: Penguin, 2004), 248, 253; Ann Stoler, *Race and the Education of Desire* (Durham, N.C.: Duke University Press, 1995), 83.
21. Quoted in Berebitsky, *Like Our Very Own*, 136.
22. Ibid., 148.
23. Michael Shapiro, ed., *A Study of Adoption Practice* (New York: Child Welfare League of America, 1955), 2: 9–10.
24. Theis quoted in Berebitsky, *Like Our Very Own*, 134.
25. Ibid.
26. Colette Guillaumin emphasizes the place of race within bourgeois projects of normalization. See *Racism, Sexism, Power, and Ideology* (New York: Routledge, 1995).
27. Rothman and Rothman, *The Origins of Adoption*, 84.
28. Ibid., 45–46.
29. Ibid., 46.
30. Melosh, *Strangers and Kin*, 103.
31. Herman, *Kinship by Design*, 57. See also Judith Modell and Naomi Dambacher, "Making a 'Real' Family: Matching and Cultural Biologism in American Adoption," *Adoption Quarterly* 1, no. 2 (1997): 3–33.

32. See Shapiro, ed., *A Study of Adoption Practice*, 1: 84.
33. Quoted in Berebitsky, *Like Our Very Own*, 142.
34. Quoted in Melosh, *Strangers and Kin*, 87.
35. Étienne Balibar, *Masses, Classes, Ideas*, trans. James Swenson (London: Routledge, 1994), 200.
36. Berebitsky, *Like Our Very Own*, 31.
37. Ibid.

# From Patton, Sandra. *Birthmarks: Transracial Adoption in Contemporary America*. NYUP, 2000.

As public discourse about transracial adoption emerged in 1993 and 1994 following the introduction of the first of several legislative proposals, a wave of television talk shows, made-for-television movies, and cinematic films began appearing in the spring of 1994 about adoption, foster care, and the relative "fitness" or otherwise of poor and middle-class mothers. However, *Losing Isaiah* was the only feature film of which I am aware specifically concerned with transracial adoption. Legislative agendas do not exist in isolation from popular culture and public opinion. As Graeme Turner explains, "What is clear is that the world 'comes to us' in the shape of stories" (Turner 1988:68). Public policy agendas draw on broader social stories about race and identity, gender and family, class and work, that are widely available in popular culture. It is through stories that political issues such as transracial adoption are given meaning for a broad segment of the public.

In popular contemporary narratives surrounding the issues of transracial adoption and welfare reform, Black women are represented as drug addicted and poor, and thus "fit" as breeders but "unfit" as mothers. Black children are shown as fragile, frail, drug addicted, unwanted, and indeed disposable. In stories like *Losing Isaiah*, Black children are uncared-for and unwanted by their Black families, and thus must be saved by those fit to save, and redeem these lost children—White women. The broader sociopolitical message is that Black families have been destroyed by the "culture of poverty" and their innocent children must be saved from the same fate. Salvation and redemption come in the form of White nuclear families, possessors of "family values."

When the film was released, the Personal Responsibility Act, part of the new Republican congressional majority's *Contract with America*, had only recently been introduced in January 1995. This original version of the bill was particularly concerned with reducing "illegitimacy," and as a means to that end, legislated the removal of all restrictions on transracial placements, prohibiting the consideration of race in placing a child for adoption. *Losing Isaiah* was certainly topical. Indeed, it went into production in 1993,

DOI: 10.4324/9781003203827-33

during the public debate over the Multiethnic Placement Act. The film was previewed for selected groups of transracial adoptees and parents, various opinion makers, social workers, and civil rights groups across the country along with the usual screenings to more general audiences. The *Los Angeles Times* reported, "In Washington, where a bill has been introduced in Congress that would make it illegal to consider race when placing children with prospective families, politicians also were invited to see *Losing Isaiah*." (Welkos 1995:Fl). A number of social workers and agency directors I interviewed reported being invited to openings in their locales.

"Illegitimacy" is consistently cited, by conservatives and centrists alike, as the primary cause for social chaos and decline, evidenced by crime, poverty, gang violence, and drug abuse, and usually represented as a primarily Black problem that has begun to spread to White families. The fact that politicians presented *transracial* adoption as a means of reducing "illegitimacy" reveals their concern with the regulation of Black women's reproductive behavior. Public discourse has been saturated with rhetoric about "family breakdown" as the cause for contemporary social ills. At the heart of this political debate is the fiercely held belief that this supposed "breakdown of the family" fails American society through a failure of *socialization*. In the most conservative version of this story, the inability of unwed mothers to properly "civilize" their "illegitimate" children threatens the demise of a free society not only by creating of a permanent "underclass," but also by failing to socialize "productive citizens" capable of ensuring U.S. competitiveness in the global market economy. Indeed, the argument posits a crisis in American democracy and locates its source in the bodies of young, poor, and primarily Black women and their children—the future citizens of this capitalist democracy.

These concerns are played out in public policy dialogues at the intersection of transracial adoption and welfare reform. Social policies regulating adoption have been discussed as a concrete means of engineering and enforcing the literal social construction of "legitimate" families and identities. The issues raised in this public discourse show how profoundly social policy shapes the identities and everyday lives of people living in the United States. Public policy is at the matrix of culture, knowledge, and power. It shapes who we become and how we live our lives.

****

Political narratives that offer explanations for social issues do not exist in isolation from other forms of public discourse. Scholars in a number of fields—perhaps most notably cultural studies and critical race theory—have applied a narrative analysis to legal and/or legislative texts as well as "fictional" stories in popular film and television.[1] Legal scholar and literary critic Laura Hanft Korobkin explains the interplay of "truth"—claiming texts and "fabricated" stories in considering legal discourse: "Coherent and effective narratives of past events will always resonate intertextually with other narratives, factual and fictional, about similar events. The circulation of influence from literature to life and back again simply brings out the narrative logic that underlies the litigative process; it does not violate it" (Korobkin 1996:232).

This understanding allows for an approach to the politics of narratives and the narratives of politics that focuses on questions of ideology, power, and representation. A common analytical tool in much of this work is the concept of *genealogical* analysis. In essence we must ask: What is the social function of a particular racial representation? What does this representation of race signify beyond the particular meanings conveyed within the given text? And, of course, we must ask: Why has this narrative appeared here and now? Cultural studies scholar Hazel Carby suggests that: "These narrative genealogies, in their production of this symbolic power, have significant political resonance when they are produced in response to a perceived crisis in the formation of a society. The process of inscribing national issues on black bodies accomplishes the ideological work that is necessary for the everyday maintenance of systems of racial injustice and inequality" (Carby 1993:236). Thus, Carby argues that popular narratives, in their allegorical power to explain sociopolitical "truths," are ideological justifications for oppression and inequality. This framework is useful in considering social narratives of adoption and welfare reform.

****

The contemporary public narrative emerged through news coverage, editorials, television talk shows and newsmagazines, fictional television dramas, cinematic films, and political rhetoric. While individual accounts varied, a generally coherent story emerged as the dominant or preferred view of transracial adoption as a social issue.[2] A range of both complementary and conflicting "facts" were presented. Some versions included critical perspectives as well as supportive views, while others insisted on the simplicity of the solution to the perceived crisis in child welfare. As the work of cultural studies scholars has demonstrated, the meanings of media texts are not inherent. Rather, they emerge through viewers' individual and collective readings. Fictional and nonfictional representations of the issue of transracial adoption are sites of struggle over the social and political meanings of race and identity, gender and family, individuals and the role of the state.

Media texts offer both the dominant readings of these issues as well as oppositional readings. Cultural studies scholar Herman Gray argues: "Because of this constantly shifting terrain of meaning and struggle, the representations of race and racial interaction in fictional and nonfictional television reveal both the elements of the dominant racial ideology as well as the limits to that ideology" (Gray 1995:431). Thus, I consider the representations of transracial adoption in public discourse—in both nonfictional and fictional texts—as a field of available readings. There are openings for resistant interpretations within any ideological narrative, but the possibilities for such opposition are circumscribed by the boundaries and logic of the story as well as the tenor and history of the power relations involved.

The dominant narrative that emerged in public discourse in roughly the first half of the 1990s begins with the assertion that the number of Black children in foster care increased dramatically in the past decade, and that race is *the* factor keeping Black children in foster care. The narrator typically bemoans the inadequate numbers of Black families able to adopt, but cites an increasing demand for "adoptable" children among Whites. The narrative continues with the information that there are plenty of White families willing to adopt Black children. People in favor of transracial adoption say the solution is simple: let White families adopt African American children. They argue that the only barriers to the implementation of this simple solution are (what they call) "racist" racial matching policies.

In a letter to the *New York Times* Elizabeth Bartholet, a law professor who has been particularly vocal in arguments against racial matching, explicated this aspect of the narrative:

> It is true that this legislation (the Multiethnic Placement Act) was originally developed in recognition of the fact that child welfare workers throughout the country are holding children of color in foster and institutional care for years at a time rather than placing them in permanent adoptive homes, solely because of their reluctance to place children transracially.
>
> (Bartholet 1993c:A24)

The contemporary public dialogue has been dominated by arguments against racial matching policies and characterizations of the National Association of Black Social Workers as the "new racists." In a *Washington Post* editorial, Ellen Goodman explained: "What keeps many children and parents apart is not the old-fangled segregation created by whites who oppose racial mixing. It's the new-fangled segregation now supported by a small but powerful group of black Americans who support 'racial matching"'(Goodman 1993:Editorial page).

The story continues with the argument that racial matching policies and practices keep African American children waiting in long-term "foster limbo" while social workers search for Black parents. This is followed by an argument in favor of transracial adoption, supported by reference to the "empirical evidence" demonstrating how well-adjusted transracial adoptees are. In a September 5, 1995 U.S. Senate discussion of the adoption legislation originally part of the welfare reform bill, Senator McCain cited the "sound research" conducted by Simon and Altstein, which concluded that "interracial adoptions do not hurt the children or deprive them of their culture." Senator McCain argued that: "By incorporating strong and reasonable antidiscrimination provisions in the Conference Report, we will help to remedy the national problem of children being held in foster care because the color of their skin does not match that of the individuals who wish to adopt them" (U.S. Senate 1995).

This narrative, while not immune to public corrections and critiques, won out as "truth" in the policy battle. This view of transracial adoption drew momentum from a number of sensationalized court battles in which White foster parents fought to adopt their Black foster children against the wishes of social service agencies; several such cases were cited in political dialogues. One of the major forces behind the crafting of this social narrative was Harvard lawyer and adoptive parent Elizabeth Bartholet. She has published widely and has been actively engaged in these legislative battles. Her 1991 and 1992 articles, "Where Do Black Children Belong?" appeared early on in the renaissance of this issue, and were successful in shaping the dominant narrative; all the basic elements of the argument were present in Bartholet's published work.[3] Along with a group of influential lawyers, she forcefully lobbied for legislation prohibiting any attention to race in the placement of a child for adoption.

The critiques and cautions about the cultural identities of Black children adopted into White families are dismissed by assertions that the "empirical evidence" of academic research demonstrates that transracial adoptees grow up well-adjusted. The "empirical evidence" directly cited by most proponents of this view is one longitudinal study conducted by Simon and Altstein. There are a number of problems with this study, chief among them the fact that the authors dismiss the concerns of the National Association of Black Social Workers as "political" in relation to their own "scientific"—and by implication apolitical—research. This dismissal correlates with a research agenda that "measures adjustment" but does not consider how transracial adoptees construct and define a sense of racial identity.[4] It is interesting that this particular study is used in the public discourse to *legitimate* the dominant public narrative advocating the promotion of "color-blind adoptions." The research was positioned and discussed as "apolitical" because it was "scientific." Yet as cultural studies scholarship of the past few decades has demonstrated, the results of science and social science research are not unproblematically "objective" and removed from power dynamics. As Mark Poster explains, "Far from neutral statements of truth, the discourses of science emerge fully implicated in practices of domination" (Poster 1993:64). This is evident in the social debate over transracial adoption.

The "scientific" research conducted by Simon and Altstein entered the political discourse through a number of channels. The final book in their study, released in 1994, stated its position in its title, *The Case for Transracial Adoption*. The authors' public comments and political actions were used in public policy dialogues as *evidence* in favor of transracial adoptions. During the early stages of congressional consideration of the Multiethnic Placement Act, which was designed to make transracial placements easier, Howard Altstein submitted a statement to sponsoring Senator Howard Metzenbaum's office in support of the bill (Altstein 1993). While Altstein sought to influence Congress, Rita Simon promoted the bill along with their new book in both scholarly and popular publications.[5] Their research was credited in the *Chronicle of Higher Education* with helping to influence the Texas legislature pass a law designed to promote transracial adoptions (Wheeler 1993).

Elizabeth Bartholet, who became one of the most vociferous opponents of racial matching after adopting two children from Peru, has relied on Simon and Altstein's work to argue for the removal of all restrictions to transracial placements. She has submitted letters to Congress, published op-ed pieces, written articles in law reviews, interdisciplinary journals, and scholarly anthologies, and published *Family Bonds: Adoption and the Politics of Parenting*, a book targeted at a general audience (Bartholet 1993a). In all her publications she draws on Simon and Altstein's longitudinal study to bolster her argument that racial matching discriminates against Black children in foster care and White parents seeking to adopt. This argument promotes "color-blind"—transracial—adoptions as the solution to largescale problems in the U.S. child welfare system. Bartholet and others suggest that White families who adopt Black and mixed-race children will solve the problems of overpopulation in the foster care system and the disproportionate representation of racial-ethnic minorities in that population. However, this argument obscures the question of why so many African American and multiracial children are channeled into the foster care system in the first place. It promotes a narrative of Black family pathology and White "family values." It obscures a systemic analysis of poverty, and of racial and gender inequality in the labor market. It promotes an *individual* solution to a *systemic* social problem.

Several racial messages emerge from this argument. Read in a social context that conflates race and class, it tells us that the "culture of poverty" has so devastated "the Black family" that African Americans cannot take care of their own children. This is ultimately a *salvation narrative*, in which White families, bearing the torch of "family values" in popular representations, are the only families—or mothers—who can *save* Black children. Yet we are told time and again that these altruistic efforts are hindered by "racist" Black social workers who value a political cause over the "best interests" of children.

If we unquestionably accept this view of transracial adoption, the logical policy initiative would be one that encourages the adoption of Black children into White families. Yet this perspective must be examined more closely in light of the political stakes driving much of the discussion, and the racial context in which these views are expressed. Legislative pressure to disregard racial matching in adoptive placements is exerted most fiercely by two primary constituencies: Whites arguing for the "right" to adopt any child they desire, and conservative policy pundits whose primary interest is, I argue, a sort of *cultural eugenics* geared toward both the regulation of poor women's reproductive capacities and the socialization of their children into "productive citizens." This by no means describes all White families hoping to adopt Black children or all the political actors involved in these debates. There are certainly participants in this dialogue who are sincere in their concern for children in foster care.

* * * *

Yet this view of the crisis has taken shape within an already existing movement primarily set in motion by legislators and prospective White adoptive and foster parents concerned with "reverse discrimination" in the adoption system. The parallels in the language of the 1996 adoption legislation with subsequent moves against supposed "racial preferences" in affirmative action are striking. The concern with "reverse discrimination" impinging on the "rights" of White families to adopt a child of color is evident in the range of sanctions the policy imposes and allows for. The federal policy

> provides that neither the State nor any other entity in the State that receives funds from the Federal Government and is involved in adoption or foster care placements may deny to any person the opportunity to become an adoptive or a foster parent, on the basis of the race, color, or national origin of the person, or of the child, involved; or delay or deny the placement of a child for adoption or into foster care, on the basis of the race, color, or national origin of the adoptive or foster parent, or the child, involved.
> (United States Congress 1996: Public Law 104–188, sec. 1808)

The law empowers individuals aggrieved by such violations to bring legal action against the state or other violating entity in any U.S. district court. States who violate this law once will receive a 2 percent deduction in state aid for that quarter, 3 percent for the second violation, and 5 percent for subsequent violations; deductions will be made each quarter until the violation is corrected. Private agencies found in violation will remit all funds received from the state.

We must read this institutionalization of a "color-blind" child welfare system in the context of contemporary racial politics. This controversial issue has emerged at a time when affirmative action is under attack as "reverse racism," the Supreme Court has issued a number of landmark rulings supporting this popular view as well as a "color-blind" legislative system in the

United States, the passage of the California Civil Rights Initiative in 1996 has legislated the dismantling of affirmative action in that state, and racist hate groups and armed militias are on the rise.

The ideological narrative of race and class in the United States posits that racial inequality existed in the past but was eradicated by the civil rights movement. This argument supports one of the central ideologies of this capitalist society, namely, that everyone has an equal chance in the economic marketplace, and that, lack of success is therefore due to individual failure rather than systemic inequality. In discussing the social and legislative gains of the civil rights movement, Howard Winant argues that:

> despite these tremendous accomplishments, patterns of institutional discrimination proved to be quite obstinate, and the precise meaning of race, in politics and law as well as in everyday life, remained undefined. The ambiguity of race in the post-civil rights period has now reached the point where any hint of *race consciousness* is viewed suspiciously as an expression of *racism*.
>
> (emphasis in original) (Winant 1994:67)

Those for whom "color blindness" is a goal may perceive attention to racial survival skills and the African American cultural identities of transracial adoptees as racist separatism. Their assumption—or at least desire—is that race does not matter and should not be highlighted; their primary explanatory category for attention to race is racism. Questions of racial identity and survival skills do not fit neatly into their racial worldview. Additionally, calls for the creation of a Black cultural identity by transracial adoptees are further devalued by the "culture of poverty" thesis that has been widely accepted by both centrists and conservatives. In a context in which U.S. poverty is largely represented as Black, "Black culture" merges with a "culture of poverty" in the popular imagination. The "culture of poverty" explanation has had a profound influence on public policy discussions in the second half of the twentieth century and has been one of the central explanatory systems drawn on in the contemporary discourse about adoption and the social welfare system. Anthropologist Oscar Lewis coined the term in his 1959 study of Mexican families, in which he argued that people living in conditions of poverty develop a culture or way of life in response to their exclusion from mainstream society. Social commentators have extrapolated Lewis's concept to explain the causes and perpetuation of poverty in general. This generic "culture" is generally said to be characterized by female-headed households, laziness, lack of motivation, lack of a work ethic, and an orientation toward the present. Sociologist Stephen Steinberg discusses Lewis's explanation for intergenerational poverty as follows:

> Once a culture of poverty is formed, he argues, it assumes a "life of its own" and is passed on from parents to children through ordinary

> channels of culture transmission. As Lewis writes: "By the time slum children are age six or seven, they have usually absorbed the basic values and attitudes of their subculture. Thereafter they are psychologically unready to take full advantage of changing conditions or improved opportunities that may develop in their lifetime" (Lewis 1966:5). The adaptations of one generation thus become the inherited culture of the next, creating a self-perpetuating cycle of poverty.
>
> (Steinberg 1989:107)

There are three particularly salient issues here. First, this formulation, as co-opted from Lewis's study, obscures the systemic causes of poverty and inequality by essentially blaming poor families for causing their own poverty through a lack of morals or good values. In the contemporary public discourse regarding family and poverty, middle-class families are cast as the indisputable possessors of good "family values," and their location in the middle class is assumed to be a result of these values. Second, this explanation suggests that public policies designed to eradicate poverty and inequality in the labor market are futile; if such a culture takes on "a life of its own" it is unlikely to be displaced by social policies. Finally, and perhaps most significant in relation to questions of adoption and race, this culture is sustained and reproduced through familial channels of socialization, leading to a "self-perpetuating cycle of poverty."

The politics of family, race, and poverty are complex issues. The dominant policy argument regarding transracial adoption asserts that the "reverse racism" of Black social workers who support and enforce racial matching policies is the only significant barrier keeping Black children from permanently leaving the "limbo" of foster care through adoption. Thus, proponents of this position argue that the solution to the problems of the U.S. foster care system is national legislation abolishing the use of race in the adoptive placement of children. This is a convenient and appealing social narrative. However, despite its attractiveness, the social workers I interviewed believed it will probably do virtually nothing to change the lives of children of color in foster care.

****

In the early years of the twentieth century these social fears led to movements for eugenic sterilization and birth control among poor women and immigrants. In the post-Holocaust and post-civil rights movement era such racist and classist inclinations must adopt a more "race-neutral" veneer. While essentialist racism—the pseudoscientific explanation of the supposed inferiority of "non-White" people—was the "legitimating" knowledge driving the eugenics of the early twentieth century, at the end of that century "cultural determinism" joined biology as the engine of racial oppression. The focus on biological heritability led to efforts to curtail the "excess" fertility of undesirables; in a framework dominated by the "culture of poverty" social engineering was envisioned through adoption. Considered in this light, policies concerning adoption—that is, which men and women the state sanctions as "fit" parents—serve both to "legitimate" children born out of wedlock and to regulate their "proper" socialization into "virtuous" citizens through the construction of "legitimate" two-parent, middle class, heterosexual families.

The construction of "legitimate" nuclear families is discussed as necessary for the good of the nation. Indeed, out-of-wedlock births are represented as a threat to Western civilization. As George Will explains: "Democracy depends on virtues that depend on socialization of children in the matrix of care and resources fostered by marriage" (Will 1993). However, underlying this concern over democratic virtue lurks the more base consideration of the future of U.S. competitiveness in the global market economy. Richard Cohen's editorial makes the connections clear: "About 1.2 million children are being born annually in single-parent homes. Without mature males as role models (not to mention disciplinarians), they are growing up unsocialized—prone to violence, unsuitable for employment and thus without prospects or hope" (Cohen 1993).

The key phrases here are "growing up unsocialized" and "unsuitable for employment." Once again, the work of Charles Murray, along with Richard Herrnstein, makes the connections clear. The central thesis of Herrnstein and Murray's *The Bell Curve: Intelligence and Class Structure in American Life* (1994) is that IQ determines economic and social success, and that the global economy is based on the manipulation of information. Thus, the future economic viability of the United States is dependent on its citizens with high IQs—what the authors of *The Bell Curve* call the "cognitive elite." From their perspective, "productive" citizens are not defined by hard work, but by superior intelligence. Unproblematically accepting the belief that IQ tests accurately and objectively measure intelligence, they argue that African Americans are less intelligent than other racial groups; they state that on average Blacks score fifteen points less than Whites on IQ tests. They use this skewed data to account for racial stratification, arguing that poverty among Blacks is due to genetic inferiority rather than discrimination and oppression.[7] In their circular logic one's socioeconomic location is also evidence of one's intelligence. Not surprisingly, they argue that women with low IQs typically have "illegitimate" children, and of course, given their hereditarian logic those children inherit their mothers' incapacity for mental achievement. "Naturally," they are destined to live on the margins of society, never achieving for themselves, forever draining government resources.

However, Herrnstein and Murray do see one glimmer of hope for these lost children. Because for them intelligence is overwhelmingly shaped by genetics (they concede a small measure of influence to the environment), they believe social programs such as Head Start are doomed to failure. Yet they see one exception, and it is here that we come back to the intersection of socialization, public policy, and adoption. They argue that adoption is the only social intervention radical enough to raise the IQs, and thus the chances for economic success, of poor "illegitimate"children. The slippery quality of their arguments is undeniable here: when the biologically determinist explanation does not suit their argument they shift their emphasis to the cultural. The added bonus, they explain, is that "In terms of government budgets, adoption is cheap; the new parents bear all the costs of twenty-four-hour-a-day care for eighteen years or so" (Herrnstein and Murray 1994:416). They continue:

> If adoption is one of the only affordable and successful ways known to improve the life chances of disadvantaged children appreciably, why has it been so ignored in congressional debate and presidential proposals? Why do current adoption practices make it so difficult for would-be parents and needy infants to match up? Why are cross-racial adoptions so often restricted or even banned? . . . Anyone seeking an inexpensive way to do some good for an expandable number of the most disadvantaged infants should look at adoption
>
> (1994:416).

In Murray's editorial on welfare reform and adoption he also provided an option for "unadoptable" children: orphanages (Murray 1993).Thus, in this social vision, children whose proper socialization cannot be ensured should be warehoused in public institutions. For those children not placed in adoptive homes Murray argued the government should "spend lavishly on orphanages." *The Bell Curve*, a racist, vitriolic book, was released shortly after Murray had laid out the basic elements of his reactionary social vision for welfare reform in the *Wall Street Journal* and in congressional testimony, and in many ways it can be read as the "scientific evidence" for his theories regarding work, poverty, and family. *The Bell Curve* is, in a sense, the "legitimating" text for Murray's draconian "solutions" to poverty, "illegitimacy" crime and "family breakdown." As Judith Stacey astutely observes social science has supplanted religion as the ultimate source of "truth" in centrist and conservative political discourse on families. However, as countless scholars from the sciences, social science, and humanities have demonstrated, this is by no means a "legitimate" scholarly work. As geneticists Joseph L. Graves and Amanda Johnson make clear:

> If a measurable depression in mean African American performance on specific cognitive tests exists, it is undoubtedly the result of the destructive physical and social environments in which the majority of African Americans have been forced to live in the United States over time. Without the elimination of the toxic conditions to which African Americans

> have been and are exposed, the debate concerning genetic differentials in generalized intelligence is scientifically meaningless.
>
> (Graves and Johnson 1995:290)

In my reading this narrative linking national economic strength, citizenship, intelligence, socialization, race, and adoption is fundamentally about what should be done with the people this information-based capitalist economy has no use for—the supposedly unintelligent masses who have become surplus labor. We continually return to the question of *socialization*. The options presented by Murray and others for the children the state removes from "unfit" unwed mothers—those unable to survive in this economy without AFDC—involve socialization and warehousing. Surplus children will be housed in orphanages or group homes, while residual adult labor will be channeled into prisons. The children placed for adoption will be raised by predominantly White, middle-class, heterosexual married couples in accordance with the "family values" of "legitimate," "productive" citizenship.

## Notes

1. See, for example, Williams (1991); Morrison (1992); Carby (1993); Gooding-Williams (1993); Delgado (1995); Morrison and Lacour (1997); Wing (1997).
2. In this section I draw on a wide range of public texts to present the dominant narrative that emerged, including Tisdale (1991); Bartholet (1991, 1992a, 1992b, 1993a, 1993b, 1993c); Kennedy (1993, 1994): Simon, Altstein, and Melli (1994); Weiss (1994); Hunt (1995); Fagan and Fitzgerald (1995).
3. See Bartholet (1991) for the version of this article that contains citations.
4. The major studies of transracially adopted individuals and their families do not address how race is defined; rather, the disciplinary and methodological boundaries o the studies rely on positivistic assumptions that translate into research practices that approach race as a "natural" fact of identity. Adoptees are unproblematically considered to "be" Black or White. Thus, rather than being seen as an "objective" framework for gathering "facts,: the assumptions of the positivisms mystify the power relations through which hegemonic definitions of race are constructed and maintained. The "scientific" methodology employed by Simon and Altstein encodes racial categories in static and immutable ways. Linguistically, race is "assigned an 'object' nature" (Van Dijk 1987: 33), bearing out Omi and Winant's assertion: "Although abstractly acknowledged to be a socio-historical construct, race in practice is often treated as an objective fact: one simply is one's race; in the contemporary U.S., if we discard euphemisms, we have five color-based racial categories: black, white, brown, yellow, or red" (Omi and Winant 1993: 10).
5. See Jeffrey (1994); Simon (1993).

****

7. For critiques of this work, see Fraser (1995); Graves and Johnson (1995); Jacoby and Glauberman (1995); Kincheloe, Steinberg, and Greeson (1996).

## Works Cited


Altstein, Howard. "Transracial Adoption: A Demonstrated Successful Alternative to Non-Permanent Options." Statement submitted to Senator Howard Metzenbaum in support of the Multiethnic Placement Act, 26 July 1993.

Bartholet, Elizabeth. "Against Racial Matching." *Reconstruction*, vol. 1, no. 4, 1992, pp. 44–55. [1992a]

———. *Family Bonds: Adoption and the Politics of Parenting*. Houghton Mifflin, 1993. [1993a]

———. "Legislating Race Separatism." *Chicago Tribune*, 5 Nov. 1993, Editorial Section. [1993b]

———. Letter to the editor. *New York Times*, 8 Dec. 1993, p. A24. [1993c]

———. "Where do Black Children Belong? The Politics of Race Matching in Adoption." *Reconstruction*, vol. 1, no 4, 1992, pp. 22–43. [1992b]

———. "Where do Black Children Belong?" *University of Pennsylvania Law Review*, vol. 139, 1991, pp. 1163–1256.

Carby, Hazel. "Encoding White Resentment: Grand Canyon—A Narrative for our Times." *Race, Identity and Representation in Education*, edited by Cameron McCarthy and Warren Critchlow, Routledge, 1993, pp. 236–247.

Cohen, Richard. "Dealing with Illegitimacy." *Washington Post*, 23 Nov. 1993, Editorial page.

Delgado, Richard. *Critical Race Theory: The Cutting Edge*. Temple UP, 1995.

Fagan, Patrick F., and William H. G. Fitzgerald. "Why Serious Welfare Reform Must Include Serious Adoption Reform." *Heritage Foundation Reports*, no. 1045, 27 July 1995, pp. 1–28.

Fraser, Steven, editor. *The Bell Curve Wars: Race, Intelligence, and the Future of America*. Basic, 1995.

Gooding-Williams, Robert. "Look a Negro!" *Reading Rodney King/Reading Urban Uprising*, edited by Robert Gooding-Williams, Routledge, 1993.

Goodman, Ellen. "Adoption—The New Racism." *Washington Post*, 11 Dec. 1993, Editorial page.

Graves, Joseph L., and Amanda Johnson. "The Pseudoscience of Psychometry and *The Bell Curve*." *Journal of Negro Education*, vol. 64, no. 3, 1995, pp. 277–29.

Gray, Herman. "Television, Black Americans, and the American Dream." *Gender, Class, and Race in Media: A Text Reader*, edited by Gail Dines and Jean M. Humez, Sage, 1995, pp. 376–386.

Herrnstein, Richard, and Charles Murray. *The Bell Curve: Intelligence and Class Structure in American Life*, Free, 1994.

Hunt, Albert R. "The Republicans Seize the High Ground on Transracial Adoption." *Wall Street Journal*, 9 Mar. 1995, p. A19.

Jacoby, Russell, and Naomi Glauberman, editors. *The Bell Curve Debate: History, Documents, Opinions*. Random House, 1995

Jeffrey, Clara. "A Question of Color." *Washington City Paper*, 28 Jan.-3 Feb. 1994, p. 21.

Kennedy, Randall. "Kids Need Parents—Of Any Race." *Wall Street Journal*, 9 Nov. 1993, Editorial page.

———. "Orphans of Separatism: The Painful Politics of Transracial Adoption." *American Prospect*, vol. 17, 1994, pp. 38–45.

Kincheloe, Joe L., et al., editors. *Measured Lies: The Bell Curve Examined.* St. Martin's, 1996.

Korobkin, Laura Hanft. "Narrative Battles in the Courtroom." *Fieldwork: Sites in Literary and Cultural Studies*, edited by Marjorie Garber, et al., Routledge, 1996.

Morrison, Toni. *Racing Justice, Engendering Power: Essays on Anita Hill, Clarence Thomas, and the Construction of Social Reality.* Pantheon, 1992.

Morrison, Toni, and Claudia Brodsky Lacour. *The Birth of a Nation 'hood: Gaze, Script, and Spectacle in the O. J. Simpson Case*, Pantheon, 1997.

Omi, Michael, and Howard Winant. "On the Theoretical Status of the Concept of Race." *Race, Identity and Representation in Education*, edited by Cameron McCarthy and Warren Critchlow, Routledge, 1993, pp. 3–10.

Poster, Mark. "Foucault and the Problem of Self-Constitution." *Foucault and the Critique of Institutions*, edited by John Caputo and Mark Yount, Pennsylvania State UP, 1993, pp. 53–69.

Simon, Rita. "Transracial Adoption: Highlights of a Twenty-Year Study." *Reconstruction*, vol. 2, no. 2, 1993, pp. 130–131.

Simon, Rita, et al. *The Case for Transracial Adoption.* American UP, 1994.

Stacey, Judith. *In the Name of the Family: Rethinking Family Values in the Postmodern Age.* Beacon, 1994.

Steinberg, Stephen. *The Ethnic Myth: Race, Ethnicity, and Class in America.* 2nd edition. Beacon, 1989.

Tisdale, Sallie. "Adoption Across Racial Lines: Is it Bad for Kids?" *Vogue*, Dec. 1991, pp. 251.

Turner, Graeme. *Film as Social Practice.* Routledge, 1988.

United States Congress. Public Law 104–188, "Small Business Job Protection Act of 1996, 1996, sec. 1808.

U.S. Senate. 141 *Congressional Record* S. 104th Congress., 13770, *S137777, 5 Sept. 1995.

Van Dijk, Tuen. *Communicating Racism: Ethnic Prejudice in Thought and Talk.* Sage, 1987.

Weiss, Michael J. "Love Conquers All." *Washingtonian*, vol. 30, no. 1, 1994, pp. 98–107.

Welkos, Robert W. "Marketing the Movie Through a Minefield." *Los Angeles Times*, 17 Mar. 1995, p. F1.

Wheeler, David L. "Black Children, White Parents: The Difficult Issue of Transracial Adoption." *Chronical of Higher Education*, 15 Sept. 1993, pp. A8–10.

Will, George. "Underwriting Family Breakdown." *Washington Post*, 18 Nov. 1993, Editorial page.

Williams, Patricia. *The Alchemy of Race and Rights: Diary of a Law Professor.* Harvard UP, 1991.

Winant, Howard. *Racial Conditions: Politics, Theory, Comparisons.* U of Minnesota P, 1994.

Wing, Adrienne Katherine. *Critical Race Feminism: A Reader.* NYUP, 1997.

# From Glaser, Gabrielle. *American Baby: A Mother, A Child, and the Secret History of Adoption.* Penguin, 2021.

While Margaret and George did not speak openly about their lost baby, others during the politically vibrant 1970s were beginning to challenge adoption's secrecy. Many adopted people and their birth mothers had begun to discuss out loud, in public, the issue of closed files and adoptee rights, and to reform the laws that kept mothers and their sons and daughters apart—especially in New York.

The highest-profile group, the Adoptees' Liberty Movement Association, or ALMA, viewed the access to original birth certificates as a fundamental civil and human right. Founded in New York in 1971, ALMA was led by Florence Fisher, an adopted woman who helped develop a registry that both adopted people and birth parents could sign into, indicating they wanted to find their mother or child—regardless of who had signed what papers when. If both parties registered with the organization, ALMA volunteers could help reunite them.

Florence had had a difficult upbringing with her adoptive parents in Brooklyn. Florence was fine-boned and small of stature, and her sturdy Russian Jewish parents, Rose and Harry Ladden, made her sleep in a crib until she was ten years old. She was a willful child, making up for her size with exuberance as a singer and dancer. Her vivacious, talkative nature annoyed her grandmother so much, she referred to her as the *momser*, Yiddish for "bastard." Florence could always sense that she wasn't like her strict, taciturn parents. She didn't look like them, and she didn't talk like them. They didn't like the same things. The differences were impossible to miss—and she began to think they were linked to a big secret.

When she was seven, Rose asked Florence to find her a handkerchief, and Florence dutifully went to her mother's dresser. In a drawer tucked beneath stockings and ironed handkerchiefs, Fisher noticed a formal looking document, a photostat. She withdrew it and read it with puzzlement. It was an adoption certificate that listed her parents' names, and the name of the girl they'd adopted, Anna Fisher.

DOI: 10.4324/9781003203827-34

When Florence returned to the kitchen with her mother's handkerchief, she asked her about it. At first her mother said the paper belonged to someone else in the family, and when Florence questioned her further, her mother slapped her. Later, Rose burned the certificate. But the name on it, Anna Fisher, had been seared into Florence's consciousness.

This was in the middle of the Depression, and formal adoption was still uncommon, so she didn't know what to make of it all. From time to time, Florence wondered about the paper, and if it could explain her parents' abusive, erratic behavior toward her. Her mother vacillated between emotional distance and hysterical possessiveness, threatening suicide whenever Florence made new playmates. "You love your friends more than you love your mother!" she'd scream, locking herself in the bathroom with a razor until Florence promised never to love anyone else. Her father was physically violent, beating the tiny girl with a belt for the slightest infraction. From the time she first found the document, she couldn't stop thinking about its mysterious provenance and dramatic disappearance, especially since her parents had made it clear that the subject was taboo.

At the end of her life, Rose had electroconvulsive therapy, which regulated her moods for the first time. For a brief period before her death in 1950, she and Florence developed a warm relationship. Florence was bereft: at twenty-one, she had finally gained a mother, only to lose her. When relatives began dividing Rose's jewelry, she felt more alone than ever. No one advocated for Florence, her own daughter, in the negotiations, and Florence realized that Rose's kin never accepted her as family. Florence confronted a cousin about the document she'd seen as a child, and she confessed the truth. Florence had been adopted as a baby.

Then a wife and mother, Florence began a twenty-year search to find her true identity, just as the postwar adoptions were in full swing. Public opinion about adoption, and the rights of adopted people to know their origins, had hewed toward complete secrecy. But Florence longed to know—*had* to know—more about her origins. So after Rose's death, she wrote to New York City for a copy of her birth certificate. Not letting on that she knew she was adopted, she used the name Anna Fisher in the correspondence. To her surprise, the ruse worked, and the clerk sent it. It listed her birth date and parents' names, Florence Cohen and Frederick Fisher.

****

Florence published a groundbreaking memoir in 1973, *The Search for Anna Fisher*. It made waves nationwide. Fisher, an attractive woman with bright brown eyes, impeccable style, and a bouffant of red hair, appeared on talk shows throughout the country, in popular magazines, and in major newspapers. She challenged the fundamental orthodoxy of adoption, which held that married parents could offer a better life than unmarried ones, by openly discussing her difficult, abusive childhood. She said repeatedly that adopted people should not be made to feel like "ingrates" for wanting to know their biological identities. Working with lawyers and legislators, she helped draft a bill to open New York's records. She placed ads in New York newspapers about her new organization, listing the group's name and post office box.

She faced the emotionally charged subject head-on: society still saw adoption as a benevolent gesture for which adoptees should feel unquestioning appreciation, she said—and this wasn't always the case. While everyone has a history and kin, Florence said, adoptees are asked to forget about them, living a contrived identity in a contrived reality. Every adoptee, she insisted, has the right to pursue the truth of his own life.

While Fisher received plenty of hate mail, she also helped start a national revolution. Virtually overnight, ALMA mushroomed to thousands of members, attracting mostly female adoptees and birth mothers. The grassroots group compiled a registry of mothers, fathers, sons, and daughter who were looking for one another. Eventually it spread to other states. Members were relentless in lobbying their legislators. In New York, the group filed a class action lawsuit that challenged the constitutionality of the closed adoption records. It argued that knowing one's original identity was a constitutional right.

Fisher was piercingly clear in her aims: Adult adoptees should demand open access to their original birth certificates and to the records of their adoptions. The legal strategy of the case emphasized the rights of adopted people to due process and equal protection under the law, and used moving testimony by adopted people that focused on the legacy of adoption secrecy, the stigma of illegitimacy, and the long-term emotional trauma brought about by the inability of adoptees to discover their original identities. Birth mothers, likewise, spoke about the weight of their loss, and the trauma of not knowing what had happened to their children. The lawsuit was dismissed, but Fisher, other advocates, and their attorney were undeterred.

Among the lawsuit's main opponents were large adoption agencies and many adoptive parents, who claimed that any search for original birth certificates was an invasion of privacy for both adoptees and birth parents. One organization called the Adoptive Parents Committee quickly grew to a thousand members. It claimed that happy adoptees would have their lives disrupted if they were contacted by their birth parents without warning, and that birth parents, likewise, would resent being reminded of their painful pasts.

But Fisher had come to believe that the happiness of an adoptive home was beside the point: adoptees, she argued, deserved to know their origins if they wanted. Objections to her argument were often hostile, and opponents were frequently cruel. Some adoptive parents called Fisher and other ALMA members "neurotic and maladjusted."

Several other voices gave momentum to the emerging adoption-rights movement of the late 1970s as well. New York adoptee Betty Jean Lifton published two memoirs that examined the emotional impact of adoption in *Twice Born: Memoirs of an Adopted Daughter* and *Lost and Found: The Adoption Experience*. In Southern California, a trio of mental health professionals who had worked in the adoption field published a seminal book that also examined the aftereffects of closed birth records. In *The Adoption Triangle*, Arthur Sorosky, a psychiatrist, and Annette Baran and Reuben Pannor, both social workers, advocated for changes in adoption practice. And Jean Paton, a Michigan-born adoptee and social worker who had first written about the adoption experience in the 1950s, argued that the tendency for society to consider adult adoptees as children obscured and diminished their lifelong struggle for identity. Together, adoption rights advocates founded the American Adoption Congress in 1978 as a national organization committed to adoption reform. At its first conference a year later, Paton, reclaiming the word so often levied at her and other adoptees, distributed buttons that read "Bastards Are Beautiful."

Birth mothers also began to demand change. In Massachusetts in the mid-1970s, Lee Campbell, who'd surrendered a son as a young woman, had attended some adoptee-support meetings and believed women like her needed their own platform. In 1976 she founded a group called Concerned United Birthparents. The organization helped popularize the term "birth parents" as a replacement for "natural mother" and "natural father," or the longstanding "real" mother and father. Campbell and other birth mothers appeared on the daytime talk show hosted by Phil Donahue, who occasionally featured tearful reunions between birth mothers and their long-lost sons and daughters. The episodes, listed in newspapers and previewed in television commercials, attracted record audiences. In 1979 journalist Lorraine Dusky wrote the memoir *Birthmark*. It detailed the wrenching surrender of her daughter, conceived during an affair with a married colleague, in 1966, and Dusky's wish to reunite with her. Its publication landed her in newspapers and magazines, and on national television shows. Birth mothers and adoptees championed her, but many adoptive parents attacked her. "You're our worse nightmare," one told her.

It wasn't just the shame that was dissolving. The fortified legal walls shielding secret adoptions were beginning to crumble too.

# From Haslanger, Sally. "Family, Ancestry and Self: What is the Moral Significance of Biological Ties?" *Adoption & Culture*, vol. 2, 2009, pp. 91–122.

## The Goods of Knowing Biological Kin

Velleman points to two different epistemic goods gained by knowing one's biological relations. First, it provides a special kind of self-knowledge based on "intuitive and unanalyzable resemblances". Second, it provides a narrative within which our actions have meaning.

Note that neither knowledge of others who are similar by virtue of biological relatedness, nor biological narratives that draw specifically on such knowledge, are necessary for developing full selfhood. So in neither case is the good in question an essential good. The question is whether the knowledge gained through contact is a basic good, understood as necessary for a good life. Knowing many adoptees whose lives seem good by any ordinary standard, some of whom have, and others don't have, contact with their birthfamilies, I find it hard to even entertain the idea that contact with birthfamilies is necessary for a good life. In fact, I think it would be insulting to adoptees I know to suggest that their lives are not good because they don't know their birthparents. Nevertheless, there may be something relevant that's easy to miss, so I will consider the issue of similarity in this section, and the issue of narrative in the next.

As Velleman points out, it is very difficult to come to know oneself simply by introspection, or by watching oneself in the mirror. The best resource, he proposes, is observation of others who are importantly similar, and the best sources for such similarity are one's biological family.

> When adoptees go in search of their biological parents and siblings, there is a literal sense in which they are searching for themselves. They are searching for the closest thing to a mirror in which to catch an external and candid view of what they are like in more than mere appearance. Not knowing any biological relatives must be like wandering in a world without reflective surfaces, permanently self-blind.
>
> (Velleman, 2005 368)

DOI: 10.4324/9781003203827-35

As mentioned before, his argument depends on not just having information about one's relatives—this is typically available even in the case of anonymous donors—but having ***acquaintance*** with them. Why? His idea is that it is only by acquaintance that we can appreciate the ***intuitive and unanalyzable*** resemblance we have to our biological relatives. We see another who is "like me". And it is this crucial to gain a sense of "deeply ingrained" aspects of my self (cf. Witt 2005).

On the face of it, however, Velleman's emphasis on biological parents and siblings is highly exaggerated. We all rely on many sources in our development of self-understanding, including friends, characters in literature and film, public figures and, in cases where biological kin are missing, custodial family members. If the crucial thing is that we have others around us who effectively mirror us to ourselves, then it isn't clear why this should be a biological relative.[9] Moreover, it is clear that self-knowledge is not *entirely* achieved by the route of mirroring Velleman describes, for if you don't have some self-knowledge prior to seeing others like yourself, then how could you tell whether they are like you or not? After all: you don't know what you are like! Given some sense of self, gained through introspection and agency, we find others to watch, to mimic, to emulate, to avoid. Although biology does sometimes provide ideal mirrors for this process, all too often it fails miserably: it is common for children to fail when they model themselves on their biological parents, and many biological parents are failures in their own lives and so are poor models even if their children could be successful.

Moreover, if the goal is to find an objective basis for self-knowledge, judgments of similarity should be viewed with caution. In the case of racial or ethnic identity, the belief in shared "blood" provides a myth of commonality. Myths of commonality run rampant in families. And such myths of commonality trace politically significant contours. For example, a female friend with two sons once commented that my son Isaac and I look alike. I was surprised since no one had ever mentioned this before. She noticed my surprise and commented: "I'm told all the time that my sons look like me. I don't think they look like me at all. They are *boys*. But that doesn't seem to matter when people are looking for parent-child similarity. People don't think Isaac looks like you because he's Black and you're White. Skin-color matters when people look for parent-child similarity. But if you actually attend to his features, he looks a lot like you." An important insight in this observation is that what similarities are salient is largely a matter of context, and some socially significant similarities are allowed to eclipse others that may be more deeply important. I don't really see our physical similarities, but Isaac and I have other emotional and temperamental similarities. This too can be easily eclipsed by our racial (and sex) difference. Social schemas tell us, among other things: Who are you allowed to look like? Who are you allowed to *be* like? (We'll return to the idea of a social schema below.)

Implicit in Velleman's discussion is a theory about why adoptees search ("they are searching for themselves") and what they find when they do ("an external and candid view of themselves"). But research on adoptees, although plagued by methodological challenges and rarely if ever reaching consensus, doesn't support this picture. Although, as Velleman notes, the number of adoptees who search has been steadily rising and may be approaching 50% (Velleman, 2005 259fn1), this is not surprising, given the opening of records and changes in adoption policy and counseling. However, this increase in numbers searching does not, by itself, support his interpretation of why adoptees search or the outcome. Although I cannot provide a literature survey in this context, there are a few points worth noting.

First, it is generally recognized that adoption is a significant factor in identity development, though whether an adoptee struggles with identity is to a significant extent a matter of context, where context includes both immediate family and society. Factors that influence identity resolution in adoptive families include: type of family relationships (e.g., authoritarian or not), ways of communicating (or not) about adoption, and parental attitudes about adoption. (Hoopes, 1990, esp. 162f; Kohler et al., 2002) Social attitudes towards adoption influence the adoptee both indirectly by influencing parents' attitudes and directly. For example:

> Problems of identity tend to arise when we have conflicting loyalties to persons, groups or associations. Identity problems arise for adoptive children not simply because they have been told they are adopted, but because there are conflicting cultural values around them, those concerned with nurturing parenthood held by their adoptors [sic], and the values concerning biological bases of kinship that are still very much alive in the culture generally.
>
> (Kirk, 1964 20, quoted in Hoopes, 1990 155)

Interestingly, and not surprisingly, adoptees who are brought up in a family which accords significant value to being reared in biological families, a value that they are obviously missing out on, are more likely to have identity problems and search for their biological relatives. Thus it would seem that Velleman's view is locally self-affirming. But adoptees who are brought in families where biology is treated as one source, but not the only source for identity, are normally able to form healthy identities without contact with their biological relatives.

Second, in carefully controlled studies, adoptees have been found to have "no significant differences between their behavior and characteristics and those of the matched group of biological children." (Borders et al., 1998, also quoted in Carp, 2002 452). In studies of adult adoptees (much of the adoption research is on youth) "while adult adoptees have had unique life experiences, in many ways they are navigating their adult years no differently than their non-adopted peers." (Borders et al., 2000 415). Remembering the distinction between PI [personal identity] and RGO [reference group orientation] in the discussion of Black identity, this research suggests that adoptees do not suffer in developing a core self measured by PI relative to non-adoptees.[10] Interestingly, however, "most of the differences found between adoptees and controls in this research could be attributed to search status. Lower self-esteem, lower family/friend support, and higher depression scores were all associated with searchers." (Borders et al., 2000 416) Whether this difference between searchers and non-searchers is the reason for, or a result of, searching is not clear. This suggests, however, that contact with biological relatives is not an assured route to a healthy identity.

Third, adoptees search for their birthfamilies for a variety of different reasons and there are many different trajectories after reunion. Recent long-term studies suggest that in most cases, even when a good relationship is established with a birthmother, the adoptee's primary relationship remains with their adoptive mother. Moreover,

> The need to have a sense of genealogical and genetic connectedness appears strong. It is part of the drive that motivates people to search. Who do I look like? Where do I come from?
>
> Whom am I like in terms of temperament and interests, skills and outlook? But although these needs trigger people to search and seek contact, they do not necessarily imply the desire for a relationship. They are information led: they are designed to meet autobiographical and identity needs.
>
> (Howe and Feast, 2001 364–65)

So even if we grant the point that it can help to gain an objective perspective on oneself through having information about or even observing biological relatives, we must ask, how much more than a glimpse is needed? How often do we need to see ourselves unexpectedly in a store window in order to form a healthy identity? Is contact needed? Apparently, an ongoing relationship is not even desired by many of those who search.

****

We should note, however, that Velleman doesn't need the claim that societies always and everywhere have organized themselves around the biological family to make his claim that this is a basic good. As noted above when considering the importance of linen shirts in 18th century England, some goods are *contextually* basic. They are necessary in a particular culture at a particular time in order to have a good life. One could reasonably claim that because the "natural nuclear family" schema is dominant in contemporary Western societies and has been for several centuries, children are harmed who are deprived of the resources to situate themselves socially using this narrative trope. Just as lacking a linen shirt in the 18th century England would be shameful and suggest a history of bad conduct, likewise admission of adoptee (or birthmother or adoptive parent) status has been considered shameful and indicative of bad conduct in our recent culture, among others. Lacking knowledge of one's biological family, one is often left without answers to questions that matter culturally, and this is stigmatizing. Given the difficulty of living a good life as a member of a stigmatized group, we owe adoptees access to their biological relatives so they have answers to questions that the natural nuclear family schema assumes they will have.

Here we have come to a point on which Velleman and I agree. The natural nuclear family schema plays an important role in forming identities—including healthy identities—in our current cultural context, and many people are stigmatized by not being able to "fit" the schema; in short, early 21st century American culture is bionormative. Being stigmatized is harmful and it is difficult to live a good life when stigmatized in this way. However, even granting the cultural significance of the natural nuclear family schema, there are two ways to combat this stigma. One is to provide resources so that everyone can come as close as possible to fitting the schema, another is to combat the dominance of the schema. Velleman prefers the former strategy; I prefer the latter. The problem, as I see it, lies in the reification of the schema as universal, necessary, and good, and not the families that fail to match it.

I take the crucial question to be whether parents, or society more generally, is obliged to provide the social bases for healthy identity formation in terms of the dominant ideology of the culture. If the obligation is simply to provide the social bases for healthy identity formation, then if there are multiple routes to this result, the obligation is only to provide one or another of these routes. For example, if the dominant schemas for identity are implicated in structures and forms of life that are unjust, the good of fitting neatly into the culture may be compromised. The best alternative may be to find or construct alternative—counter-hegemonic—identities and narratives that complicate gender, race, ethnicity, family, etc. In a context in which the dominant schema is biological/genetic determinism, it is useful to be acquainted with one's biological relations. But this is a conditional good and is not good by virtue of the biological relations alone. Anonymous gamete donation may make telling a life-story that fits with the dominant family schema difficult, but likewise children of interracial partnerships have (or had) more difficulty telling a life-story that fits with the dominant schema of the Black-White racial binary. This doesn't mean that interracial couples are (or were) doing something immoral by having a child. Providing our children the social bases for alternative family schemas may be not only permissible, but morally good; it may even be a moral duty to combat bionormativity. In particular, constructing and teaching narratives that normalize adoption and schemas that challenge the assumption that our biological inheritance defines who we are, may not be to spread lies (Velleman, 2005 378), but to provide the resources to build a more just society.

In the case of the natural nuclear family schema, much more would have to be said to determine whether and to what extent its dominance is implicated in structures of injustice. Insofar as the schema underwrites traditional gender roles and heteronormative models of the family, I take it to be morally problematic. But this is a large debate that goes beyond the opportunities this paper provides. My argument is more limited. I believe that knowing one's biological relatives can be a good thing, and that contact is valuable in the contemporary cultural context largely because this context is dominated by the natural nuclear family schema. Even in this context, the formation of a full self and the formation of a healthy identity do not require contact with, or even specific knowledge of, biological relatives. Identities are formed in relation to cultural schemas, and fortunately our culture provides a wealth of schemas that sometimes fit with and sometimes run counter to the dominant ideology. Living under the shadow of the natural nuclear family schema, it is reasonable to provide children with information about or contact with their biological relations, if and when this becomes an issue in their forming a healthy identity. However, if we are to avoid harming our children, then rather than enshrining a schema that most families fail to exemplify and which is used to stigmatize and alienate families that are (yes!) as good as their biological counterparts, we should instead make every effort to disrupt the hegemony of the schema.[15]

## Notes

9. Although Velleman's emphasis on narrative suggests a sympathy with a psychoanalytic notion of self, the "self psychology" of Kohut employs the notion of "mirroring" in a way that seems relevant to but different from Velleman's notion of mirroring. (Baker and Baker, 1987) On Kohut's view, in developing a healthy self it is crucial that the primary caretaker "mirror" the child by providing empathetic and appropriate responses to his/her affective states. Whether the primary caretaker is capable of this has little to do with his/her similarities with the child, but depends more on their own narcissistic tendencies. Insofar as narcissistic projection and a failure to recognize the child as a fully separate person is more tempting with a biological child, it may even be that a non-biological parent or care-taker is better suited to this mirroring role than a biological parent.
10. This data is not exactly what is needed to respond to Velleman's argument because the data doesn't distinguish adoptions in which there is contact with

biological relations from adoptions in which there isn't. Because until recently there were very few fully open non-kin adoptions, however, the question is whether the data is primarily drawn from non-kin or kinship adoptions.

****

15. Thanks to Lawrence Blum, Jorge Garcia, Heather Paxson, Brad Skow, Natalie Stoljar, Charlotte Witt, and Stephen Yablo for helpful discussion of the issues in this paper. I presented drafts of this paper at the University of Massachusetts, Boston Philosophy Department, the Centre de Recherche en Éthique de L'Université de Montréal, McGill University Center for Research and Teaching on Women, and Encountering New Worlds of Adoption Conference at the University of Pittsburgh. Thanks to the participants at these sessions and to Marianne Novy and an anonymous referee for valuable feedback.

## Works Cited

Baker, Howard S., and Margaret N. Baker. "Heinz Kohut's Self Psychology: An Overview." *American Journal of Psychiatry*, vol. 141, no. 1, 1987, pp. 1–9.

Borders, L. DiAnne, et al. "Are Adopted Children and Their Parents At Greater Risk of Negative Outcomes?" *Family Relations*, vol. 47, no. 3, 1998, pp. 237–241.

Carp, E. Wayne. "Adoption, Blood Kinship, Stigma, and the Adoption Reform Movement: A Historical Perspective." *Law and Society Review*, Special Issue on Nonbiological Parenting, vol. 36, no. 2, 2002, pp. 433–460.

Hoopes, Janet L. "Adoption and Identity Formation." *The Psychology of Adoption*, edited by David M. Brodzinsky and Marshall D. Schechter, Oxford UP, 1990, pp. 144–66.

Howe, David, and Julia Feast. "The Long-Term Outcome of Reunions Between Adult Adopted People and Their Birth Mothers." *British Journal of Social Work*, vol. 31, no. 3, 2001, pp. 351–368.

Kohler, Julie K., et al. "Adopted Adolescents' Preoccupation With Adoption: The Impact on Adoptive Family Relationships." *Journal of Marriage and Family*, vol. 64, no. 1, 2002, pp. 93–104.

Velleman, David J. "Family History." *Philosophical Papers*, vol. 34, no. 3, 2005, pp. 357–378.

Witt, Charlotte. "Family Resemblances: Adoption, Personal Identity, and Genetic Essentialism." *Adoption Matters: Philosophical and Feminist Essays*, edited by Sally Haslanger and Charlotte Witt, Cornell UP, 2005, pp. 13–45.

# From Jacobson, Heather. *Labor of Love: Gestational Surrogacy and the Work of Making Babies.* Rutgers UP, 2016.

I see three basic assumptions driving the chilly reaction described by Sherry. The first is the assumption that surrogates are parting with their own children. As I will show in this chapter, this is a common conception surrogates confront. The second assumption is the idea that pregnancy and birth hold no pleasure in and of themselves and are painful, unpleasant experiences best avoided—unless you *really* want a baby. With these two assumptions, surrogacy is framed as both morally suspect and illogical. This brings us to the third assumption: that people do not engage in painful, immoral behavior for the benefit of others unless they are immoral themselves or are pressured to do so. Surrogacy only makes sense, from this perspective, if women are coerced into surrogacy by their own greed (or others') or by their own desperate needs.

The image of surrogates that these assumptions evoke is of women somehow lost (or "cold," as Sherry put it), unmoored from what is seen to be the natural relationship between women and the children they bear, coerced by financial reasons to behave unnaturally. Surrogacy challenges basic cultural ideologies of motherhood—those deeply held, socially constructed cultural beliefs that women are the mothers of the children they gestate, that women bond deeply with their gestating babies and newborns, and that women who birth children want to mother them. This idealized model of mothering, popular since the early twentieth century and continuing to intensify (but seen to be "natural, universal, and unchanging") places "responsibility for mothering . . . almost exclusively on one woman (the biological mother), for whom it constitutes the primary if not sole mission during the child's formative years" (Glenn 1994, 3; see also Hays 1996). Surrogacy deeply challenges these notions. With gestational surrogacy, the concept of a unified mother (genetic, gestational, and social) is parceled into distinct and separate bodies, identities, and relationships: three possible women (egg donor, gestational carrier, and intended mother), three bodies, three relationships to the fetus or child (Hartouni 1997; Teman 2010). With commercial surrogacy, not only is reproduction separated from sexual

DOI: 10.4324/9781003203827-36

intercourse, but also the act of carrying a pregnancy and birthing a child is divorced from the intimacy of the family and placed within the market. Commercial surrogates are paid to gestate and bear babies and not bond with them in what is thought to be a "motherly way," to not see themselves as the mothers of those infants, and to not engage in the infants' social mothering.

The movement of reproduction into the market and the commercialization of mothering activities have raised deep social, legal, and ethical concerns about surrogacy for the last four decades. These concerns are reflected in court cases, media stories, and public opinion on surrogacy. Surveys since the 1980s have consistently found that most people do not approve of surrogacy, finding it the least acceptable route to family expansion (Dunn et al. 1988; Edelmann 2004; Krishnan 1994; Poote and van den Akker 2009; Weiss 1992). Media stories reflect this repulsion and frame surrogacy as freakish and unnatural, intending to provoke scorn and outrage about these arrangements.

As I explore in this chapter, in public presentations of surrogacy, we can see an intense anxiety about women who engage in third-party pregnancy. Part of this anxiety is about how to delineate exactly what surrogates are doing and why they are doing it. When a woman gestates and bears a child for a family member without pay, that gesture is often framed not as labor, but as a gift given out of familial love. But when a woman makes such an arrangement with strangers for pay—and does it again and again—that labor has the potential to blur the culturally constructed boundaries between work and family. When pregnancy becomes something akin to employment, do families become work?

In this chapter, I also explore how women come to work in the highly contentious field of surrogacy, both the initial seed of inspiration and the motivations that draw them to this practice. I am centrally interested in how surrogates think about the labor in which they engage: Do they consider it employment? Moreover, how do the negative images of surrogacy shape how they think about their work and the interactions they have with others? How do they negotiate the negative cultural discourse around the commodification of their labor? In exploring the process through which women become surrogates and analyzing the ways in which surrogates talk about their work, I examine how surrogates confront and negotiate assumptions about surrogacy and the negative image of their work. In doing so, I describe the actual labor involved in surrogacy and contemplate links between surrogacy and other forms of feminized labor in the United States.

****

These archetypes cast surrogates negatively as workers: either they are capitalizing on their fertility to swindle as much money as possible out of vulnerable IPs, or they are forced by the larger structural forces of poverty and gender inequality to capitalize on their reproductive abilities to feed their own children. How do surrogates deal with these insinuations about their character? How do women who are contemplating surrogacy react to these assumptions? Through my interviews, it became clear to me that surrogates are aware of these negative images and work hard to dispel them. As this chapter explains, they largely do so by attempting to undermine the three popular assumptions of surrogates discussed above: (1) the assumption that they are parting with their own children; (2) the idea that pregnancy and birth hold no pleasure in and of themselves and are painful, unpleasant experiences best avoided—unless you really want a baby or are desperate for money; and (3) people do not engage in painful, immoral behavior for the benefit of others unless they are greedy or pressured to do. The pushback against these assumptions begins early in the career of a surrogate and can be seen in the ways in which women frame their initial motivations to engage in third-party pregnancy.

****

The concept of "reproductive labor" is helpful here. Feminists scholars used this term to capture and make visible "women's nonmarket activities—house work, child care, the servicing of men, and the care of the elderly—and [to define] all those activities as *labor*" (di Leonardo 1987, 441; see also DeVault 1991; Hartmann 1976; Oakley 1974). Many scholars today use the term "care work" in place of reproductive labor and have added relational aspects (such as "the activity of attending to others and responding to their emotions and needs" [Coltrane and Galt 2000, 16]) to hands-on care to more fully understand this kind of work. Though there is some variation in how scholars conceptualize care work and some debate about which occupations should be included in this category, interestingly the gestation and birth of children is often not included; the laboring activities listed by many scholars center on the care of people who have already been born. I argue that the work of human reproduction—that is, the gestating and birthing of children—should be seen as a kind of reproductive labor or care work inasmuch as gestating and birthing children is care of children (and of embryos and fetuses), part of the social reproduction of families, and an essential activity for ongoing human existence. World overpopulation aside, as a species, we need children to be born. And in twenty-first-century America, the gestation and birth of children can take considerable mental, physical, and emotional effort.

Those who have studied various forms of care work have shown that women's caring labor is devalued (not seen as real work), as evidenced by low wages and little prestige, which is made possible especially because this labor often occurs in the home or in homelike settings (such as nursing homes) and is therefore often hidden from public view (Abel 2000; Daniels 1987; Fisher 1990; Glenn 1992; MacDonald 2010; Romero 1992). Wages are also kept low because this labor is often framed not as work that requires skill, but as that which makes use of feminine abilities that arise naturally in women (England 2005). Women are seen to be ideally suited for caring work, and the caring occupations are dominated by women (Dodson and Zincavage 2007; Duffy 2005; Folbre 2001).

The notion that women are inherently better at caregiving presupposes that men and women are inherently different. As gender scholars have shown, the idea of essentialized gendered difference creates hierarchies of power and privilege (Hartmann 1981). The gendered division of labor disadvantages women, both in the home and in the workplace (DeVault 1991). Ironically, it is a rhetoric of love and sacrifice—of care—that enables this inequality because it permeates understandings of women's work, allowing low wages, little prestige, and lessthan-ideal working conditions. As Pierrette Hondagneu-Sotelo argues in her work on immigrant domestics caring for children in Los Angeles, "parents want someone who will really 'care about' and show preference for their children; yet such personal engagement remains antithetical to how we think about much employment" (2001, 10). Normative ideas about work and family and the divide conceptualized between the two position carework in a liminal state: not quite family love and not quite paid employment. When it comes to caring work, then, wages are kept low because the work is meant to be a calling and done out of love. High wages are seen as representative of noncaring employees—and when care is the service, the use of noncaring employees is seen to equate to lower quality service. In a capitalistic society in which value is designated monetarily, the low wages in female-dominated occupations are framed as a badge of maternal sacrifice, displaying workers, commitments to care and the way we like to think about that care as genuine, as love. Paula England and Nancy Folbre (1999) write about this as a care penalty. Just as unpaid work in the home is viewed as unskilled drudgery, so, too, is paid care work of a similar nature (Daniels 1987). Caring labor is infused with contradictions: it is given lip service as valuable (at least by those needing it), yet ultimately seen as unskilled; it is culturally valorized, yet not adequately compensated—precisely because it is labor engaged in by women and seen as an expression of inherent female skills, interests, and abilities; work that is hidden because it is family work.

Surrogates frame their work as sacrifice, neatly positioning surrogacy alongside other forms of female-dominated labor. Their work is meant to be a labor of love, arising out of their nature and womanly skills. Of course, while some men have entered other female-dominated fields, especially the older markets of nursing and primary-school education, being a surrogate mother is impossible for men. Because of this, surrogacy is perhaps the most uniquely feminine of all the female-dominated occupations. The rhetoric that undergirds surrogacy—one of self-sacrifice and altruism—is, therefore, inherently gendered, with ideas about women and reproduction used to support the industry. It is a familiar narrative, allowing the system to function.

Like other care workers, surrogates call on the rhetoric of self-sacrifice and love in framing their labor. However, they emphasized that they—and their families—deserve compensation not only because of the time demands involved but also because of the bodily risks they take and the specialized skills they bring to the market. But the intrusion of the market into reproduction that surrogacy represents—the outsourcing of making babies, among our most intimate interactions—provokes general anxiety and, as survey research implies, is repugnant to many (Edelmann 2004; Hochschild 2012; Krishnan 1994; Weiss 1992). This anxiety can be seen in the attention surrogacy garners in the press and in Hollywood, despite the relative low estimated numbers of surrogate births per year. To neutralize that anxiety, the strongest marker of the market, compensation, while essential for the market to operate, needs to be obscured for that market to be culturally palatable. The surrogacy market depends on surrogates; yet, ironically, cultural anxieties about the commodification of reproduction and children have resulted in a marketing and cultural discourse that either largely obscures the actual labor (including the attached compensation) or pathologizes it. Surrogacy in the United States is therefore seldom acknowledged as a legitimate and culturally sanctioned form of paid employment—even, as this chapter has explored, by those engaging in it. The obscuring of surrogacy as work plays out in various dimensions including, as the following chapter shows, the relationships that surrogates in the United States create with their IPs.

## Works Cited

Abel, Emily. "A Historical Perspective on Care." *Care Work: Gender, Labor, and the Welfare State*, edited by Madonna Herrington Meyer, Routledge, 2000, pp. 8–14.

Coltrane, Scott, and Justin Galt. "The History of Men's Caring: Evaluating Precedents for Father's Family Involvement." *Care Work: Gender, Labor, and the Welfare State*, edited by Madonna Herrington Meyer, Routledge, 2000, pp. 15–36.

Daniels, Arlene Kaplan. "Invisible Work." *Social Problems*, vol. 34, no. 5, pp. 403–415.

DeVault, Marjorie. *Feeding the Family: The Social Organization of Caring as Gendered Work*. U of Chicago P, 1991.

Di Leonardo, Micaela. "The Female World of Cards and Holidays: Women, Families, and the Work of Kinship." *Signs*, vol. 12, no. 3, 1987, pp. 440–453.

Dodson, Lisa, and Rebekah M. Zincavage. "'It's Like a Family': Caring Labor, Race, and Exploitation in Nursing Homes." *Gender & Society*, vol. 21, no. 6, 2007, pp. 905–28.

Duffy, Mignon. "Reproducing Labor Inequalities: Challenges for Feminists Conceptualizing Care at the Intersections of Gender, Race, and Class." *Gender & Society*, vol. 19, no. 1, 2005, pp. 66–82.

Dunn, Patricia, et al. "College Students' Acceptance of Adoption and Five Alternative Fertilization Techniques." *Journal of Sex Research*, vol. 24, no. 1, 1988, pp. 282–287.

Edelmann, Robert J. "Surrogacy: The Psychological Issues." *Journal of Reproductive and Infant Psychology*, vol. 22, no. 2, 2004, pp. 123–136.

England, Paula. "Emerging Theories in Care Work." *Annual Review of Sociology*, vol. 31, no. 1, 2005, pp. 381–399.

England, Paula, and Nancy Folbre. "The Cost of Caring." *Annuals of the American Academy of Political and Social Science*, vol. 561, no. 1, 1999, pp. 39–51.

Fisher, Berenice. "Alice in the Human Services: A Feminist Analysis of Women in the Caring Professions." *Circles of Care: Work and Identity in Women's Lives*, edited by Emily K. Abel and Margaret K. Nelson, SUNY P, 1990, pp. 108–131.

Folbre, Nancy. *The Invisible Heart: Economics and Family Value*. New, 2001.

Glenn, Evelyn Nakano. "From Servitude to Service Work: Historical Continuities in the Racial Division of Paid Reproductive Labor." *Signs*, vol. 18, no. 1, 1992, pp. 1–43.

———. "Social Constructions of Mothering: A Thematic Overview." *Mothering, Ideology, Experience, and Agency*, edited by Evelyn Nakano Glenn, et al., Routledge, 1994, pp. 1–29.

Hartmann, Heidi. "Capitalism, Patriarchy, and Job Segregation by Sex." *Signs*, vol. 1, no. 3, 1976, pp. 137–169.

———. "The Family as Locus of Gender, Class, and Political Struggle." *Signs*, vol. 6, no. 3, 1981, 366–394.

Hartouni, Valerie. *Cultural Conceptions: On Reproductive Technologies and the Remaking of Life*. U of Minnesota P, 1997.

Hays, Sharon. *The Cultural Contradictions of Motherhood*. Yale UP, 1996.

Hochschild, Arlie Russell. *The Outsourced Self: Intimate Life in Market Times*. Metropolitan, 2012.

Hondagneu-Sotelo, Pierrette. *Domestica: Immigrant Workers Cleaning and Caring in the Shadows of Influence*. U of California P, 2001.

Krishnan, Vijaya. "Attitudes toward Surrogate Motherhood in Canada." *Health Care for Women International*, vol. 15, no. 4, 1994, pp. 333–357.

MacDonald, Cameron Lynn. *Shadow Mothers: Nannies, Au Pairs, and the Micropolitics of Mothering*. U of California P, 2010.

Oakley, Ann. *Women's Work: The Housewife, Past and Present*. Vintage, 1974.

Poote, Aimee, and Olga van den Akker. "British Women's Attitudes to Surrogacy." *Human Reproduction*, vol. 24, no. 1, 2009, pp. 139–145.

Romero, Mary. *Maid in the U. S. A.* Routledge, 1992.

Teman, Elly. "The Social Construction of Surrogacy Research: An Anthropological Critique of Psychosocial Scholarship on Surrogate Motherhood." *Social Science & Medicine*, vol. 67, no. 7, 2010, pp. 1104–1112.

Weiss, Gregory. "Public Attitudes about Surrogate Motherhood." *Michigan Sociological Review*, vol. 6, 1992, pp. 15–27.

# From Latchford, Frances J. "Reckless Abandon: The Politics of Victimization and Agency in Birthmother Narratives." *Adoption and Mothering*, edited by Frances J. Latchford, Demeter, 2012, pp. 73–87.

In the film *Then She Found Me* (2007), written and directed by Helen Hunt, a successful talk show host, Bernice Graves, is confronted by her birth-daughter as to the reason for her relinquishment. In the conversation that ensues, Bernice admits honestly, "you're right, I wanted a life more than I wanted you." What mother today could confess such feelings to her birth child and not raise the alarm and ire of anyone within earshot? Bernice, nevertheless, manages to avoid this censure. She does so, in part, because *Then She Found Me* is a comedy and as such, Bernice's confession, the cultural horror it would normally elicit, is contained by the absurd; unlike other genres, comedy facilitates the safe exploration of unthinkable ideas, events, or human acts that, in the real world, trouble us emotionally and psychically primarily because they threaten our sociocultural norms. She also does so because Bette Midler, the actor who plays Bernice, is the consummate comedienne. Indeed, Midler, I suspect, is one of only a handful of women who could get away with, and really be forgiven for, not wanting to raise the child she bore. Her character on and off screen embodies an extraordinarily uncommon balance between traditional femininity and autonomy and, in so doing, she wins the sympathy of a heteronormative audience and enables it to understand and accept her as an "individual" who has a right to choose a life apart from motherhood. This is the genius of casting Midler as Bernice, because neither Midler nor her characters kid around when it comes to what they want, and this is why audiences admire her. Midler's persona renders bearable and intelligible the idea that a woman, genuinely and justifiably, could *choose* not to rear her birth child. She allows us to accept Bernice and not condemn her as "selfish," as I think Hunt intends, when she challenges her daughter with a real, but rarely articulated, truth: some women who relinquish their children are genuinely autonomous agents: they make independent decisions to place a child for adoption.

The discourse of naturalized motherhood that surrounds birthmothers enables us to look at how women's agency is effaced by bio-essentialist

DOI: 10.4324/9781003203827-37

views of motherhood within and without adoption, search, and reunion discourse. In the simplest terms, it is a mode of knowledge that casts women as innately driven toward motherhood and bio-narcissistic nurturing. It understands women primarily in relation to their reproductive biology, and its success or failure, which is treated as the cause of women's natural inclination toward motherhood. It exiles from intelligibility critical questions asked by Judith Butler regarding the normative production of sex: "to what extent does a body get defined by its capacity for pregnancy? Why is it pregnancy by which that body gets defined?" (Butler 33). Naturalized motherhood is a discourse governed by bio-essentialist and heteronormative ideals of sex and reproduction, the family, gender, and sexuality, all of which continue to curtail women's freedoms. It holds that reproduction and bio-narcissistic nurturing are a kind of nuclei around which a woman's identity, as normal or pathologically abnormal, is centered. Thus, even as it is more acceptable for women today to pursue maternity and motherhood later in life, women *qua* women remain subject to the imperative of naturalized motherhood. Indeed, its contemporary impact on women's lives is clearly evident in the stigma to which childless women continue to be subject; these women are treated as suspect, social pariahs, and/or in denial of the natural aims of their biological make-up as women. For instance, in a recent study on "voluntary childlessness," Sarah L. Pelton and Katherine M. Hertlein found that women who refuse childbirth and the role of motherhood outright are typically characterized as "selfish, deviant, immature, and unfeminine," because society still "equates motherhood with womanhood" or female adulthood (43). In effect, only women that utilize their reproductive organs and, further, assume bio-heteronormative maternal roles are read as normal. In adoption, search and reunion discourse, naturalized motherhood also informs the pathology that surrounds birthmothers. The pathology of these women stems from trauma that surrounds their inability, or perceived failure, as women and *ipso facto* as mothers to nurture the children they bear. Depicted almost exclusively as victims of coercion and trauma who must come to terms with the meaning of their biological motherhood, birthmothers are pathologized as incapable of either inner peace and/or a normal sense of self because they are denied a social role and recognition as mothers.

This paper interrogates the bio-essentialism of the dominant birthmother narrative: it examines its relationship to entrenched notions of feminine gender, and its re-inscription of a naturalized imperative of motherhood that forecloses women's possibilities and freedoms. It does *not* deny the real grief and loss experienced by so many birthmothers. Nor does it deny a history soaked with the tears of women who have been coerced into giving up their children for adoption. On the contrary, it assumes that too many surrenders have been compelled by systemic injustices due to class, family, peers, religion, racism, and/or the institution of adoption and social work, although this is not its central focus. Instead, it argues that birthmothers, like Bernice, who *are* agents in relinquishing their children, are the unacknowledged secret of the dominant birthmother narrative. It suggests that insofar as the stories of autonomous birthmothers are erased, so too is the political import of their decisions and experiences as sites of resistance against imperatives of naturalized motherhood and bio-essentialist notions of family. It contends not only the reality, but the validity of these choices is disavowed by the dominant discourse that positions birthmothers *as* fundamentally traumatized and bereaved women. It argues that a woman's complete social equality turns on a social and political understanding of herself as a free agent: she has a right to choose whether or not to mother her biological child, just as a pregnant woman has a right to choose whether or not she carries a child to term. It has implications for the subjectivity and rights of birthmothers as they are currently understood: it implies that to secure their rights as "mothers," birthmothers should not be forced to portray relinquishment as a phenomenon that is always and only intelligible when it is the result of some form of coercion. It concludes that in adoption, search and reunion discourse, birthmothers will be better served if and when maternal work replaces coercion and biological motherhood as the foundation that best sustains their identities and rights as mothers, their choices as women, and, ultimately, their access to their children.

* * * *

What does the profound commitment to grief and victimization as the central object of study in the literature on birthmother experience say about the operations of naturalized motherhood as a normative meaning in adoption? What is the effect of the rhetorical reiteration of qualifiers in adoption literature that obfuscate the agency of these women? What purpose is served, for instance, when J. A. Aloi writes, "[t]he decision to place a child for adoption is *almost always* a heart-wrenching one; and, with it, some of the most significant losses that one can face" (27)?[10] And what of the birthmothers who neither experience themselves as victims, nor grieve the choice to relinquish, so much as they grieve the pain of an obligatory secret that is necessitated by a real choice, one that nevertheless must remain a secret to avoid being cast as monsters and retain their identities as "women" and/or "mothers"?

Within the discourse of adoption, search and reunion, the logic of naturalized motherhood, which informs the birthmother's pathology due to coerced separation, also functions as the naturalized basis for a right-the right of access to her birthchild. The political strategy that adoption experts and search activists have derived from this logic is umbilically bound to a broader bio-genealogical imperative that already naturalizes Western ideals about "family" and familial rights *as* biological in origin.[11] This strategy helps to establish the birthmother's access to her child insofar as her biological tie already operates as the material foundation for other rights in our culture. In addition to this, it institutionalizes the birthmother's right *as* the cure for her pathology. Still, it traps the birthmother in the horns of a dilemma: her right is only deemed valid where she identifies as a birthmother who is also a victim of pathology and coercion. This identification, within naturalized motherhood, is what proves that the materiality of her biological tie and/or her motherhood is real, which is the foundation upon which her right depends. It does so because naturalized motherhood undercuts the possibility that a "mother" is ever free to relinquish a child; where autonomy is claimed, the bio-logic of naturalized motherhood necessarily denies a birthmother's access to the identity of "mother." Nevertheless, to identify as the "birthmother coerced" renders a woman's motherhood and rights suspect too because *as* any kind of birthmother she still has relinquished a child, which remains contrary to the rule of bio-narcissistic nurturing entailed by naturalized motherhood. There is then a great price to be paid by the birthmother whose relinquishment *within* the discourse of naturalized motherhood is openly coerced *or* secretly chosen.

To solve this dilemma, the naturalized basis upon which the birthmother lays claim to her rights to child access and knowledge must change: to prevent her victimization and coercion, to minimize her grief, to ensure her access, and to instate her autonomy. To resist naturalized motherhood entails the rejection of the biological tie, in and of itself, as proof that the right to the child is real. But if we refuse the edict of naturalized motherhood, how does this alter the meaning and dimensions of the birthmother's right? Does it mean she will lose this right? And if not, how is the right to be retained? What, in effect, would a new right that insures access to the child while resisting naturalized motherhood look like?

An alternative basis upon which to establish the birthmother's right is her work; her care and activity in pregnancy, her labour, birth, and the physical, perhaps even the psychic aftermath of reproduction. All of these can operate as the ground for a newly conceived right to child access. Indeed, some birthmothers already argue the process of reproduction is a kind of nurture and parenting, precisely, to respond to arguments that claim "parenting" *is* solely the work of *extra utero* nurture as a means to exclude birthmothers from the right to access.[12]

## Notes

10. Italics mine.
11. This imperative (which I investigate in my forthcoming monograph, *Steeped in Blood: Crimes Against the Family Under the Tyranny of a Bio-genealogical Imperative*) plays a role in over-determining family bonds as biological bonds and has various implications for the subjectivity of birthmothers, adoptees, and adoptive parents alike, although I do not discuss them here. Where biological bonds are set-up as ontologically superior in (modern Western) discourse and knowledge, the self that is a birthmother, is adopted, or adopts is prone to measure "family" experience against the presence or absence of biological ties. The effects of this discourse on one's subjectivity can manifest, therefore, as grief and loss on the part of all members of what is commonly referred to as the adoption triad: the birthmother and adoptee because their biological tie is severed and the adoptive parent because her tie is not biological. This raises the question of whether or not these experiences are actually rooted in either the absence or severing of biological ties *per se* (i.e., the *Cri du Sang*) or in a totalizing and socially constructed meaning of family that is attached to biological ties.
12. This argument has been made to me in conversations I have had with different birthmothers.

## Works Cited

Aloi, J. A. "Nursing the Disenfranchised: Women Who Have Relinquished an Infant for Adoption." *Journal of Psychiatric and Mental Health Nursing*, vol. 16, 2009, p. 29.

Butler, Judith. "Gender as Performance: An Interview with Judith Butler." *Radical Philosophy*, vol. 67, 1994, pp. 32–39.

Pelton, Sarah L., and Katherine M. Hertlein. "A Proposed Life Cycle for Voluntary Childfree Couples." *Journal of Feminist Family Therapy*, vol. 23, 2011, pp. 39–53.

*Then She Found Me*. Dir. Helen Hunt. Perf. Helen Hunt, Bette Midler, Colin Firth, Matthew Broderick. Killer Films, John Wells Productions, Blue Rider Pictures, 2007.

# Index

*Note*: References following "n" refer notes.

9781032067827